*Peter Porcupine
in America*

WILLIAM COBBETT

PETER PORCUPINE IN AMERICA

Pamphlets on Republicanism and Revolution

EDITED WITH AN INTRODUCTION BY

DAVID A. WILSON

CORNELL UNIVERSITY PRESS

ITHACA AND LONDON

A volume in the series
Documents in American Social History,
edited by Nick Salvatore

Copyright © 1994 by Cornell University

All rights reserved. Except for brief quotations in a review, this book, or
parts thereof, must not be reproduced in any form without permission in
writing from the publisher. For information, address Cornell University Press,
Sage House, 512 East State Street, Ithaca, New York 14850.

First published 1994 by Cornell University Press.

Printed in the United States of America

⊚ The paper in this book meets the minimum requirements
of the American National Standard for Information Sciences—
Permanence of Paper for Printed Library Materials, ANSI Z39.48-1984.

Library of Congress Cataloging-in-Publication Data
Cobbett, William, 1763–1835.
 Peter Porcupine in America : pamphlets on Republicanism and
revolution / William Cobbett ; edited with an introduction by David A. Wilson.
  p.   cm. — (Documents in American social history)
Includes bibliographical references and index.
ISBN 0-8014-2839-4 (alk. paper)
 1. United States—Politics and government—1789–1897—Sources. 2. Cobbett,
William, 1763–1835. 3. Pamphleteers—United States—Biography. I. Wilson,
David A., 1950– . II. Title. III. Series.
E311.C658 1994
973.4—dc20   93-33875

To
George A. Rawlyk
and
Donald H. Akenson
for all their help through the years.

Contents

Illustrations ix

Acknowledgments xi

Some Explanatory Notes xiii

Introduction 1

[1]
Observations on the Emigration of Dr. Joseph Priestley 50

[2]
A Bone to Gnaw, for the Democrats 87

[3]
A Kick for a Bite 119

[4]
The Bloody Buoy 137

[5]
The Life and Adventures of Peter Porcupine 155

[6]
History of the American Jacobins 182

[7]
Pen Portraits 217

[8]
Detection of a Conspiracy 239

[9]
Farewell Address 258

Notes 261

Index 281

Illustrations

The Life of William Cobbett   9

The Providential Detection   16

Second Street North, Philadelphia, 1799   54

The Friends of the People   69

The Times: A Political Portrait   141

A Peep into the Antifederal Club   186

What a Beastly Action   225

A Political Sinner   237

Acknowledgments

To begin at the beginning: I thank Cornell University Press editor Roger Haydon for his initial interest in and continuing enthusiasm for this project; it has been a pleasure working with him. At the University of Toronto, William H. Nelson gave me much encouragement and strongly supported my application for a Humanities and Social Sciences Committee Research Grant, which the university awarded me in 1990–91. I could not have had a better research assistant than Martha Smith; she transferred Cobbett's pamphlets to the word processor with a conscientiousness above and beyond the call of duty, and always brightened the room with her cheerfulness. Billy G. Smith of Montana State University, Nick Salvatore of Cornell University, and Al Young of Northern Illinois University read the Introduction and suggested several changes that were incorporated into the final version; the usual disclaimers apply.

The difficult task of tracking down Cobbett's numerous references in the pamphlets was made easier by the help of scholars on both sides of the Atlantic. In particular, I thank Geoffrey Carnall of the University of Edinburgh; Susan R. Gannon of Pace University; Maldwyn Mills of the University of Wales in Aberystwyth; Pat Rogers of the University of South Florida; and Tom Good and John Beattie of the University of Toronto.

A special word of thanks is due to Ann Dooley, Máirín Nic Dhiarmada, and Jean Talman of the Department of Celtic Studies at St. Michael's College for being such delightful colleagues and good friends. Thanks also go to Jane Hunt for her superb copyediting—especially for sorting out the "thats" from the "whiches"—and to Liz Holmes for her equally skillful part in the production of the book.

Finally, I thank Zsuzsa for her support and sound advice in all things, for the love and the laughter, and for simply being there.

D. A. W.

Some Explanatory Notes

COBBETT'S VOLUMINOUS AMERICAN WRITINGS BETWEEN 1794 AND 1800 can be divided broadly into two categories—the pamphlets, most of which were written between 1794 and 1796, and the newspaper articles in *Porcupine's Gazette*, which appeared between 1797 and 1799. I have decided to focus on the pamphlets, since it is here that we get the most sustained exposition of Cobbett's views and arguments. His newspaper pieces frequently take the form of asides and brief comments on reports from other papers, correspondents, and congressional debates. Cobbett's comments make no sense when divorced from these documents; to include the documents to which Cobbett was responding would expand the text to lengths that might endanger the sanity of the reader. With this in mind, I have limited the extracts from the *Gazette* to some of Cobbett's more colorful attacks on the personalities of his opponents. I have chosen some of Cobbett's most popular pamphlets and have tried to capture the central themes and spirit of each one. In editing the pamphlets, I have cut out sections containing lengthy quotations from other sources and omitted material that is excessively repetitive (such as the description of revolutionary atrocities in "The Bloody Buoy") or that becomes bogged down in detail (such as Cobbett's financial relationship with his publishers as described in "The Life and Adventures of Peter Porcupine").

The footnotes in the text are written by Cobbett; the endnotes, delineated by numbers in square brackets, contain explanatory comments on the text.

On the occasions when Cobbett quotes other authors and inserts his own comments in the text, his remarks have been placed in {braces}. My own editorial insertions in Cobbett's writings are delineated by square brackets. I have used "[sic]" only for words that might be mistaken for modern typographical errors.

*Peter Porcupine
in America*

Introduction

ICONOCLASTIC, EGOTISTICAL AND ARROGANT, OFTEN OUTRAGEOUS, and usually entertaining, William Cobbett was one of the most powerful political writers in the English-speaking world during the late eighteenth and early nineteenth centuries. Born into the family of a small farmer and innkeeper in southern England in 1763, he described himself as "one of those, whom the spirit-stirring circumstances of these awful times have drawn forth from their native obscurity."[1] Cobbett is best known today for the persistent and determined verbal guerrilla warfare which he waged against the British government during the first decades of the nineteenth century, as he poured out close to fifteen million words in eighty-eight volumes of his weekly *Political Register* against corruption, oppression, and injustice in the new England of the Industrial Revolution. In the process, he revolutionized journalism by pioneering the use of editorials, began to publish parliamentary debates (today's *Hansard* is a direct offshoot of *Cobbett's Parliamentary Debates*), wrote extensively on subjects ranging from agricultural improvements to the nature of the Protestant Reformation, and established himself as one of the founders of the popular radical tradition in Britain. At the center of Cobbett's work was his *Rural Rides*, an evocative "condition of England" travelogue that has been compared to George Orwell's *Road to Wigan Pier* and has become

---

[1] William Cobbett, "Preface" to *Political Register* (henceforth *PR*), vol. 8, July-December 1805.

a classic text in English political literature. He was larger than life, taller than a myth. Karl Marx, who was hardly a supporter of Cobbett, called him "the greatest pamphleteer England has ever possessed." *The Times*, pilloried by Cobbett as "The Bloody Old Times," wrote on the occasion of his death in 1835 that he was "in some respects a more extraordinary Englishman than any other of his time." Cobbett himself had no doubt about his own importance. "Mine is the most curious history," he immodestly wrote in 1828, "that has ever recorded the life and actions of man."[2]

What is less known about that history—and what has sometimes embarrassed his English admirers—is that the man who became a leading radical publicist in monarchical Britain began his literary career as a High Tory pamphleteer and journalist in republican America, writing under the pseudonym of Peter Porcupine. And despite, or more probably because of, his determination to fight against "all the hell of democracy" on both sides of the Atlantic, Cobbett emerged as the most widely read political writer in the United States during the French Revolution.[3] Between 1794 and 1800, when Americans were locked in a crisis of identity over the meaning of liberty and the destiny of empire, when the new republic was buffeted by the rival claims of competing British, French, and Spanish imperialisms, Cobbett above all appealed to a sense of "Englishness" within the American consciousness. He called for a renunciation of the "spirit of 1776" and evoked a remarkable response. "It is astonishing, but not less astonishing than true," he told the English anti-Jacobin writer William Gifford in 1799, "that it was I, and I alone, that re-exalted the character of Great Britain in America."[4] His enemies—of whom there were many—accused him of wanting to "assimilate our government to that of Great Britain" and to "establish a monarchy instead of a republic"

---

[2] Karl Marx, *Collected Works*, vol. 11 (New York, 1979), p. 498; *The Times*, June 20, 1835; *PR*, January 12, 1828. On Cobbett's literary output, see George Spater, "The Quest for William Cobbett: A Revisionist View of an English Radical," *Times Higher Educational Supplement*, September 18, 1981, pp. 12–13. For an interesting comparison of Cobbett and Orwell, see George Woodcock, "Introduction" to Cobbett, *Rural Rides* (Harmondsworth, 1977), pp. 10–11.

[3] Cobbett, *An Antidote for Tom Paine's Theological and Political Poison* (Philadelphia, 1796), p. 52. On the sales of his writings in America, see Pierce W. Gaines, "William Cobbett's Account Book," *Proceedings of the American Antiquarian Society* 78 (1968), pp. 299–312.

[4] Quoted in George Spater, *William Cobbett: The Poor Man's Friend* (Cambridge, Mass., 1982), vol. 1, p. 86.

in America.⁵ And they were right; it takes no great effort of imagination to understand their horror and alarm at Cobbett's popularity.

For Cobbett's contemporaries, his writings were a force to be reckoned with; for us, they provide a fascinating insight into American political and social attitudes in the early national period. His pamphlets record the optimism with which many Americans greeted the French Revolution, with its apparent promise of a new world order based on individual rights, social justice, and economic opportunity. Through Cobbett, we learn about democratic attempts to revolutionize the customs and manners of the American people, to create a new language for the New World, and to address the issue of women's rights in the republic. But his pamphlets also register the conservative backlash against such changes, as Cobbett articulated an antidemocratic ideology whose emphasis on traditional Christian virtues and family values in some ways anticipates the attitudes of the present-day religious right in the United States.

Cobbett's American career appears all the more remarkable when one realizes that he initially arrived in the United States in 1792 as a republican émigré from Britain. "Ambitious to become the citizen of a free state," he informed Secretary of State Thomas Jefferson, "I have left my native country, England, for America: I bring with me youth, a small family, a few useful literary talents and that is all."⁶ Far from pointing in the direction of Toryism, Cobbett's early attitudes and experiences seemed to place him in that first wave of transatlantic "Jacobins" who left benighted Britain for the land of liberty during the 1790s. Before he settled in the United States, Cobbett had fought against corruption in the British army, had written a popular pamphlet on the subject, and had been an admirer of Thomas Paine's *Rights of Man*. "I had imbibed principles of republicanism," he told his American readers in 1796, "and . . . I thought that men enjoyed here a greater degree of liberty than in England; and this, if not the principal reason, was at least one, for my coming to this country."⁷ To understand both Cobbett's early radicalism and his conversion to conservatism in America, we need to examine his formative years as a plowboy in rural England and as a soldier in the British army.

⁵ Samuel Bradford, *The Imposter Detected, or a Review of Some of the Writings of 'Peter Porcupine'* (Philadelphia, 1796), pp. xii, xiii.
⁶ Quoted in Mary Clark, *Peter Porcupine in America* (Philadelphia, 1939), p. 7.
⁷ Cobbett, "Life and Adventures of Peter Porcupine," this volume, p. 171.

Early Life

When he recalled his upbringing in the prosperous hop-growing area around Farnham, Cobbett's mood was nostalgic, idyllic, and lyrical. He wrote of holidays, hunting, healthy work, and happy days in an England where decency, honesty, and self-respect were recognized and rewarded. Throughout his later writings, the idealized memory of his youth became a unifying symbol in his thought; his romantic identification with Old England was central to his self-perception and served as a yardstick against which he would measure democratic politics in America or governmental corruption at home. "All that I can boast of in my birth, is, that I was born in Old England," he informed his American audience in 1796. "I wish to see," he told his British readers eleven years later, "the poor men of England what the poor men of England were when I was born."[8]

Beneath this retrospective idealization of his early life, there were deep undercurrents of restlessness. He ran away from home to see Kew Gardens in London when he was only a boy, tried to join the Royal Navy after being filled with "astonishment and admiration" at the sight of the fleet off Spithead, and left Farnham for good at the age of twenty. Despite Cobbett's romantic nostalgia, the real world of rural England was too small for him. Books and politics pulled him outward and began to expand his horizons. He recalled going without supper at the age of eleven to buy a copy of Jonathan Swift's *Tale of a Tub* and described the experience as a "sort of birth of intellect." When the American Revolution brought politics into the English countryside, he listened attentively while his father defended the Patriots against the arguments of the local gardener, "a shrewd and sensible old Scotchman." "Had my father been on the other side," he added, "I should have been on the other side too." Farnham could not hold him. Like many other young men of the time, Cobbett wound up in London, looking for work. After toiling fifteen hours a day as an attorney's clerk ("when I think of the *saids* and *soforths*, and the counts of tautology that I scribbled over . . . my brain turns"), he escaped by joining the army.[9]

---

[8] Cobbett, "Life and Adventures," p. 157; *PR*, February 28, 1807. On the influence of the Surrey countryside on Cobbett's later outlook, see James Sambrook, *William Cobbett* (London, 1973), pp. 31–36, and Daniel Green, *Great Cobbett: The Noblest Agitator* (Oxford, 1985), pp. 24–37.

[9] Cobbett, "Life and Adventures," pp. 160–62, 165.

For the next eight years, from 1784 to 1791, he served with His Majesty's 54th Regiment of Foot; after thirteen months of training in England, he joined his regiment in the "woods and snows of Nova Scotia and New Brunswick." Reading voraciously, memorizing Bishop Lowth's *Grammar*, and mastering the plain style of writing, Cobbett emerged as a hardworking and self-disciplined soldier who quickly impressed his superiors. Among other things, he handled the administrative work of the regiment, designed and supervised the building of a barrack for four hundred men, wrote a short book on arithmetic for his fellow soldiers, helped introduce to the regiment a new system of drilling and weapons handling, and wrote up a report for the Loyalist Claims Commission in New Brunswick. Not surprisingly, he won rapid promotion to the rank of regimental sergeant major. "In my regiment," he boasted, "I was every thing: the whole corps was under my controul.... the fame of my service and talents ran through the whole country."[10]

At the same time, though, Cobbett felt a galling sense of resentment toward the society and the situation in which he found himself. He wrote scathingly about the social pretensions of the Loyalist elite in New Brunswick, and supported the popular party in the colony's first election at Saint John in 1785. And it grated to take orders from officers of higher birth but lower talent. "Those who were commanding me," he recalled, "... were, in everything except mere authority, my inferiors; and ought to have been commanded by me."[11] His anger reached the boiling point when he discovered that some of his officers were not only incompetent, but also practicing peculation. After his initial attempts to expose such corruption met with a hostile reaction, Cobbett decided to prepare secretly a case against the worst offenders, get safely out of the army, and then take legal action against them. The opportunity arose in the winter of 1791–92, when the regiment was sent back to England.

His return coincided with dramatic new developments in British political life. Inspired by the French Revolution and groaning under what Thomas Hardy called "the heavy pressure of the daily accu-

---

[10] *PR*, June 17, 1809. See also *PR*, December 6, 1817; November 21, 1818; November 22, 1828. Cobbett's career in Nova Scotia and New Brunswick is discussed in Wallace Brown, "William Cobbett in the Maritimes," *Dalhousie Review* 56 (1976), pp. 448–61.

[11] *PR*, June 17, 1809. On Cobbett's attitude to the Saint John election, see *PR*, December 13, 1817, and D. G. Bell, *Early Loyalist Saint John* (Fredericton, N.B., 1983), pp. 130–31, 142–44.

mulating taxes, and the consequent rise in the prices of all the necessaries of life," unprecedented popular radical democratic societies were beginning to organize themselves into a significant political force. "It was in 1792," wrote historian Gwyn Williams, "that 'the people' entered politics." And the ordinary tradesmen, shopkeepers and mechanics who formed the backbone of the societies derived much of their political vocabulary from Thomas Paine's enormously influential *Rights of Man*, a book that A. J. P. Taylor has called "the best statement of democratic belief in any language." The winter of 1791–92 witnessed the birth of the democratic movement in Britain.[12]

In this atmosphere, Cobbett secured an honorable discharge from the army and initiated court-martial proceedings against four of his former officers. Almost immediately, serious obstacles were put in his way: the government initially tried to hold the court-martial at the army base in Portsmouth rather than the more neutral location of London; the judge advocate general reduced the scope of the inquiry; and Cobbett's request that a key witness be discharged from the army was denied. In the middle of all this came the bombshell: the Secretary at War, Sir George Yonge, delivered a speech in Parliament that indicated the government tolerated corruption in the army and would rather increase the pay of common soldiers through raising taxes than reform the system. Beside himself with anger, Cobbett decided to take the issue to the public. The result was *The Soldier's Friend*, a remarkable (but anonymous) pamphlet that marked his entry into the field of political literature.[13]

In what would become classic Cobbett style, the pamphlet launched a stinging and sarcastic attack on the hypocrisy of the government for condoning in practice the corruption it condemned in theory. He exposed Yonge's cover-up of abuses in the army, explained the mechanics of peculation to his civilian readers, wrote with contempt of corrupt officers, and identified with the condition of the common

---

[12] Thomas Hardy, *Memoirs of Thomas Hardy* (London, 1832), p. 10; Gwyn A. Williams, *Artisans and Sans-Culottes* (London, 1968), p. 4; A. J. P. Taylor, quoted in Michael Foot and Isaac Kramnick, "Introduction" to *The Thomas Paine Reader* (Harmondsworth, 1987), p. 33. On the British popular radical movement of the 1790s, see E. P. Thompson, *The Making of the English Working Class* (Harmondsworth, 1970), and Albert Goodwin, *Friends of Liberty* (London, 1979).

[13] See *PR*, June 17, 1809, for Cobbett's own description of these events; for the views of one of his opponents, see Anon., *The Rival Imposters* (London, 1809). The best modern account of the affair is in Spater, *William Cobbett*, pp. 30–36.

soldier. Above all, Cobbett became politicized. If he had previously believed that corruption in the army was the exception rather than the rule, his experiences in England changed his mind. It now seemed clear that his personal grievances were the product of the political system. The government's refusal to remedy abuses, he wrote,

> points out in the clearest light the close connection that exists between the *ruling Faction* in this Country and the military Officers: and this connection ever must exist while we suffer ourselves to be governed by *a Faction*. If any other body of men had thus impudently set the laws of the land at defiance, if a *gang of robbers*, unornamented with red coats and cockades, had plundered their fellow citizens, what would have been the consequence? They would have been brought to justice, hanging or transportation would have been their fate; but it seems, the Army is become a *sanctuary* from the power of the law.

While the "ruling Powers" looked after themselves, he argued, the burden of looking after the ordinary soldiers fell on the ordinary people. No wonder, then, that there existed an "enormous load of taxes, that press out the very vitals of the People."[14]

In one sense, Cobbett's position can be seen as traditional and even conservative; he wanted the government to follow its own laws and to practice what it preached. By highlighting the discrepancy between the ideal and the real, he hoped to prevent the kind of misuse and abuse of power he had experienced in the army. Yet the pamphlet was also distinctly Paineite in tone—so much so, in fact, that at least one contemporary suspected it had been written by Paine himself.[15] Such suspicions were understandable; as Cobbett later admitted, writing from a Tory perspective, "I had not only been a republican, but an admirer of the writings of PAINE. The fault, therefore, if there was any, was in the head, and not in the heart; and, I do not think, that even the head will be much blamed by those who duly reflect, that I was, when I took up PAINE's book, a novice in politics, that I was boiling with indignation at the abuses I had witnessed, and that, as to the powers of the book itself, it required first a proclamation, then a law, and next the suspension of the *habeas-corpus* act, to counteract

---

[14] Cobbett, *The Soldier's Friend* (London, 1792), pp. 17, 20–21, 4.
[15] George Chalmers, *The Life of Thomas Pain* (London, 7th ed., 1793), p. 25.

them." The *Rights of Man* helped shape both the style and the content of *The Soldier's Friend*.[16]

By the standards of the day, Cobbett's pamphlet was almost certainly seditious. It was republished in 1793 at the price of twopence, cheap enough for most people to purchase; it was condemned by Lord Melville as "fraught with ten times more mischief than Paine's Rights of Man," and it was described as "a considerable source of the naval mutiny at the Nore" in 1797.[17] Had the government identified Cobbett as the author, he would have been in serious trouble; his publisher, James Ridgway, got four years in jail in 1793 for printing radical literature, and Cobbett could have expected a similar sentence. At the same time, his attempt to court-martial his officers threatened to backfire on him. Just before the trial, Cobbett learned that several soldiers from his regiment intended to give evidence that he had "damned and drunk to *the destruction of the House of Brunswick.*"[18] Under these circumstances, he decided that it was too dangerous to stay in England. In March 1792, he left for revolutionary France; six months later he was on his way to the United States.

Conversion to Conservatism

If we were able to cut ourselves off from the dubious wisdom of hindsight and were asked to predict Cobbett's future career in the United States, our conclusions would be clear: he would become a prominent Jeffersonian journalist, working with the many other British and Irish radicals who crossed the Atlantic during the 1790s to escape governmental repression. To make our case, we could point to several aspects of his early experiences and attitudes in England: his identification with a rural way of life, his hostility to the misuse and abuse of power, his tendency to contrast the real with the ideal, his treatment at the hands of the government, and his support for Paineite principles. And yet, we would be completely wrong. Within eighteen months of his arrival in the United States, Cobbett had reappeared on the other extreme of the political spectrum as an

---

[16] *PR*, October 5, 1805.

[17] The attacks are quoted in *PR*, October 5, 1805. On the general question of political radicalism in the army at this time and on the particular impact of Cobbett's pamphlet, see Clive Emsley, "Political Disaffection and the British Army in 1792," *Bulletin of the Institute of Historical Research* 48, no. 118 (1975), pp. 230–45, esp. p. 232.

[18] *PR*, June 17, 1809. On Ridgway's prosecution, see Goodwin, *Friends of Liberty*, p. 272.

The Life of William Cobbett, from James Gillray's version of Cobbett's life, published in 1809. During his court-martial proceedings in 1792 against his former officers, Cobbett had assured Sir Charles Gould, the judge advocate general, that if his charges were not well founded, he should burn in hell. Gillray takes Cobbett at his word. (Courtesy of the Trustees of the British Museum.)

aggressive conservative writer who denounced democracy, republicanism, Paine, and the rights of man with unparalleled ferocity. It was one of the most sudden, unexpected, and remarkable transformations of its time. What happened?

Part of the explanation lies in Cobbett's personal reactions to the United States. Having read positive accounts of the country by people like the Abbé Raynal, William Winterbotham, and Paine himself, Cobbett had expected to find a land of liberty, virtue, and simplicity. Instead, he discovered a wide gap between the America of his imagination and the America of his experience. The United States, he informed an English friend, was "exactly the contrary of what I expected it. The land is bad, rocky.... The seasons are detestable.... The people are worthy of the country—[a] cheating, sly, roguish gang."[19] Cobbett was not alone in his disillusionment; many other transatlantic radicals found Americans to be self-centered and avaricious. Wolfe Tone, the Irish revolutionary who took temporary refuge in the United States, commented in 1795 that the country was "like a beautiful scene in a theatre; the effect at a proper distance is admirable, but it will not bear a minute inspection."[20] But while most "ideological immigrants" eventually came to terms with their new environment, formed their own political networks, and pushed for greater democracy in the United States, Cobbett's initial impressions hardened into an enduring sense of anger and betrayal. Connecting the personal with the political, he rooted his negative reaction to the country in its republican form of government. "The truth is," he wrote in 1805, "the change in my way of thinking was produced by experience. I had an opportunity of *seeing* what republican government was; this experience overcame prejudice; I followed the dictates of truth and reason. Instead of that perfect freedom, of which PAINE had given me so flattering a description, I found myself placed under a set of petty, mean, despots, ruling by a perversion of the law of England."[21] The real contradicted the ideal; in the United States, Cobbett found corruption, self-aggrandizement, and the lust for power masquerading under the banner of liberty.

---

[19] Cobbett to Rachel Smither, July 7, 1794, in Lewis Melville, ed., *The Life and Letters of William Cobbett in England and America* (London, 1913), vol. 1, p. 87.

[20] Quoted in Michael Durey, "Thomas Paine's Apostles: Radical Emigrés and the Triumph of Jeffersonian Republicanism," *William and Mary Quarterly* 44 (October 1987), p. 673.

[21] *PR*, October 12, 1805.

This sense of the gap between republican professions and republican practice was intensified by the news coming across the Atlantic from revolutionary France. Under the pressures of external war and internal counterrevolution, radical politicians in August 1792 linked up with the Parisian sansculottes and provincial *fédérés* to sweep aside the monarchy and establish Europe's first democratic republic. As the military situation deteriorated and food shortages worsened, rumors of a counterrevolutionary "prison plot" precipitated the September Massacres, which resulted in the indiscriminate killing of well over a thousand prisoners. With the defeat of the invading armies at Valmy later that month, the immediate threat was over. But the entry of Britain into the war in February 1793, the French military reverses that spring, the effects of soaring inflation, and the growing tensions between Paris and the provinces all pushed the Revolution further to the left. In May and June, a Jacobin coup ousted the relatively moderate Girondins on the grounds that desperate circumstances demanded desperate measures. By September 1793, terror had become the order of the day.

Cobbett was shocked by this sequence of events. He had left France during the republican revolution of August 1792, and must have heard about the September Massacres shortly after arriving in the United States. Working initially in Wilmington, Delaware, as a teacher of English to émigrés from France and San Domingo, Cobbett was in close contact with people whose lives had been turned upside down by the revolution. The first thing he published in the United States was the translation of a French pamphlet on the impeachment of the Marquis de Lafayette, the French nobleman who had fought with Washington in the American War of Independence and helped to establish a constitutional monarchy in France, but who pulled back from the brink of republican democracy. There was no commentary; for once in his life, Cobbett allowed the story to speak for itself.[22] But the impeachment documents clearly revealed the existence of intolerance, judicial persecution, and popular intimidation in the name of liberty. Cobbett had already attacked the abuse of power in England; now he must have felt that the cure of republican democracy was far worse than the disease.

---

[22] *Impeachment of Mr. Lafayette. . . . Translated from the French by William Cobbett* (Philadelphia, 1793); see also Spater, *William Cobbett*, pp. 47–48.

Disillusioned with America and disgusted with France, Cobbett began to transform his deep attachment to rural England into a political identification with the land of his birth. What had not been apparent in his brief phase as a Paineite in England—and what Cobbett had probably not realized himself—was the depth of his English patriotism. It was only when he was outside his country (or his country's empire) that his latent patriotism became manifest. When he read or heard criticism of England, Cobbett bristled with rage. He had, in his own words, "long felt a becoming indignation at the atrocious slander that was continually vomitted forth against Great Britain"; by 1794 he could take it no longer and lashed out at the revilers of his country. His sense of Englishness, his affronted nationalism, overrode everything else. "Though I had been greatly disgusted at the trick played me in England, with regard to a court-martial," he recalled, "I forgot every thing when the honour of England was concerned." And even later in life, after he had come to reject the British "system" and transformed himself into a political radical, Cobbett never felt any reason to apologize for his patriotism in America; on the contrary, he remained proud of it. The problem, he wrote in 1817, was that he had confounded "the *government* of my country with *my country herself*."[23]

From this perspective, Cobbett's conversion to conservatism is not as puzzling as it first appears. The powerful patriotism that had been invisible at home was brought into sharp relief in America. The tension between the ideal and the real that had radicalized him in Britain lay behind his rejection of republicanism in America, as he attacked the United States for failing to live up to its reputation as the land of liberty. The blurring of the political and the personal, which had made him connect his treatment in the army with the system of government in Britain, drove him toward Toryism in America, as he equated his own negative experiences in the United States with democratic individualism. And the hostility he had displayed in England to the misuse and abuse of power made him turn against the revolution in France, where he believed the language of liberty concealed the reality of democratic tyranny. These attitudes—patriotism, idealism, the personalization of politics, and a strong but selective sense of justice—remained central and permanent features of Cobbett's outlook. In 1792, these views had impelled him toward Paineite repub-

---

[23] Cobbett, *The Democratic Judge* (Philadelphia, 1798), p. 7; *PR*, February 19, 1820; *PR*, January 4, 1817.

licanism, and in the early nineteenth century they would lead him in the direction of a socially conservative brand of political radicalism back in Britain. But for six crucial years in America, from 1794 to 1800, they turned him into a populist Tory writer who commanded the largest audience in the country.

Federalists and Republicans

Cobbett's American career coincided with deep divisions over the definition and direction of the new republic; the 1790s was one of the most polarized decades in the country's history. Against the background of the French Revolution and European war, the United States was faced with severe external pressures and internal tensions; at times, the very survival of the republic seemed in doubt. To the west, the United States was confronted by the presence of the British and Spanish empires. Britain controlled the St. Lawrence, maintained a military presence in the American Northwest, and tried to build up a Native American buffer state south of the Great Lakes to hold back the United States. Spain controlled the Mississippi, encouraged secessionist movements in Kentucky and Tennessee, and worked with the Creeks and Cherokees to contain the republic between the Atlantic and the Alleghenies. In the Atlantic, the United States was faced with the naval strength and unprecedented economic power of Britain as it began its take-off into the new world of the Industrial Revolution; in fact, the Anglo-American connection in the late eighteenth century constituted one of the first neocolonial relationships in history. In addition to the economic hammerlock of Britain, the United States also had to deal with the ideological and strategic imperatives of revolutionary France. Appealing to a common Franco-American republican consciousness, and attempting to use the United States as a base of operations against the British and Spanish empires, France hoped to recover the continental ground it had lost after the Conquest of 1760.[24]

[24] On the conflict of rival imperialisms for hegemony in North America, see Richard Van Alstyne, *The Rising American Empire* (Oxford, 1960); William Appleman Williams, *The Contours of American History* (Chicago, 1961); John C. Miller, *The Federalist Era* (New York, 1960); R. R. Palmer, *The Age of the Democratic Revolution: The Struggle* (Princeton, 1964), pp. 509–46; Samuel Flagg Bemis, *Pinckney's Treaty* (New Haven, 1960); J. Leitch Wright, Jr., *Britain and the American Frontier, 1783–1815* (Athens, Ga., 1975), pp. 66–102; Arthur Whitaker, *The Mississippi Question, 1795–1803* (Gloucester, Mass., 1934).

These external pressures interlocked with internal divisions, as Americans attempted to realize their own vision of continental and maritime power and to develop republican institutions that would consolidate the achievements of the revolution—to build, in short, their own empire of liberty. The stakes were high; many Americans were convinced that the decisions they made in the first years of the republic would decisively affect its future character. "Now is the seed time of continental union, faith and honour," Paine had written back in 1776. "The least fracture now will be like a name engraved with the point of a pin on the tender rind of a young oak; the wound will enlarge with the tree, and posterity read it in full grown characters."[25] By the 1790s, in the context of the polarization and politicization generated by the French Revolution, Americans split into two loose-knit but fiercely opposed political parties, the Federalists and the Republicans. Each accused the other of wounding the tree.

The Federalists, in power until 1800, were convinced that the greatest internal threat to the new republic came from excessive liberty, from the influence of the "people" on the government. In their view, the crust of the earth was very thin; beneath the surface of civil society, they believed, lurked dangerous passions and violent tendencies which could easily be exploited by unscrupulous and ambitious demagogues. "Our disease," wrote Federalist politician Fisher Ames, "is democracy. It is not the skin that festers—our very bones are carious, and their marrow blackens with gangrene."[26] To inoculate the United States against this potentially fatal illness, the Federalists attempted to build a strong central government based on the rule of the wealthy and respectable members of society. Right from the start of the Federalist era, men like John Adams had stressed the need to foster habits of deference to authority and wanted Americans to address their head of state as "His Elective Majesty" or "His Excellency," in imitation of British forms. Similarly, Alexander Hamilton maintained that the new government should use a mixture of patronage and power to inculcate a sense of obedience and should encourage religious beliefs that supported law and order.[27] But the key to the Federalist empire-

---

[25] Thomas Paine, *Common Sense*, in Philip S. Foner, ed., *The Complete Writings of Thomas Paine* (New York, 1945), vol. 1, p. 17. See also John R. Howe, Jr., "Republican Thought and the Political Violence of the 1790s," *American Quarterly* 19 (1967), pp. 147–65.

[26] Quoted in Miller, *Federalist Era*, p. 120.

[27] On the debate over titles in the new federal government, see Miller, *Federalist Era*, pp. 7–10; for Hamilton's views, see John R. Nelson, Jr., *Liberty and Property* (Baltimore, 1987), pp. 23–28, 32.

building strategy lay in its fiscal program. Above all, Hamilton's policies of funding the national debt, assuming state debts, and establishing a national bank were designed to bind the commercial elite and its economic dependents to the central government. In this way, power would be protected from the pressures of public opinion.

Central to this program were close economic and political ties with Britain. The revenues needed to finance Federalist fiscal policies came largely from Anglo-American trade, and the government's principal creditors were merchants whose livelihood depended on Anglo-American commerce; both the government and its creditors had an obvious interest in maintaining a harmonious relationship with the former Mother Country. And on the political level, conservative American politicians found much to admire in the British system of government; in 1787, for example, Hamilton described the British Constitution as "the best in the world." During the 1790s, in the context of international revolution and war, Britain appeared to many Federalists as a bastion of ordered, civilized, and constitutional government standing against the horrors of a democratic bloodbath. From the Federalist perspective, any disruption of the Anglo-American relationship would not only bring their entire empire-building strategy crashing down, but also increase the influence of French Jacobin principles in the United States. Not surprisingly, then, the Federalists preferred cooperation to confrontation with Britain.[28]

Such policies commanded considerable support in the United States. The Federalist program particularly appealed to the established elite in New England, the politically insecure tidewater planters of South Carolina, and the landed and mercantile aristocracy of the middle states. There was a strong Federalist presence in Cobbett's Philadelphia, where much of the merchant community had close commercial connections with Britain. But Federalism was by no means confined to the upper classes in America; it was embraced by a wide variety of social, regional, religious, and ethnic groups, including frontier farmers who depended on a powerful national government for protection, the inhabitants of the Potomac watershed who anticipated significant benefits from the location of the federal capital in Washington, the rural Anglicans and Methodists of southern Delaware, and many—but not all—immigrants from England throughout

---

[28] For an excellent analysis of Federalist political economy, see Nelson, *Liberty and Property*, pp. 22–65. See also Richard Buel, *Securing the Revolution: Ideology in American Politics, 1789–1815* (Ithaca, N.Y., 1972); Miller, *Federalist Era*, pp. 33–69, 99–125, 140–54; Williams, *Contours of American History*, pp. 162–70.

The Providential Detection, a typical Federalist view of Thomas Jefferson as an American Jacobin, prepared to sacrifice American independence to the Satanic forces of revolutionary France. Cobbett's own writings both reflected and reinforced this image of Jefferson. (Courtesy of the Library Company of Philadelphia.)

the country. Nor was Federalism an ideological monolith; it contained many shades of opinion and differences of emphasis, which would become increasingly apparent during the debates of the 1790s. At any rate, Federalism was sufficiently broad and variegated to ensure that many of its adherents would be attracted to at least some aspects of Cobbett's conservatism.[29]

Against these forms of Federalism stood the Republicans, who believed that the United States had more to fear from excessive power than excessive liberty, and who accused the Federalists of creating an aristocracy of wealth in a republic of supposed equals. The Republicans were strongest in the South, where a relatively cohesive white society rested on the foundation of slavery, where planters feared that an Anglo-American rapprochement would force them to pay back their prerevolutionary debts, and where Hamilton's fiscal program was rejected as a scheme to enrich northern stockholders at the expense of the rest of the country. But there was also an increasingly important urban wing of Republicanism, supported by manufacturers and mechanics who wanted protection from British imports and by the growing number of merchants who traded outside the British Empire. As the international war produced new commercial opportunities for men on the make, and as more and more farmers were drawn into new transatlantic trading networks, the Republicans reaped the benefits. "The strength of the Jeffersonian movement," observed Joyce Appleby, "was precisely in the fast-growing areas." And these areas included the politically crucial states of New York, Pennsylvania, and Maryland.[30]

From the Republican perspective, the Federalist vision of empire resulted in policies that perpetuated America's neocolonial status, supported Anglo-American commercial interests at the expense of domestic manufacturing, and aligned the United States with counterrevolutionary Britain against the "sister republic" in France. To establish the conditions for prosperity, stability, and liberty, argued the Republicans, the United States must break both the British economic

---

[29] Buel, *Securing the Revolution*, pp. 72–90; Alfred Young, *The Democratic-Republicans of New York* (Chapel Hill, N.C., 1967), pp. 566–75; Roland Baumann, "The Democratic-Republican Societies of Philadelphia: The Origins, 1776–1797" (Ph.D. dissertation, Pennsylvania State University, 1970), p. 411; Norman K. Risjord, *Chesapeake Politics, 1781–1800* (New York, 1978), pp. 396–400; John A. Munroe, *History of Delaware* (Newark, 1979), p. 86.

[30] Buel, *Securing the Revolution*, pp. 72–90; Nelson, *Liberty and Property*, pp. 80–99; Joyce Appleby, *Capitalism and a New Social Order* (New York, 1984), p. 48.

stranglehold and the domestic dominance of wealthy speculators. As a result, leading Republicans such as Thomas Jefferson and James Madison advocated commercial discrimination against Britain, demanded the development of a more diversified economic system, pushed for the democratization of the political process, and remained broadly receptive to the ideology of republicanism in France.[31]

Among the strongest supporters of the French Revolution were the Democratic Societies, which emerged in 1793 to protect the United States from international counterrevolution and internal "monarchical" and "aristocratic" tendencies. Emanating from Philadelphia, and drawing considerable support from the "middling" orders of society, the societies stood for human rights, universal white male suffrage, economic liberty, and social justice.[32] Embracing the style and slogans of revolutionary France, the democrats went around greeting each other as "citizens," wore caps of liberty, sported red, white and blue cockades, attended "civic feasts" celebrating the triumph of French armies over the "leagued despots" of Europe, and injected a spirit of secular millenarianism and egalitarianism into American politics. In imitation of the French revolutionary calendar, in which 1792 became Year 1 of the Republic, the secretary of Philadelphia's Democratic Society began to date resolutions from America's own Year 1, 1776; thus 1794 became also the Eighteenth Year of American Independence. Taken together, the American and French revolutions would begin the world over again and sweep away the accumulated rubbish of errors of the past; in Philadelphia, there were even ritual reenactments of the guillotining of Louis XVI. "He was guillotined in effigy, in the capital of the union, twenty or thirty times every day, during one whole winter, and part of the summer," wrote Cobbett, who was incensed by the spectacle.[33] Indeed, Cobbett's writings are one of our best sources on the activities of the American democrats.

The Democratic Societies were forming at precisely the time that Citizen Edmund Genet, the new foreign minister from republican France, arrived in the United States. Genet realized that the United States was determined to stay out of the widening international war, and he pushed for an American definition of neutrality that would, in

---

[31] Nelson, *Liberty and Property*, pp. 66–171; Appleby, *Capitalism and a New Social Order*, pp. 51–105.

[32] The best study of the Democratic Societies remains Eugene P. Link, *Democratic-Republican Societies, 1790–1800* (New York, 1942). But see also Philip S. Foner, ed., *The Democratic-Republican Societies, 1790–1800: A Documentary Source-Book* (Westport, Conn., 1976).

[33] Cobbett, "History of the American Jacobins," this volume, p. 200.

practice, benefit France at the expense of Britain. He set out to launch French privateers from American ports, organize expeditions against the British and Spanish colonies on the continent, and arrange for the export of American grain to feed the French Revolution. The United States and France would both gain, he maintained: the ties between the "sister republics" would be strengthened, Britain's dominance in the Atlantic would be reduced, the encirclement of the older powers in the West would be broken, and Britain's attempt to starve the revolution into submission would be thwarted.[34]

Within America's growing radical movement, these proposals had considerable appeal. Although Genet in no sense "created" the Democratic Societies, he did serve as a source of inspiration, as a symbol around which they could rally. From the moment he landed at Charleston, Genet was given a hero's welcome; he was swept on a wave of democratic republican enthusiasm to Philadelphia, where he was greeted by large crowds and wined and dined by the local Republicans. For a few brief weeks, it looked as if Genet's presence would strengthen popular opposition to Federalist policies. Jefferson certainly thought so; in his view, pro-French feeling would reinforce the position of Republicans in Congress and thus provide a counterweight to Hamilton's influence in the government.[35]

But it did not turn out that way. The crunch came when Washington, fearful that Genet's activities would plunge the United States into an unwanted war with Britain, ordered the French minister to put a stop to privateering. Convinced that public opinion was behind him, Genet not only refused to comply, but also threatened to take his case directly to the people over the head of the President. In taking this stand, however, Genet overreached himself; in effect, he became a victim of his own popularity. Moving in for the kill, Hamilton and the Federalists immediately accused him of trying to use democratic sentiment to subvert the institutions of the United States and portrayed the Republicans as agents of French revolutionary imperialism. Under these circumstances, most of Genet's former supporters abandoned him as quickly as possible. The Republicans and Genet each had tried to use the other for their own ends; neither had succeeded. The result was a crack in pro-French sentiment that people like Cobbett would attempt to widen and deepen.

If the Genet affair revealed the possibilities—and the limitations—

---

[34] On Genet's mission, see Harry Ammon, *The Genet Mission* (New York, 1973).
[35] Ammon, *Genet Mission*, pp. 62–64.

of a conjuncture between French emissaries and American democrats, the Whiskey Rebellion of 1794 appeared to confirm Federalist fears about the fragility of the social order in the United States.[36] A reaction against administration attempts to enforce the excise on whiskey in western Pennsylvania, the rebellion was part of a wider movement for frontier autonomy in early national America, and was rooted in long-standing western grievances against the eastern establishment. Westerners needed access to the Mississippi as an outlet for their produce; the federal government appeared to be dragging its feet on the issue, and powerful eastern mercantile interests were manifestly opposed to rapid western expansion. Westerners wanted strong military action against the Native Americans in the area, but the campaigns by Generals Harmar and St. Clair in 1790 and 1791 had been badly organized and failed miserably. Westerners were mired in poverty while wealthy eastern speculators—including President Washington himself—owned vast tracts of land. Into this tense social environment came the excise on whiskey, which ran into popular traditions of hostility to "internal" taxes and threatened to damage the only successful industry in the region. It is no wonder that the Westerners resisted.

What is particularly striking about the Whiskey Rebellion is the speed at which it spread. From a minor skirmish with excise officers, it quickly escalated into massive protest meetings, interception of the federal mail, dark threats to government informers signed by "Tom the Tinker," and talk about taking Pittsburgh (which was described as a latter-day Sodom) and marching on to Philadelphia. At the Braddock's Field demonstration of August 1, attended by some 7,000 people, a six-striped flag for an independent western state was raised; amid rumors that the rebels were negotiating with Britain and Spain for assistance in a separatist revolution, signs of unrest appeared throughout the western frontier. Under these circumstances, the government took vigorous action to contain and crush the rebellion. Fearing the contagion of disaffection, the dangers of democracy, and the breakup of the country, Washington organized an army of 13,000 men—larger than any he had commanded against the British during the War of Independence—to impose federal authority in the West. And in November, after the rebellion had been defeated, he accused

---

[36] The best modern treatments of the Whiskey Rebellion are Stephen Boyd, ed., *The Whiskey Rebellion: Past and Present Perspectives* (Westport, Conn., 1985), and Thomas Slaughter, *The Whiskey Rebellion: Frontier Epilogue to the American Revolution* (New York, 1986).

"certain self-created societies"—the Democratic Societies—of fomenting revolt in the region.

In truth, the relationship between the societies and the Rebellion was complex and ambiguous. The Mingo Creek Society in western Pennsylvania, described by one contemporary as "the cradle of the insurrection," may actually have been a moderating influence; on the other hand, the very existence of such societies in the West probably contributed to antigovernment and antieastern sentiment. In Philadelphia, the Democratic Society opposed both the excise on whiskey and the armed action against it; when a resolution that described the westerners' behavior as "an outrage upon order and democracy" was introduced, the society split down the middle. Meanwhile, many of the state's militia officers and leading Republican politicians wavered before coming down on the government's side. Taking advantage of such division and indecision, the Federalists attempted to isolate and politically destroy the democratic opposition. In the short run, at least, they were successful.[37]

Along with the twin threats of popular unrest and French revolutionary imperialism, the Federalists were also faced in 1794 with the alarming prospect of an economic or even a military confrontation with Britain. In the Atlantic, the Royal Navy was seizing American ships that carried French goods; in the Northwest, Britain appeared to be encouraging the Native Americans to fight the United States. Desperate to avoid a conflict that would leave its empire-building strategy in ruins, the American government decided to send John Jay across the Atlantic to open up negotiations with Britain. There, in London, Jay bowed to George III, praised the king's "justice and benevolence," kissed the hand of the queen, hobnobbed with lords and ladies, and acted on the principle that "the quarrel between Britain and America was a family quarrel, and it is time that it should be made up."[38] And there, in London, he succeeded in his attempt to defuse Anglo-American tensions and win the agreement that bears his name—Jay's Treaty.[39]

---

[37] Slaughter, *Whiskey Rebellion*, pp. 164–65; Link, *Democratic-Republican Societies*, pp. 145–48; Foner, *Democratic-Republican Societies*, pp. 27–30; William Miller, "The Democratic Societies and the Whiskey Insurrection," *Pennsylvania Magazine of History and Biography* 62 (1938), pp. 324–49; Baumann, "Democratic-Republican Societies of Philadelphia," pp. 471–93.

[38] Quoted in Miller, *Federalist Era*, p. 164.

[39] The classic work is Samuel Flagg Bemis, *Jay's Treaty: A Study in Commerce and Diplomacy* (New York, 1924); see also Jerald A. Combs, *The Jay Treaty: Political Battleground of the Founding Fathers* (Berkeley, 1970).

The great strength of the treaty, from the Federalist viewpoint, was that it secured Anglo-American peace and a British promise to pull out of the American Northwest. But the price was high; the United States gave up the principle of freedom of the seas and agreed to conduct its trade along lines approved by Britain. Among other things, the treaty prevented the United States from discriminating against British imports and British ships, established procedures to settle prerevolutionary debts owed to Britain, and severely restricted American commerce with France. When the terms were leaked to the press in the summer of 1795, there was a storm of protest. The treaty not only threatened the economic interests of small producers, southern planters, and merchants who traded with Britain's enemies; it also appeared as a betrayal of both the "sister republic" and the "spirit of 1776." "A Treaty with Great Britain," wrote Alexander Dallas, regarding British political influence as a kind of economically transmitted disease, "is in every view unfriendly to *the People* of the United States; because, it will give her an influence upon our Government hostile to liberty; for a nation so debauched and corrupt, must communicate her debauchery and corruption to those with whom her intercourse is easy and familiar."[40]

For over a year, the fate of the treaty hung in the balance, as President Washington weighed its advantages and disadvantages. What tipped the scales was Britain's release in the summer of 1795 of intercepted French documents that indicated Secretary of State Edmund Randolph had been involved in intrigues with Genet's replacement, Joseph Fauchet. "The truth is," commented John C. Miller, "Randolph's actions convinced the President that French influence was rife even in the highest councils of the government and that unless a settlement was made with Great Britain the United States stood in grave danger of being converted to a French satellite."[41] In August 1795, Washington signed. During the spring of 1796, the battle over the treaty's implementation shifted to the House of Representatives, where the congressmen were evenly divided. The tie was broken by Frederick Muhlenberg, the chairman of the House and a Republican; to everyone's surprise, he cast his vote in favor. It cost him; a few days later he was stabbed by his brother-in-law for his "base desertion" of the cause.

[40] [Alexander Dallas], *Letters of Franklin on the Conduct of the Executive* (Philadelphia, 1795), pp. 15–16.
[41] Miller, *Federalist Era*, p. 171.

Domestically, the debate over the treaty hastened the development of party politics, as Federalists and Republicans organized themselves against each other; internationally, it plunged Franco-American relations into crisis. Internal and external forces increasingly came together, as Citizen Adet, the new French minister to the United States, supported the Republican attempt to block the treaty in the House of Representatives and tried to sway the 1796 presidential election against the Federalist John Adams and toward the Republican Thomas Jefferson. With the failure of these efforts, Franco-American relations rapidly deteriorated; France began to seize American ships in the Atlantic and explored ways to reassert itself in the continental North and West. Then, in April 1798, came the shock of the so-called XYZ affair, when President Adams publicized the French attempt to bribe three American commissioners sent to Paris for negotiations. For the next few months, the United States succumbed to a species of war fever; John Adams was kept so busy writing replies to the anti-French addresses pouring into his office that his wife began to fear for his health. In this situation, Congress passed the Alien and Sedition Acts, which were designed to prevent the emergence of a Jacobin International in the United States, muzzle Republican journalists, and consolidate the position of the Federalists in power.[42]

And yet, the Quasi-War between France and the United States did not turn into a full-scale conflict, and the Republican press was not politically destroyed. As France's international position weakened after the disastrous Egyptian campaign in 1798, its government sent out peace feelers to the United States. In what he would later regard as the most courageous decision of his political career, Adams responded by reopening negotiations with Paris. His decision outraged the Hamiltonian Federalists, who had wanted the United States to join Britain in an anti-Jacobin crusade that would make the world safe from democracy. During the election campaign of 1800, Adams was hit from both sides—from Republicans who accused him of being a power-hungry crypto-monarchist, and from Hamiltonians who accused him of attempting to win popular approval by abandoning his principles and becoming a dupe of France. The Federalist party fell apart at the seams, opening the way for the Republican victory which Jefferson described as the "revolution of 1800."

[42] On the deterioration of Franco-American relations, see Van Alstyne, *Rising American Empire*, pp. 74–76; Miller, *Federalist Era*, pp. 132–39; Palmer, *Democratic Revolution: The Struggle*, pp. 516–43; Mason Wade, "Quebec and the French Revolution of 1789:

Cobbett's Toryism

Cobbett was in the thick of these political controversies, responding to the immediacy of events, exorcising the spectre of Jacobinism, and extolling the virtues of true British liberty. Pragmatic rather than philosophical, he was more concerned with winning arguments than winning prizes for intellectual consistency. If lying through his teeth or concealing his real opinions would help him advance the cause of Britain in America, then Cobbett would lie through his teeth or conceal his real opinions. When he began his career as a Tory journalist in Philadelphia, he pretended to be an American to increase the acceptability of his ideas. When the Federalists were in power, Cobbett described his purpose as "keeping alive an attachment to the Constitution of the United States"; but after the Republicans took over, he dismissed that same constitution as "impractical nonsense." And when he learned of the efforts of men like William Blount and William Bowles to increase Britain's influence in America, Cobbett publicly dissociated himself from their actions while privately hoping that they would succeed.[43] For Cobbett, the means were justified by the end; he used every available weapon to discredit the democrats and was not particularly squeamish about contradicting himself in the process. Nevertheless, through even his most polemical writings it is possible to detect certain broad patterns of thought that characterized his conservatism.

The main thrust of his thought was negative; Cobbett was happier attacking democracy than praising monarchy and happiest of all when he was needling his Jacobin opponents. His anti-Jacobin posi-

---

The Missions of Henry Mezière," *Canadian Historical Review* 31 (1950), pp. 345–68; T. S. Webster, "A New Yorker in the Era of the French Revolution: Stephen Thorn, Conspirator for a Canadian Revolution," *New York Historical Society Quarterly* 53 (1969), pp. 251–72; Jeanne A. Ojala, "Ira Allen and the French Directory, 1796: Plans for the Creation of the Republic of United Columbia," *William and Mary Quarterly* 36 (1979), pp. 436–48; Whitaker, *Mississippi Question*, pp. 101–29. On the Alien and Sedition Acts, see John C. Miller, *Crisis in Freedom: The Alien and Sedition Acts* (Boston, 1951), and James Morton Smith, *Freedom's Fetters: The Alien and Sedition Laws and American Civil Liberties* (Ithaca, N.Y., 1956).

[43] Cobbett, "A Bone to Gnaw, for the Democrats," this volume, p. 98; "Life and Adventures," p. 178; *PR*, July 10, 1802. On the Blount conspiracy, see *Congressional Records of 1797* in *Porcupine's Works* (henceforth *PW*), vol. 9, pp. 135–80; on Bowles, see Elisha Douglass, "The Adventurer Bowles," *William and Mary Quarterly* (1949), pp. 3–23. For Cobbett's views, see Cobbett to William Windham, 1803, in Melville, *Life and Letters*, vol. 2, pp. 181–82, and *The Porcupine*, July 21, 1801.

tion repeated standard Anglo-American Loyalist arguments, but was no less powerful for that; indeed, his lack of originality was an asset rather than a liability, as he struck deep chords in the American consciousness. In Cobbett's view, democracy was a utopian attempt to impose abstract theories on complex realities, with disastrous results. As he argued in his first American pamphlet, "Observations on the Emigration of Dr. Joseph Priestley," democrats were "system mongers" who tried to make circumstances conform to their "visionary" theories, instead of making their theories conform to circumstances. "They do not consider what *can* be done, but what they think ought to be done," wrote Cobbett. "They have no calculating principle to direct them to discover whether a reform will cost them more than it is worth or not. They do not set down to count the cost; but, the object being as they think desirable, the means are totally disregarded."[44]

The inevitable result of such an approach, Cobbett contended, was revolutionary terror—the oppression of the people in the name of the People. Arguing that political actions should be judged by their probable effects rather than their intentions, Cobbett criticized people like Priestley for failing to cope with the consequences of their philosophy. "Either he saw the consequences of the French revolution or he did not foresee them," wrote Cobbett of Priestley. "If he did not, he must confess that his penetration was far inferior to that of his antagonists, and even to that of the multitude of his countrymen; for they all foresaw them. If he did foresee them, he ought to blush at being called the 'friend of human happiness;' for, to foresee such dreadful calamities and to form a deliberate plan for bringing them upon his country he must have a disposition truly diabolical. If he did not foresee them, he must have an understanding little superior to that of an idiot: If he did, he must have the heart of a *Marat*. Let him choose."[45] Among Priestley's "antagonists," of course, was Edmund Burke, whose *Reflections on the Revolution in France* (1790) had predicted that France would slide into increasing chaos and violence. When Cobbett wrote, it was as if Burke had crossed the Atlantic, recast his arguments in the plain style, and tapped into the reservoir of populist Toryism in the United States.

Equally Burkean was Cobbett's view that democracy would culminate in the tyranny of the majority. The rule of the mob, Cobbett

---

[44] Cobbett, "Observations on the Emigration of Dr. Joseph Priestley," this volume, pp. 64–66.
[45] Ibid., pp. 67–68.

argued, would result in the disruption of the entire system of property relations that held society together. "When once the lower orders of the people, those who have nothing, begin to give law to those who have something, a state of anarchy is at no great distance," he wrote. "This dreadful scourge now menaces the United States, and the only way of avoiding it is for every honest man, every man of property, to give his hearty and sincere support to the General Government." Not only did the majority lack property; it also lacked reason. "We are afraid to put men to live and trade each on his own private stock of reason," Burke had written, "because we suspect that this stock in each man is small." Cobbett agreed; he spoke scathingly of the "CRAWLING DEMAGOGUES" and "popular parasites" who pandered to "jealousy, envy, revenge, and every passion that can disgrace the heart of man," and who would willingly "sacrifice truth, honour, justice, and even common sense, to the stupid stare and momentary huzza of the populace." He was in no doubt that democracy would destroy both freedom of property and freedom of expression—a view that had also been expressed by many of the Founding Fathers at the Constitutional Convention back in 1787.[46]

Just as democracy disrupted property relations in society, argued Cobbett, it also undermined the Christian basis of morality that was essential to civilized behavior. Operating from the premise that civil order and religious order were inseparable, he pointed out that a disproportionate number of Jacobins were dissenters, deists, or atheists—people who rejected all authority, secular or spiritual. "His religion is exactly of a piece with his politics," Cobbett commented after reading Thomas Paine's deist *Age of Reason*, the book that had poured scorn on scriptural revelation; "one inculcates the right of revolting against government, and the other that of revolting against God. Having succeeded against the Lord's anointed [Louis XVI] . . . he turned his impious arms against the Lord himself. The process is perfectly natural, as has been exemplified in the conduct of others as well as that of Paine." And the process, Cobbett believed, was producing entirely predictable results; lacking a strong religious foundation, the United States was becoming a corrupt, immoral and dishonest

---

[46] Cobbett, *A Little Plain English* (Philadelphia, 1795), p. 110; Edmund Burke, *Reflections on the Revolution in France* (London, 1790; reprint, Harmondsworth, 1968), p. 183; Cobbett, "Preface" to *Plain English*, p. 6; *Plain English*, p. 3; Nelson, *Liberty and Property*, pp. 11–15.

society. "In such a state of morals," he wrote, "there can be *no real public liberty*."⁴⁷

One of the most disturbing aspects of this development, in Cobbett's view, was its effect on the traditional family values that underpinned the social order. Again, one is reminded of Burke, who had written in his *Reflections* that "to love the little platoon we belong to in society, is the first principle (the germ as it were) of public affections." In his autobiography, Cobbett had romanticized his upbringing in England; in later years, he continued to write in idealistic terms about his own family life, even though his wife had attempted suicide and his children had turned against him. According to the ideal that he held with such tenacity, the mutual obligations, duties and feelings of affection that ought to exist between husband and wife served as a model and exemplar for social relations in general. The husband provided for and protected the wife, and the wife honored and obeyed the husband; each respected and loved the other. But democratic ideology and irreligion, he believed, were subverting these reciprocal relations and eroding established gender roles. In this respect, his imagery is illuminating; France was variously portrayed as a "whore," as "guilty of poligamy," and as a "cruel spouse" attempting to seduce John Bull. "How happy were we in escaping a marriage with a termagent like this," he wrote. Any talk of women's rights appeared particularly threatening; the spheres would be thrown out of joint, and chaos would follow. With this outlook, Cobbett scornfully dismissed the feminism of Mary Wollstonecraft, ridiculed the writings of Susanna Rowson, and sneered at the idea of women in politics.⁴⁸

Without stable property relations, established religious values, and traditional familial and communal loyalties, felt Cobbett, there could be no social cohesion; without social cohesion, there was only the war of all against all. From this perspective, democracy was the very antithesis of liberty, the ingratiating mask that concealed the reality of narrow self-interest and ambition. "*Liberty*, according to the Demo-

---

⁴⁷ Cobbett, *Political Censor* (henceforth *PC*), May 1796, pp. 196–97; see also "Pen Portraits," this volume, p. 219; *PR*, April 2, 1808; August 22, 1807. See also *Porcupine's Gazette* (henceforth *PG*), September 26, 1797; October 4, 1797; *PW*, vol. 9, pp. 3–6; *PR*, October 12, 1805.

⁴⁸ Burke, *Reflections*, p. 135; Cobbett, *A Bone to Gnaw, Part II* (Philadelphia, 1795), pp. 59–61; "A Kick for a Bite," this volume, pp. 128–34; "Bone to Gnaw," pp. 89–90. On the gap between the ideal and the real in Cobbett's own family life, see Spater, *William Cobbett*, pp. 518–19.

cratic Dictionary," Cobbett remarked, "does not mean *freedom from oppression*; it is a very comprehensive term, signifying, among other things, *slavery, robbery, murder*, and *blasphemy*." The democrats who volunteered to fight for Genet against Spain and Britain were a case in point: "For one of them, who was actuated by a love of liberty," he wrote, "there were five hundred who were actuated by a love of plunder. Some of them longed for a dive into the Spanish mines, and, in idea, already heard the chinking of the doubloons; while others were eyeing the British merchant-men with that kind of savage desire, with which the wolf surveys a herd of fat oxen." But the clearest example of democratic hypocrisy, in Cobbett's view, lay in the contradiction between the language of liberty and the reality of slavery in the American republic. Not that Cobbett himself favored emancipation; on the contrary, he adopted a crude form of racism that makes for extremely unpleasant reading. His purpose was not to help black slaves, but to expose the emptiness of all that democratic cant about liberty and equality. When he saw advertisements in democratic newspapers for slaves, Cobbett went for the jugular: "And these are the people, my God!" he exclaimed, "who talk about the *natural* and *unalienable* rights of man—and who make such a boast of the purity of their principles. Never was there any thing in the world, that exhibited such a base, odious, and disgusting contrast as the professions and the conduct of this race of patriots."[49]

Democracy, then, was associated with hypocrisy, unbridled ambition, the breakdown of the family, the tyranny of the majority, and terror. If anyone wanted "a striking and experimental proof of the horrible effects of anarchy and infidelity," he continued, they need only cast their eyes across the Atlantic to France. In France, he argued, the ties of obligation, duty, respect, and honor had been severed; unscrupulous and unprincipled Jacobin demagogues mouthed the slogans of liberty while ruthlessly crushing their enemies, suppressing freedom of expression, and practicing the politics of plunder. Instead of Christianity, there was the bizarre spectacle of the Cult of the Supreme Being and the worship of Robespierre; instead of order, there were unparalleled horrors and atrocities that turned the country into "a gloomy wilderness watered with rivers of human

---

[49] Cobbett, "Bone to Gnaw," p. 95n; "History of the American Jacobins," p. 189; *PW*, vol. 8, pp. 122–23. For Cobbett's racism, see *PR*, July 28, 1804.

blood." And what had happened in France could also occur in the United States, where there existed "a hardened and impious faction, whose destructive principles, if not timely and firmly opposed, may one day render the annals of America as disgraceful as those of the French revolution." The conclusion was clear: the "just and humane people in the United States of America" must destroy the scourge of Jacobinism before it destroyed them.⁵⁰

If France symbolized for Cobbett all the evils of democracy, Britain represented the benefits of monarchy; if France stood as a clear and terrible warning to the United States, Britain was a model of peace, order, and good government. As he took on the Jacobins in America, Cobbett increasingly came to see himself as the personification of Englishness. "Almost as often as I have mentioned Old England," he wrote in 1798, "I have boasted of its being my native country. I have a thousand times expressed my attachment to it, and my respect and veneration for the King's Government, family, and person. . . . Where is the unnatural brute who would caress me for disowning the land where I first drew my breath, where my forefathers lie buried, and where my parents yet live? What! forswear my kindred, my country, and my King!—I would almost as soon forswear my God."⁵¹

When Cobbett thought of Old England, he thought of a hierarchical, organic society bound together by benevolent rulers and loyal subjects. "As the state cannot, by its own arbitrary will, withhold that protection which is the birthright of any individual subject," he wrote, "so no subject can, by his arbitrary will, alienate that allegiance which is the right of the state." The state was symbolized by the person of the monarch, whose central concern was "the advancement and the preservation of the power and glory of the nation, and *the happiness of his subjects in general.*" The British Constitution was seen as a harmonious whole in which the different orders complemented rather than competed with each other. While democratic republicans challenged the concept of constitutional checks and balances from the left, Cobbett attacked it from the right. "Nothing is more invidious, nothing more repugnant to the principles of the monarchy, nothing more dangerous and leading to consequences more destructive," he maintained, "than this whiggish doctrine of *separate powers*, acting in opposition to

---

⁵⁰ Cobbett, "The Bloody Buoy," this volume, p. 154; see also *Bone to Gnaw, Part II*, p. 42.
⁵¹ *PW*, vol. 8, pp. 14–15.

each other." Like the prominent English Loyalist John Reeves, Cobbett believed in monarchical rather than mixed government.[52]

Because Britain's system of government rested on the accumulated wisdom of the ages, felt Cobbett, it had succeeded in securing prosperity, justice, and *"real* liberty" for its subjects. Just as he judged democracy in France by its negative consequences, Cobbett assessed monarchy in Britain by its positive results. In Britain, he wrote, "the granaries were full"—and the ability of a government to feed its people would remain Cobbett's principal criterion of political success. (Later in life, long after he had returned to radicalism, he debated with a fellow reformer who wanted to educate working people in the scientific principles of Francis Bacon; the only "bacon" the people needed, argued Cobbett, was bacon in their bellies.) In Britain, according to Cobbett, an independent and impartial judicial system guaranteed each individual security from oppression—anyone who doubted that need only remember that two loyal church-and-king supporters had recently been hanged for their part in rioting against the disloyal dissenter Joseph Priestley in 1791. And in Britain, Cobbett maintained, there was more freedom of the press than anywhere else in the world—certainly more than in America, where the democrats acted as if "the press is free for them, and them alone."[53] This portrait of the old country, it is clear, reveals more about the condition of Cobbett's mind than the condition of England. But then, for Cobbett, the England that existed in his imagination was the only one that really counted.

From this broad pro-British and anti-Jacobin perspective, Cobbett grappled with the particulars of American politics, the "details and local circumstances" at which he excelled.[54] In the world according to Cobbett, the Democratic Societies, Genet's mission, and the Whiskey Rebellion were the visible manifestations of a Franco-American Jacobin conspiracy. The French government, he argued, wanted to control the United States and bring it into the war against Britain. To accomplish its aims, France sent Genet to America with instructions to

---

[52] Cobbett, *PC*, November 1796, p. 32; *PW*, vol. 8, p. 136; *PG*, August 24, 1797; for Cobbett's ideological affinity with Reeves, see *PR*, January 29, 1803.

[53] *PW*, vol. 11, p. 139; Cobbett, "Observations on the Emigration," pp. 84, 56; Cobbett, *The Scare-Crow* (Philadelphia, 1796), p. 19.

[54] The phrase comes from William Hazlitt, "Character of Cobbett," in P. P. Howe, ed., *Complete Works of William Hazlitt*, vol. 8, p. 52. Although Hazlitt was commenting on Cobbett's English writings, his remark applies equally well to Cobbett's American career.

Introduction [31]

link up with the American democrats, those "men of bad moral characters" who were hostile to any form of authority. "They are a sort of flesh flies," he wrote, "that naturally settle on the excremental and corrupted parts of the body politic." This unholy union between Genet and disaffected Americans produced the Democratic Societies, which existed "for the express purpose of clogging the wheels of government, weakening its power, and exciting a spirit of discontent among the people, that might acquire strength enough to force it into a war on the side of France, or totally annihilate it." In this view, American democrats appeared as either knaves or dupes—or, more probably, a combination of both.[55]

Only against this background, Cobbett continued, was it possible to understand the Whiskey Rebellion of 1794. The insurrection, he insisted, was "fomented by democratic fuel, [and] paid for with French gold"; it was part of the grand plan to destroy the government and turn the United States into a French satellite. "During two years had the Western complaints existed," Cobbett observed; "the complainants had often assembled, and had passed resolves without number about their detestable drink; but never till now did they join their cause to that of France: never till now did they wear national cockades, or rally under the *tree of liberty* mounted with a bloody Parisian cap. Will any man in his senses believe that these were mere whims, freaks of fancy, that came athwart their brains by chance, without the least advice or prior instruction from their friends in the East?" It was this conjunction of western grievances and French revolutionary ideology that was so dangerous, in Cobbett's view, and that fully justified Washington's firm action against the rebels. He believed that the government's vigorous response had gone far toward breaking the Jacobin conspiracy; it had not only defeated the rebellion, he argued, but also divided and discredited the democrats, who were now becoming "less daring and insolent" than before.[56]

Just as Cobbett supported the government's suppression of dissent at home, he welcomed its increasing alignment with Britain abroad. In particular, he embraced Jay's Treaty as a means of restoring good Anglo-American relations, isolating revolutionary France and further undermining American democrats. Against Republican arguments that the treaty was unnecessary and unjust, Cobbett replied

---

[55] Cobbett, "History of the American Jacobins," pp. 185–86, 215.
[56] Ibid, pp. 206, 211. See also "Bone to Gnaw," pp. 99–102.

that it was essential to regulate the growing volume of Anglo-American trade, to "terminate all differences in an amicable manner," and to secure the northwest posts that Britain had held since 1783. If the terms of the treaty were not as advantageous as Americans might have wished, he added, they were as good as a relatively weak and economically dependent republic could expect to extract from the most powerful nation in the world. Against the Republican view that the treaty would infect the United States with British "debauchery and corruption" and subversive "monarchical principles," Cobbett reminded his readers that American law and government already rested on British foundations and quoted extensively from Burke's parliamentary speeches to underline the point. And against Republican complaints that America was abandoning France, Cobbett rejoiced that the United States was finally shaking itself free of pernicious French influences. One of the principal benefits of the treaty, in his view, was that it protected Americans from French attempts to embroil the United States in a diversionary war against Britain, "at the expense of your prosperity, and even your very existence as a nation."[57]

For eight critical months before and during the congressional debate over the treaty's implementation, Cobbett repeated these arguments in a relentless barrage of words directed against the Republicans. Later in life, he insisted that without his efforts the treaty would never have been ratified; for that reason, he wrote in his usual modest and unassuming manner, it should really have been called "Cobbett's Treaty."[58]

Cobbett had every reason to feel triumphant in 1796. The Democratic Societies had run out of steam, Genet's mission had backfired, the Whiskey Rebellion had been defeated, and Jay's Treaty—or Cobbett's Treaty—had brought the United States closer to Britain. But he did not regard the Anglo-American commercial treaty as an end in itself; rather, he saw it as an important first step in the direction of a full-scale military alliance between Britain and America against France. Such an alliance, he argued, would "cut off the cankering, sans-culotte connexion, and leave the country once more sound and *really independent*." It would put an end to French revolutionary imperialist designs on the North American continent, and enable Britain

[57] Cobbett, *Plain English*, pp. 9, 48, 62, 86, 96.
[58] *PR*, August 22, 1829; see also *PR*, January 29, 1825.

and the United States—who were, after all, natural allies—to clear the Spanish out of the New World. "America and Great Britain might bid defiance to the world," he wrote. "The map of this continent and its islands lies open before them: they might cut and carve for themselves, and sit down in the quiet enjoyment of their conquests."[59]

In taking this position, Cobbett initially found himself on the far right of the political spectrum. "Let not the reader start," he wrote immediately after his call for war against France, anticipating the shock. "He must accustom himself to think and talk on the subject, and the sooner he begins the better." During 1797 and 1798, as Franco-American relations deteriorated into the Quasi-War, more and more Americans did indeed think and talk on the subject. In the context of French attacks on American shipping and French plans to control the West, Cobbett was able to revive traditional American fears about French "encirclement" and to insist that the "French Regicides" were following the same policy that the French monarchists had adopted earlier in the century—to "cut off all communication between this country and Great Britain, as the only effectual means of rendering us totally dependent on themselves."[60]

Under these circumstances, Cobbett's writings in the *Porcupine's Gazette* repeatedly struck the resonant frequency. He articulated the growing American apprehension about France's continental ambitions, expressed and exploited the rising American anger about "French piracy on American commerce," and appealed to the American sense of pride and honor. No truly independent nation, he argued, would submit to such humiliating treatment; war was essential to preserve America's dignity. The XYZ affair appeared to confirm Cobbett's image of France as a corrupt and arrogant power; the hard line of the French government had played straight into his hands. During the war fever of 1798, Cobbett reached the peak of his popularity in the United States.[61]

All this popular attention seemed to augur well for the hidden agenda that lay beneath Cobbett's calls for an Anglo-American

---

[59] *PW*, vol. 8, p. 65; *PC*, December 1796, p. 46.

[60] Cobbett, *PC*, November 1796, p. 73; *PC*, January 1797, p. 18; see also Cobbett, *The Scare-Crow*, p. 12; *PG*, September 8, 1797; *PC*, November 1796, pp. 53–54, 66–67.

[61] For some examples of Cobbett's comments on France's continental ambitions, see *PG*, March 13, 1797; March 30, 1797; April 6, 1797; September 8, 1797. His accounts of "French piracy" can be found in *PG*, March 15, 1797; March 16, 1797; June 10, 1797, and *PW*, vol. 8, pp. 321–480. Typical appeals to American pride and honor are in *PG*, April 28, 1797; May 16, 1797; July 15, 1797, and *PW*, vol. 6, p. 29.

alliance—to lock the United States firmly into the British sphere of influence, and to replace the threat of French encirclement with the reality of British encirclement. That was why Cobbett privately supported British attempts to strangle the development of American manufactures and keep the United States economically dependent on the former mother country; that was why he secretly hoped Britain would reestablish itself in East Florida and Louisiana.[62] And, without a doubt, Cobbett preferred monarchical government to the "many-headed hydra" of republicanism. "For my part," he wrote in 1797, "I never hear talk of a *sovereign people* . . . without laughing." "Damn them," he was reported to have said of the Americans at much the same time, "no curse bad enough can happen to them, for their infamous declaration of independence; but I hope soon to see the two countries united together again."[63] Cobbett never forgot that he was an Englishman; his country always came first.

It was precisely the fear of being drawn into the British orbit that prompted President Adams to pull back from the brink of war with France. When Cobbett heard that the United States was reopening negotiations with France, he reacted with disbelief and anger; he dismissed Adams as "a precipitate old ass," and accused Adams's moderate Federalist supporters of "having abandoned every idea of consistency, and every principle of honour and freedom." As the Federalists split on the question of peace, Cobbett became increasingly isolated. Like the Hamiltonian Federalists whom he had supported, he was rapidly losing his influence. Indeed, the sales of his *Porcupine's Gazette* are an accurate barometer of the political fortunes of the Hamiltonians; the paper was widely read during the Quasi-War, ran into trouble during the peace talks of 1799, and folded completely in January 1800. By the end of the year, Jefferson had become President, the Federalists were heading for political oblivion, and Cobbett had left for England, "where neither the moth of *Democracy*, nor the rust of *Federalism* doth corrupt."[64]

---

[62] Cobbett's attitude to American manufactures is described in Richard Twomey, "Jacobins and Jeffersonians" (Ph.D. dissertation, University of Northern Illinois, 1974), pp. 153–54.

[63] *PW*, vol. 5, p. 168; Matthew Carey, *The Porcupiniad, Canto I* (Philadelphia, 1799), p. ii.

[64] *PW*, vol. 9, p. 4; vol. 10, p. 108; vol. 12, p. 110; see also *PW*, vol. 9, pp. 186–87; vol. 10, pp. 148–50; vol. 11, p. 42.

Readers' Reactions

In the course of his brief but brilliant American career, Cobbett had apparently pulled off the impossible; this thinly disguised English Tory had become the most popular pamphleteer and journalist in the United States. His pamphlets went into numerous editions and circulated throughout the country. At its peak, his *Porcupine's Gazette* reached over 3,000 subscribers, far outstripping the sales of his closest competitors. Cobbett employed a small army of "barrow boys" to distribute his works and issued a special *Country Porcupine* to reach rural districts.[65] He was read avidly by closet Loyalists like Elizabeth Drinker, who felt that at some level she knew the man, and by Federalists like Alexander Graydon, who had been converted to conservatism (much to his own surprise) after reading Burke's *Reflections*.[66] Cobbett's account book reveals that he had customers right across the continent, from Republican Georgia to Loyalist Nova Scotia. But his writings were particularly popular in Pennsylvania, New York and Maryland—states where the Republicans were rising most rapidly—rather than in Federalist strongholds like New England.[67] At first sight, this seems surprising; one is reminded of Hazlitt's observation that Cobbett's enemies enjoyed reading him the most.[68] And yet, there is a certain logic in the pattern of his readership. Cobbett's appeal was greatest in areas where politics were polarized, where the Republicans were successfully challenging established authority, and the Federalists were being forced onto the defensive. His uncom-

---

[65] Pierce Gaines, *William Cobbett and the United States* (Worcester, Mass., 1971); Clark, *Porcupine in America*, p. 95; Karen List, "The Role of William Cobbett in Philadelphia's Party Press, 1794–1799" (Ph.D. dissertation, University of Wisconsin-Madison, 1980), pp. 263–71. See also Donald Stewart, *The Opposition Press of the Federalist Period* (Albany, 1969), and Frank Mott, *American Journalism* (New York, 1931).

[66] List, "Role of William Cobbett," p. 272; Elaine Forman Crane, ed., *The Diary of Elizabeth Drinker* (Boston, 1991), vol. 3, p. 1305; Alexander Graydon, *Memoirs of a Life, Chiefly Passed in Philadelphia* (Edinburgh, 1822), pp. 375–76, 427.

[67] Gaines, "William Cobbett's Account Book," pp. 299–312.

[68] Hazlitt, "Character of Cobbett," p. 52, commented that "even those he abuses read him. The Reformers read him when he was a Tory, and the Tories read him now that he is a Reformer." Much the same point was made by James Thomson Callender, who observed in 1796 that "The reception of his writings has been extremely favourable, and even those who profess to dislike his opinions, and his attachments, have often paid a tribute of admiration to the superiority of his talents." See *British Honour and Humanity, or, the Wonders of American Patience* (Philadelphia, 1796), p. 3.

promising anti-Jacobinism and his aggressive tone perfectly matched the mood of people who feared that they were being cornered.

Such readers were attracted more by Cobbett's denunciation of democracy and democrats than by his pro-British position. Indeed, the characteristic Federalist response to his writings was one of ambivalence. George Washington rather liked Cobbett's attack on Citizen Adet's intervention in the American election of 1796, but felt compelled to make "allowances for the asperity of an Englishman." Abigail Adams believed that Cobbett was a useful antidote to the democratic republicanism of Benjamin Franklin Bache's *Aurora*, but added that "he frequently injures the cause he means to advocate for want of prudence and discretion." Similarly, Fisher Ames commented that Cobbett was a "writer of smartness," but noted that he "might do more good, if directed by men of sense and experience—his ideas of an intimate connection with Great Britain justly offend correct thinkers."[69] Not only did most Federalists stop short of supporting a full-scale alliance with Britain; they also wanted to distance themselves from Republican accusations that they were crypto-monarchists. They welcomed Cobbett's anti-Jacobinism but were embarrassed by his Toryism.

Nevertheless, many Americans found his Toryism anything but embarrassing. There remained in the United States a concealed but considerable Loyalist presence after the War of Independence. Despite the exodus of émigrés to British North America, the vast majority of Loyalists stayed in the United States, kept their opinions to themselves, and tried to adjust to the new order. Many of them resurfaced as Federalists; Jefferson in 1793 numbered the "old tories" among his opponents, and radical writers like James Thomson Callender agreed. This was not merely Republican propaganda; it is clear that former Loyalists voted for and sometimes assumed leadership roles in the emerging Federalist party. But whether or not they were directly associated with the Federalists, they constituted a natural and receptive audience for Cobbett's writings. Benjamin Rush recalled that the

---

[69] George Washington to David Stuart, in John C. Fitzpatrick, ed., *The Writings of George Washington* (Washington, 1931–44), vol. 35, p. 360; Abigail Adams to Mary Cranch, March 13, 1798, in Stewart Mitchell, ed., "New Letters of Abigail Adams," *American Antiquarian Society* 55 (1945), pp. 321–22; Fisher Ames to Alexander Hamilton, January 26, 1797, in Harold C. Syrett, ed., *The Papers of Alexander Hamilton* (New York, 1967), vol. 20, pp. 488–89.

"tory citizens of Philadelphia" read Peter Porcupine, and Noah Webster remarked that Cobbett had "the countenance and support of British subjects and some Americans who were unfriendly to the American Revolution." Cobbett himself attributed his success in the United States to his courage in articulating feelings of "affection for England" which many held in private but few would express in public.[70]

Another reason for his success, of course, was his forceful, energetic and direct writing style; the medium was at least as important as the message. Combining Burkean politics with Swiftian satire, Cobbett carried his arguments along in an apparently inexhaustible stream of personal invective, sheer vindictiveness, and scurrilous character sketches. His readers across the political spectrum registered the shock effect of his language. Robert Liston, the British minister to the United States, unsuccessfully attempted to persuade Cobbett to tone down the "gross personal abuse" that ran through his pamphlets. Socially respectable Federalists found him grating on the ears; Washington disapproved of his "strong and course expressions," and Abigail Adams found a "strange mixture" in him. "He can write very handsomely," she commented, "and he can descend and be as low, and vulgar as a fish woman." Elizabeth Drinker, with her pronounced Loyalist sympathies, still found his "Kick for a Bite" to be "rather Scurrilous." And yet, despite the disclaimers, they continued to read him; Liston admired Cobbett's "uncommon ability and strength of mind," Adams referred to him regularly in correspondence with her sister, and Drinker bought his pamphlets and subscribed to *Porcupine's Gazette*. One suspects that he attracted such a large readership pre-

---

[70] Jefferson to Madison, May 12, 1793, in Paul L. Ford, ed., *The Writings of Thomas Jefferson* (New York, 1892–99), vol. 6, p. 251; James Thomson Callender, *History of the United States for 1796* (Philadelphia, 1797), p. 45; Rush to Jefferson, December 17, 1811, in L. H. Butterfield, ed., *The Letters of Benjamin Rush* (Princeton, N.J., 1951), vol. 2, p. 1112; *PR*, September 29, 1804; January 29, 1805; Webster to Priestley, January 20, 1800, in Harry R. Warfel, ed., *Letters of Noah Webster* (New York, 1953), p. 205. For modern scholarship on the Loyalist-Federalist connection, see William H. Nelson, *The American Tory*, 2d ed. (Boston, 1992), pp. x–xi; Harold B. Hancock, *The Loyalists of Revolutionary Delaware* (Newark, 1977), pp. 97–101, 112–17; Young, *Democratic Republicans of New York*, pp. 566–67; Jacob E. Cooke, *Tench Coxe and the Early Republic* (Williamsburg, Va., 1978); Elizabeth P. McCaughey, *From Loyalist to Founding Father: The Political Odyssey of William Samuel Johnson* (New York, 1970); George A. Rawlyk, "The Federalist-Loyalist Alliance in New Brunswick, 1784–1815," *Humanities Association Review* 27 (1976), pp. 142–60.

cisely because of his "strong and course expressions." Cobbett's writings both shocked and titillated; many of his readers found the combination irresistible.[71]

As might be expected, Republican reactions to his language were much harsher. Thomas Paine, now one of Cobbett's principal targets, described *Porcupine's Gazette* as a mixture of "wit" and "*blackguardism.*" Matthew Carey, another of Cobbett's opponents, was particularly scathing in his judgment. "The style of Porcupine's Gazette is unquestionably the most base and wretched of any newspaper in Christendom," he wrote.

> I believe there never was a Gazette so infamous for scurrility, abuse, cursing, swearing, and blasphemy, except that of Hebert, the pere Duchene, who figured on the stage in the early part of the French revolution. Cobbett, when hard pressed in an argument, calls his opponent, rascal, scoundrel, villain, or thief, or desires him to '*go to the devil.*' By this eloquent mode he doubtless carries conviction to his readers, and triumphs over his adversaries. '*In the devil's name,*' may be found in his paper fifty times. That phrase, '*what the devil,*' and '*by heaven!*' are as commonly introduced to fill up chasms, as they are in the familiar conversation of the residents of St. Giles's and Billingsgate.[72]

In one important respect Carey's account is misleading; Cobbett's skill lay in combining argument with abuse, rather than substituting abuse for argument. But the notion of Cobbett as a kind of Hébert of the right is worth considering, especially in the light of his later career as a populist radical in England. Mary Wollstonecraft had made a similar point about Burke: "Reading your *Reflections* warily over," she remarked, "it has continually struck me, that had you been a Frenchman, you would have been, in spite of your respect for rank and antiquity, a violent revolutionist."[73] There were indeed latent radical tendencies within Cobbett, which would become manifest when he confronted the "Pitt system" in his native land. Cobett's anger at the

---

[71] Liston is quoted in Bradford Perkins, *The First Rapprochement* (Berkeley, 1967), pp. 9–10; Washington to Stuart, in Fitzpatrick, *Writings of George Washington,* vol. 35, p. 360; Mitchell, "New Letters of Abigail Adams," pp. 207, 213, 321–22, 347, 375; Crane, *Diary of Elizabeth Drinker,* vol. 1, p. 660; see also vol. 1, p. 725, and vol. 2, p. 910.

[72] Paine, "To the Citizens of the United States," in Foner, *Complete Writings,* vol. 2, p. 924; Carey, *The Porcupiniad,* pp. 13–14.

[73] Quoted in Conor Cruise O'Brien, "Introduction" to Burke, *Reflections,* p. 20.

misuse of power, his nose for hypocrisy, his jovial ferocity, his combative language, and his refusal to defer to anyone or anything were all carried through to his nineteenth-century radical writings. Cobbett's style did not change after he returned home; only the targets changed.

Carey was also right to point out that Cobbett's language drew on the conversation of the street. It was exactly this sensitivity to the vernacular that made him such an effective writer. Cobbett strove for clarity of expression and believed that "perspicuity is so essential a quality in every writer, that hardly any thing can make up for the want of it." "I beg leave to observe to you," he told one literary and political adversary, "that, though tropes and figures are very useful things, when they fall into skillful hands, they are very dangerous, when they fall into those of a contrary description. When I see you flourishing with a metaphor, I feel as much anxiety as I do when I see a child playing with a razor."[74] Through plain language, Cobbett appealed to the common sense, the ordinary understanding, of his readers.

Within this approach, there was a strong populist streak. He preferred useful mechanics to useless intellectuals and wrote that "a cobler with his hammers and awls, is a more valuable acquisition than a dozen philosophi-theologi-politi-cal empiricks with all their boasted apparatus."[75] Yet there were certain ironies here. In adopting the plain style, Cobbett was part of a broader eighteenth-century "revolution in rhetoric" that embraced writers like Jonathan Swift, Oliver Goldsmith, and Thomas Paine, and that had been strongly influenced by the scientific revolution. Back in 1667, Thomas Sprat had written that the founders of the Royal Society, dedicated to the pursuit of scientific knowledge, consciously rejected "swellings of style" and preferred "the language of Artizans, Countrymen, and Merchants, before that, of Wits, or Scholars."[76] There was nothing here with which Cobbett could disagree; the only trouble was that the source of these words in particular, and the movement toward the plain style in general, emanated from precisely those scientific and intellectual circles that Cobbett attacked—in the plain style.

It is also ironic that Cobbett was in effect appealing to the people to reduce the influence of the people on government. Apart from any-

---

[74] Cobbett, "A Kick for a Bite," p. 126.
[75] Cobbett, "Observations on the Emigration," p. 82.
[76] Wilbur Howell, *Eighteenth-Century British Logic and Rhetoric* (Princeton, N.J., 1971); Thomas Sprat, *The History of the Royal Society of London* (London, 1667), p. 113.

thing else, his American career clearly demonstrates that there was no automatic connection between the plain style and democratic politics. Nevertheless, there was a tension between his populism and his Toryism, one that sometimes pushed him in unusual directions. When he learned in 1798 that the Earl of Exeter had burned his copies of the works of Voltaire, Rousseau, Raynal, Volney, and Bolingbroke, Cobbett predictably condemned the books "which have produced the mischief, which now threatens to overwhelm the world." But he then went on to argue that "it would be a happy thing, if the accursed art of printing could be totally destroyed, and obliterated from the human mind."[77] These are unorthodox opinions for a journalist.

Given the unhappy fact that the art of printing was here to stay, Cobbett was determined to use it for his own ends. In a Federalist literary culture whose dominant image was the "Voyage to Laputa," with its satire on impractical scientific experiments and visionary philosophical "projects," Cobbett's Swiftian approach perfectly matched the current mood. "Every one will, I hope, have the goodness to believe that my grandfather was no philosopher," he wrote in his autobiography. "Indeed he was not. He never made a lightning rod, nor bottled up a single quart of sun-shine, in the whole course of his life." Anyone who united the new science with the new politics ran the risk of his ridicule. Joseph Priestley, whose scientific accomplishments included the discovery of oxygen, did more than bottle up quarts of sunshine, wrote Cobbett; he "set to work bottling up his own f–rts, and selling them for superfine inflammable air." Benjamin Franklin was nicknamed "old Lightning-Rod" for his experiments with electricity, and caricatured as "a whore-master, a hypocrite and an infidel." Benjamin Rush, the revolutionary Philadelphia doctor who believed in bleeding as a cure for the yellow fever, was called "Doctor Sangrado" and accused of unleashing a medical terror that slew thousands of Americans. By the time Cobbett had finished, there was hardly a Republican reputation left intact.[78]

Some of Cobbett's victims took this kind of thing in their stride. In 1800, Joseph Priestley could still inform a friend that Cobbett was "by far the most popular writer in this country, and, indeed, one of the

---

[77] *PW*, vol. 9, p. 204.

[78] Cobbett, "Life and Adventures," p. 158; "Observations on the Emigration," p. 86; *The Scare-Crow*, p. 18; *PG*, September 18 and 19, 1797. For Cobbett's pen portrait of Rush, see Chapter 7, this volume. On the image of Laputa in Federalist writings, see Linda K. Kerber, *Federalists in Dissent* (Ithaca, N.Y., 1970), pp. 1–22.

Introduction   [41]

best in many respects."⁷⁹ But others did not. Outraged by Cobbett's accusations of medical malpractice, Benjamin Rush decided to sue for libel. Thomas McKean, the chief justice of Philadelphia whom Cobbett had earlier caricatured as a corrupt, henpecked alcoholic, made sure that the case would be tried in the state, rather than the federal, courts. By the time of the trial, in 1799, McKean had been elected governor of Pennsylvania. The verdict was a foregone conclusion: the presiding judge, Edward Shippen, was a friend of McKean; the jury lists were drawn up by Shippen's son-in-law; Rush's chief counsel was McKean's nephew. What was unexpected was the severity of the punishment; Cobbett was fined $5,000, which was as unprecedented as it was ruinous. Four days later, McKean appointed Shippen chief justice of Pennsylvania.⁸⁰

Cobbett never forgot and never forgave this example of "democratic justice"; it not only confirmed his feelings about republicanism, but prompted him to leave the political cesspool of the United States. He vented his anger in a periodical whose title said it all: "The American Rush-Light; by the help of which, Wayward and Disaffected Britons may see a Complete Specimen of the Baseness, Dishonesty, Ingratitude, and Perfidy of Republicans, and of the Profligacy, Injustice, and Tyranny of Republican Governments." The bitterness would frequently resurface later in his life; in 1808, for example, he wrote of his "hatred" for the people responsible, and in 1824 he could still fume about the "blackest villany" of the "corrupt and tyrannical" government of Pennsylvania. And the anger fueled his earliest writings back in Britain, where he was determined to save his country from the fate of the United States. Cobbett's attitude to American republicanism and his political purpose in Britain were clearly set out in the prospectus of the daily newspaper, *The Porcupine*, which he launched in 1800.

> Having, in America, witnessed the fatal effects of revolution; having seen piety give place to a contempt of religion, plain-dealing exchanged for shuffling and fraud, universal confidence for universal suspicion and distrust; having seen a country, once the seat of peace and good neighbourhood, torn to pieces by faction, plunged, by

⁷⁹ Priestley to T. Lindsay, May 1, 1800, in Melville, *Life and Letters*, vol. 1, p. 109.
⁸⁰ For Cobbett's comments on McKean, see *PW*, vol. 3, p. 437; vol. 4, p. 365; vol. 6, pp. 80, 94–95n, 329, and Chapter 7, this volume. See also Spater, *William Cobbett*, pp. 103–4.

intriguing demagogues, into never-ceasing hatred and strife; having seen a people, once too fond of what they called liberty to bear the sway of a British King, humbly bend their necks to the yoke, nay, to the very foot, of a set of grovelling despots; having, in short, seen the crime of rebellion against monarchy punished by the tormenting, the degrading curse of republicanism, it is with the utmost astonishment and indignation that I find many of those, who have the press at their command, endeavouring to bring down on my native country the very same species of calamity and disgrace.

Upon reading this, his Tory supporters must have added a hearty Amen.[81]

Return to Radicalism

It seemed, then, that Cobbett's return home would be characterized by continuity—except that he could now reveal his true feelings about the "crime" of the American Revolution. He increasingly described the revolution as the "American rebellion (for, I love to call things by their right names)."[82] And yet, Cobbett in England was actually moving into a new phase of his career—one that would take him through disillusionment with Britain's system of government toward a populist brand of socially conservative political radicalism.

The process of change was a molecular one that in many ways paralleled his earlier conversion from Paineite republicanism to High Toryism. The man who had attacked the American government for refusing to declare war against France now found, in 1801, that his own government was negotiating peace terms with France; for someone who viewed the conflict as a holy war against the evil of French republicanism, such negotiations were a form of apostasy. The man who had associated America with the rule of the mob now found himself being victimized by an English mob for refusing to illuminate his house during the celebrations for peace in 1802; not only that, but the government supporters regarded the affair as an "excellent joke." The man who in America had praised the impartiality of the English

---

[81] *PW*, vol. 11, p. 209; *PR*, March 26, 1808; January 24, 1824; January 31, 1824; January 25, 1825; November 2, 1833; Cobbett, *Prospectus of a new Daily Paper, to be entitled The Porcupine* (London, 1800), pp. 1–2.

[82] *PR*, December 19, 1807.

judicial system now ran up against the practice of packed juries and received a fine of £500 for criticizing the administration of government in Ireland. The man who had portrayed England as a land where the granaries were full returned home to find out that they were empty. And the man who had written about "*real* English liberty" became increasingly disgusted with the whole network of patronage and corruption that enveloped the entire political system. It was not the England of "grovelling statesmen," of William Wilberforce's shallow humanitarianism, of newfangled Methodists and weak-minded tea drinkers, but the England of his imagination, that Cobbett had defended against American Republicans and that he would continue to defend against its modern enemies at home.[83]

The more he thought about it, the more he became convinced that the "degeneration" of England was the result of commercialism in general and the financial system in particular. Looking back to an idealized past in which honor, virtue, and personal connections meant more than profit, self-interest, and the cash nexus, Cobbett drew on the Country Party writings of Bolingbroke, Swift, and Pope to diagnose the British disease. He concluded that the growth of paper money, the stock market, banks, and the national debt were producing a new class of "moneyed men" who used their financial power to control the government and corrupt the members of Parliament. Searching for further information, he turned to Paine's *Decline and Fall of the English System of Finance* and "soon arrived at a conviction of this truth; that, the nation must destroy that monster the Debt; or that the monster must destroy this form of government."[84] Cobbett would spend the rest of his life trying to roll back the financial revolution and restore England to its true spirit and character.

As he moved into this new trajectory, Cobbett found himself coming closer to the reformers whom he had previously attacked. He

---

[83] Cobbett, *Letters to the Right Honourable Lord Hawkesbury* (London, 1802); *Porcupine*, October 12, 1800; *PR*, February 6, 1802; May 1, 1802; Cobbett, *The Scare-Crow*, p. 20; "Observations on the Emigration," pp. 58, 84; *The Democratic Judge* (Philadelphia, 1798); Spater, *William Cobbett*, pp. 125–26; Roger Wells, *Wretched Faces: Famine in Wartime England, 1793–1801* (New York, 1988); *PR*, October 19, 1805.

[84] *PR*, December 21, 1822; see also *PR*, July 6, 1811, and December 18, 1819. On the financial revolution and Country Party reactions to it, see Peter Dickson, *The Financial Revolution in England* (London, 1967); Isaac Kramnick, *Bolingbroke and His Circle* (Cambridge, Mass., 1968); Bolingbroke, *The Works of Lord Bolingbroke* (Philadelphia, 1841), vol. 2, pp. 443, 451, 458; Jonathan Swift, *The Prose Works of Jonathan Swift* (Oxford, 1939–68), vol. 2, p. 124. See also Paine, *The Decline and Fall of the English System of Finance*, in Foner, *Complete Writings*, vol. 2, pp. 651–74.

initially looked for allies among the "ancient country gentry," believing them to be the repository of traditional English values. By 1805, he was supporting parliamentary reformers like Francis Burdett and aligning himself with "the people who are in the middling walks of life, who have property to preserve and who have judgment to direct their actions." A few years later he hoped that the Prince Regent would behave like a patriot king and implement reform from above. It was not until 1816, after all these tactics had failed and after he had spent two years in Newgate Prison for seditious libel, that Cobbett cast his lot with the common people, wrote explicitly for "journeymen and labourers," and became a democrat.[85]

In the process, his views of the United States gradually began to change. During his first decade back in England, Cobbett continued to criticize American "liberty" and to urge vigorous measures against the rising American empire; even after his conversion to political radicalism, Cobbett's anti-Americanism remained so intense that it offended his new allies.[86] But by 1811, when he was serving time in prison, a new outlook emerged. Cobbett wrote approvingly about American methods of reducing the national debt; there was a lesson here for the British government, he believed. Similarly, he praised New York's libel laws, in which truth was a central defense against conviction; if Britain had followed this example, Cobbett was convinced, he would not have been incarcerated in Newgate. He increasingly pointed out that the United States was not encumbered by placemen, sinecures, tithes, and oppressive taxation, nor were Americans degraded by deference—"in that country poor men do not, to be sure, crawl almost upon their bellies before the rich." In short, Cobbett had come to feel that the example of the United States provided British reformers with a powerful weapon against the whole system of financial corruption and political oppression—or "the Thing," as he called it—that was destroying Old England.[87]

From this perspective, Cobbett began to view Anglo-American relations in a new light. He had previously argued that American neu-

---

[85] *PR*, April 27, 1805; March 15, 1806; April 15, 1809; November 2, 1816.

[86] See, for example, Thomas Hardy to Thomas Paine, October 15, 1807, in the Place Papers (British Library, London), Add. Ms. 27818, f. 72.

[87] For Cobbett's changing views on American financial policies, see *PR*, March 9, 1805; October 19, 1805; September 15, 1810; September 29, 1810; April 13, 1811; and April 17, 1811. On his attitude to New York's libel laws, see *PR*, September 15, 1810. For examples of his new opinions about cheap government and egalitarianism in America, see *PR*, March 6, 1811; August 15, 1812; September 7, 1811; June 13, 1812.

trality in the war between Britain and France was a cover behind which the United States was building up its merchant marine to challenge Britain's traditional dominance in transatlantic commerce, and he had fully supported vigorous search and seizure measures against the American navy. But now, in 1811, he believed that Britain's policy toward America was motivated less by the need to keep down a rival imperial power than by the desire to destroy the American source of inspiration for the British reform movement. Consequently, he saw the War of 1812 as a struggle between liberty and tyranny rather than a conflict of empire. Convinced in 1814 that liberty had triumphed, Cobbett rejoiced at the result, which he called "an event of infinitely greater importance to the world than any that has taken place since the discovery of the Art of Printing."[88]

This view of the United States persisted through the postwar radical agitation of 1816–17, when sales of Cobbett's writings shot through the roof. Faced with governmental repression, the suspension of habeas corpus, and the prospect of further imprisonment, he chose exile over martyrdom and sought refuge in America—not unlike those British and Irish democrats of the 1790s who had fled William Pitt's crackdown on radicalism and had been among the principal victims of Cobbett's earlier attacks. The man who had dismissed those democrats as "trans-Atlantic traitors" and "Emigrated Patriots" was now an emigrated patriot himself. He admitted to his former antagonists that he had been mistaken, shook hands with old enemies like Matthew Carey and William Duane, and continued to focus his attention on British rather than American politics. His positive image of the United States and his negative feelings toward the British government and its supporters were powerfully expressed in one of his articles for consumption back home: "And then," he wrote, "to see a free country for once, and to see every labourer with plenty to eat and drink! Think of *that*! And never to see the hang-dog face of a tax-gatherer. Think of *that*! No Alien Acts here. No long-sworded and whiskered Captains. No Judges escorted from town to town and sitting under the guard of dragoons. No packed juries of tenants. No Crosses. No Bolton Fletchers. No hangings and rippings up. No Castles and Olivers. No Stewarts and Perries. No Cannings, Liverpools, Castlereaghs, Eldons, Ellenboroughs or Sidmouths. No Bankers. No

---

[88] *PR*, January 14, 1815. See also *PR*, August 8, 1812; January 2, 1813; April 23, 1814; June 11, 1814; December 10, 1814.

Squeaking Wynnes. No Wilberforces. Think of *that*. No Wilberforces!"[89]

Nevertheless, beneath the surface, Cobbett's attitude to America was deeply ambivalent. On the one hand, he saw American liberty as a means of boosting the reform movement in Britain, with the end of restoring old English honor, glory, and strength. On the other hand, he continued to regard the rising American empire as a threat to England's traditional power and international prestige. Cobbett's attitude to the "Empire of Liberty" oscillated between qualified approval and straightforward hostility, between hope and fear; American imperial power contradicted the ends that he wanted the example of American liberty to serve in Britain. He was torn between his belief that, had Britain won the War of 1812, "it would have been better to be a dog than an Englishman" and his "mortification" at the "demonstrations of triumph" he read in American newspapers celebrating the end of the war. He was torn, in short, between siding with American liberty against the British government and urging the British government to check and challenge the American empire. "This is a very cruel dilemma to be reduced to," he wrote in 1825, "but, reduced to it I am, and so is every Englishman, who is not content to be a slave himself, and to leave his children slaves behind him." It was a dilemma that he was never able to resolve.[90]

American Legacies

It is clear that Cobbett was primarily concerned with the condition of his own country; he was first and foremost an Englishman who thought and felt in national terms. But the American dimension of his career was critically important. In the United States, Cobbett established himself as one of the best political writers in the Atlantic world and acquired a reputation that carried him into the mainstream of English journalism. In the United States, he exercised the talent for plain speech, biting satire, argument, and abuse that characterized his later writing in Britain. In the United States, he discovered and articulated the patriotic pride that remained central to his cast of mind. When in 1804 his enemies in the British government accused him of

[89] *PR*, October 3, 1818.
[90] *PR*, June 13, 1815; September 3, 1825.

being "an *American* and a *traitor*," Cobbett replied that he had "exhibited a perfect consistency" based on "the principles of loyalty and patriotism, which I had inculcated and practiced in America." And in the United States he developed the deep distrust of democratic theory and organization that remained with him for the rest of his life. Cobbett's radicalism was grounded on self-made myths of the past rather than on abstract notions about the "rights of man." Even in the political storm-zones of 1816–17 and 1830–32, he argued against the formation of radical clubs and societies, preferring to put his faith in the "free, unpacked, unbiassed" power of public opinion.[91]

Just as the United States provided the context in which Cobbett could develop his distinctive outlook and style, Cobbett's writings played an important part in the conflict over the character of America during the 1790s. "I do not know how it is," he wrote in 1795, "but I have strange misgivings hanging about my mind, that the whole moral as well as political world is going to experience a revolution."[92] From the hostile vantage point of his blue-painted Philadelphia print shop, with its juxtaposed pictures of Franklin and Marat peering from the window, Cobbett reported and ridiculed the revolution in political and social attitudes that swirled around him. He provided vivid images of pro-French festivals of fraternity, exuberant celebrations of equality, and optimistic affirmations of American destiny. He registered the growing influence of British and Irish radicals who pushed for greater democracy, social reform, and the abolition of slavery. He watched the first glimmerings of the movement for women's rights, expressed in Susanna Rowson's semihumorous inversion that "Women were born for universal sway, Men to adore, be silent and obey."[93] For Cobbett, this really was the world turned upside down; he responded with a mixture of magnificent sarcasm and bitter invective in what amounted to a verbal "White Terror."

His wide readership is striking testimony to the fear and anxiety that these changes generated in the United States. In this sense, Cobbett spoke to the condition of "old tories" and new Federalists who felt threatened by change and wanted to roll back the revolution in attitudes. It is no coincidence that he was most popular in those states where the Federalists were losing their grip on power.

[91] *PR*, September 29, 1804; March 1, 1817.
[92] Cobbett, "Kick for a Bite," p. 131.
[93] Ibid., p. 130. For a particularly striking example of this kind of inversion, see the *Aurora*, January 20, 1790.

But although the Federalists ultimately went down to defeat, and Cobbett left the country in disgust, the populist Toryism that his writings both reflected and reinforced did not disappear from the American political scene; indeed, it persisted well into the nineteenth century and beyond. There was the straightforward anti-intellectualism, a kind of right-wing common sense that egalitarians could—and often did—approach from the opposite direction. There was the emphasis on traditional Christian family values and the hostility to women's rights, the mocking male voice that echoed down the decades. There was the virulent nativism that manifested itself in Cobbett's anti-Irish writings during the Alien and Sedition Acts and would become a powerful political force—again with the Irish as the principal target—in the Know-Nothing Party half a century later. And there was the Anglophilia that became increasingly "respectable" toward the end of the nineteenth century and continues to permeate American popular culture. This is not to say that Cobbett himself initiated traditions that were transmitted and transformed into modern America; that would be to exaggerate his significance out of all proportion. But it is to argue that, even though Cobbett was clearly outside the liberal mainstream, many of his attitudes still remained deeply ingrained in the American consciousness.

In many respects, this is disturbing; certainly, there is nothing to admire in Cobbett's chauvinism and nativism or their modern manifestations—although it is obviously important to recognize the existence of such attitudes and understand their character if they are to be confronted and challenged. In other ways, however, Cobbett's writings contain some sharp social and political insights that cannot be easily dismissed. His belief that actions must be assessed according to their probable consequences rather than first principles, for example, is an important reminder of the dangers of dogmatism. Similarly, his critique of Jacobinism, for all its wild distortions and distensions, did detect totalitarian tendencies within democratic ideology—although we must also bear in mind the different dangers of his own absolutist thinking.

But perhaps Cobbett's greatest legacy was his attack on hypocrisy, grounded on his insistence that Americans should "look to the characters and actions of men, and not to their professions."[94] His sense of the contradiction between people's professions and practices was ex-

---

[94] Cobbett, "Bloody Buoy," p. 152.

traordinarily acute; the gap between the Republican ideology of liberty and support of slavery was only the most glaring example of a much broader phenomenon. Precisely because Cobbett exaggerated so much and presented his readers with the verbal equivalent of James Gillray's cartoons, there is a tendency to treat him as a congenital liar and disbelieve almost everything he wrote. Yet there was often a core of truth beneath his caricatures. To understand Cobbett's anger, we must remember what he was angry about—the behavior of a Republican politician like Thomas McKean, who was indeed a political crook; the self-serving actions of a self-proclaimed democrat like John Swanwick, who had indeed feathered his own nest while serving the patriot cause during the War of Independence; the position of Southern planters, whose opposition to Jay's Treaty related directly to their degree of indebtedness to British merchants; more generally, the pro-French American radicals who condemned violence on the right while condoning far greater violence on the left. The gap between profession and practice appeared particularly wide in the United States, with its public attachment to high ideals and its private pursuit of the main chance. That tension, mirroring the tension between the ideal and the real within Cobbett himself, has not gone away; if anything, it has become magnified in our own time. And although Cobbett's solutions should be thrown on the scrap heap of history, his awareness of the problem and his relentless attack on its symptoms are not entirely without contemporary relevance.

[1]

Observations on the Emigration of Dr. Joseph Priestley

THIS PAMPHLET, WRITTEN IN THE SUMMER OF 1794, MARKED Cobbett's entry into American politics. It was occasioned by the arrival in New York of Joseph Priestley, the English scientist, Unitarian, and democrat whose house and laboratory had been destroyed by a church-and-king crowd three years earlier, in the Birmingham Riots of 1791. American democrats, together with the "Republican Natives of Great Britain and Ireland" who lived in New York, embraced Priestley as a refugee from the "corrupt and tyrannical government" of Britain, and welcomed him to the land of liberty. In his reply, Priestley rejoiced that he had found an "asylum from persecution" in the United States, spoke warmly of the "wisdom and happiness of republican governments," and attacked the "evils" of hereditary rule.

All of this infuriated Cobbett. He had already become disillusioned with democratic ideology, and he was smoldering with rage about attacks on his native country in the American press. Cobbett's sense of anger may well have been intensified by his personal situation; his first child had just died at the age of seventeen months, and he was deeply depressed. At any rate, Priestley's reception forced into the open Cobbett's growing hostility to republican notions of liberty and equality. And although the "Observations" lacked the biting humor of his later writings, it did articulate many of the central themes that would characterize Cobbett's American career—including his hostility to abstract first principles, his opposition to religious dissent, his view that radicals like Priestley were self-righteous, devious, and untrustworthy, and his idealization of Old England as a land of justice, freedom, peace, and plenty.

The "Observations" also sheds some light on radical democratic attitudes in the United States. The democratic addresses to Priestley contain interesting examples of the internationalist, antihistorical, egalitarian, and optimistic elements of American Jacobinism. Similarly, the letter of "Agricola" cited on p. 81 is a classic statement of the view that the ordinary people—"farmers, mechanics, and labourers"—who made the American Revolution were being excluded from its benefits.

What struck Cobbett's contemporaries, of course, was the sheer power of the pamphlet's anti-Jacobinism. The publisher, Thomas Bradford, would not put his name to the first edition, for fear of the consequences. As Cobbett wrote of his first two pamphlets: "They were thrown upon the parish like foundlings; no soul would own them, till it was found that they possessed the gift of bringing in the pence." And bring in the pence they did; the "Observations" quickly went into five Philadelphia editions and was reprinted in New York, London, and Birmingham.

OBSERVATIONS ON THE EMIGRATION OF DR. JOSEPH PRIESTLEY: TO WHICH IS ADDED, A COMPREHENSIVE STORY OF A FARMER'S BULL.

WHEN THE ARRIVAL OF DOCTOR PRIESTLEY IN THE UNITED STATES WAS first announced, I looked upon his emigration (like the proposed retreat of Cowley, to his imaginary Paradise, the Summer Islands)[1] as no more than the effect of that weakness, that delusive caprice, which too often accompanies the decline of life, and which is apt, by a change of place, to flatter age with a renovation of faculties, and a return of departed genius. Viewing him as a man that sought repose, my heart welcomed him to the shores of peace, and wished him, what he certainly ought to have wished himself, a quiet obscurity. But his answers to the addresses of the Democratic and other Societies at New York, place him in quite a different light, and subject him to the animadversions of a public, among whom they have been industriously propagated.

No man has a right to pry into his neighbour's private concerns; and the opinions of every man are his private concerns, while he keeps them so; that is to say, while they are confined to himself, his family, and particular friends: but when he makes those opinions public—when he once attempts to make converts, whether it be in religion, politics, or anything else—when he once comes forward as a candidate for public admiration, esteem or compassion, his opinions, his principles, his motives, every action of his life, public or private, become the fair subject of public discussion. On this principle, which the Doctor ought to be the last among mankind to controvert, it is easy to perceive that these observations need no apology.

His answers to the addresses of the New York societies are evidently calculated to mislead and deceive the people of the United States.[2] He there endeavours to impose himself on them for a sufferer in the cause of Liberty; and makes a canting profession of moderation, in direct contradiction to the conduct of his whole life.

He says, he hopes to find here, "that protection from violence, which laws and government promise in all countries, but which he has not found in his own." He certainly must suppose that no European intelligence ever reaches this side of the Atlantic, or that the inhabitants of these countries are too dull to comprehend the sublime events that mark his life and character. Perhaps I shall show him, that it is not the people of England alone who know how to estimate the merit of Doctor Priestley.

Let us examine his claims to our compassion: let us see whether his charge against the laws and government of his country be just, or not.

On the 14th of July, 1791, an unruly mob, assembled in the town of Birmingham, set fire to his home and burnt it, together with all it contained.[3] This is the subject of his complaint, and the pretended cause of his emigration. The fact is not denied; but in the relation of facts, circumstances must not be forgotten. To judge of the Doctor's charge against his country, we must take a retrospective view of his conduct, and of the circumstances that led to the destruction of his property.

It is about twelve years since he began to be distinguished among the dissenters from the established church of England. He preached up a kind of *deism*[1] which nobody understood, and which it was thought the Doctor understood full as well as his neighbours. This doctrine afterwards assumed the name of Unitarianism, and the *reli-*

---

[1] This is one of those "hazarded assertions" alluded to in the introductory address. But how is it hazarded? The Doctor says, in his answer to Paine's Age of Reason, that "the doctrines of *atonement, incarnation*, and the *trinity*, have no more foundation in the scriptures, than the doctrine of *transmigration*." Is not this a kind of *deism*? Is it not *deism* altogether? Can a man who denies the divinity of Christ, and that he died to save sinners, have any pretensions to the name of *Christian*?

SECOND STREET. North from Market S.t w.th CHRIST CHURCH. PHILADELPHIA.

Second Street North, Philadelphia, in 1799, from William Birch's engravings of Philadelphia in the late 1790s. Between 1796 and 1800, Cobbett ran his bookselling, publishing, and printing shop on this street, opposite Christ Church. (Courtesy of the Free Library of Philadelphia.)

gieux of the order were called, or rather they called themselves, Unitarians.[4] The sect never rose into consequence; and the founder had the mortification of seeing his darling Unitarianism growing quite out of date with himself, when the French Revolution came and gave them both a short respite from eternal oblivion.

Those who know anything of the English dissenters, know that they always introduce their political claims and projects under the mask of religion.[5] The Doctor was one of those who entertained hopes of bringing about a revolution in England upon the French plan; and for this purpose, he found it would be very convenient for him to be at the head of a religious sect.[6] Unitarianism was now revived, and the society held regular meetings at Birmingham. In the inflammatory discourses, called sermons, delivered at these meetings, the English constitution was first openly attacked. Here it was that the Doctor beat his drum ecclesiastic, to raise recruits in the cause of rebellion. The press soon swarmed with publications expressive of his principles. The revolutionists began to form societies all over the kingdom, between which a mode of communication was established, in perfect conformity to that of the Jacobin Clubs in France.

Nothing was neglected by this branch of the Parisian *Propagande* to excite the people to a general insurrection. Inflammatory hand-bills, advertisements, federation dinners, toasts, sermons, prayers; in short, every trick that religious or political duplicity could suggest, was played off to destroy a constitution which has borne the test, and attracted the admiration of ages; and to establish in its place a new system, fabricated by themselves.

The fourteenth of July, 1791, was of too much note in the annals of modern regeneration to be neglected by these regenerated politicians. A club of them, of which Doctor Priestley was a member, gave public notice of a feast, to be held at Birmingham, in which they intended to celebrate the French revolution. Their endeavours had hitherto excited no other sentiments, in what may be called the people of England, than those of contempt. The people of Birmingham, however, felt, on this occasion, a convulsive movement. They were scandalised at this public notice for holding in their own town a festival, to celebrate events which were in reality a subject of the deepest horror: and seeing in it at the same time an open and audacious attempt to destroy the constitution of their country, and with it their happiness, they thought their understandings and loyalty insulted, and prepared to avenge themselves by the chastisement of the English revolutionists, in the midsts of their scandalous orgies. The feast nevertheless took place; but the Doctor, knowing himself to be the grand projector, and consequently the particular object of his townsmen's vengeance, prudently kept away. The cry of *church and king* was the signal for the people to assemble; which they did to a considerable number, opposite the hotel where the convives were met. The club dispersed, and the mob proceeded to breaking the windows, and

[56] *Peter Porcupine in America*

other acts of violence incident to such scenes; but let it be remembered, that no personal violence was offered. Pe[r]haps it would have been well, if they had vented their anger on the persons of the revolutionists; provided they had contented themselves with the ceremony of the horse-pond or blanket. Certain it is, that it would have been very fortunate if the riot had ended this way; but when that many-headed monster, a mob, is once roused and put in motion, who can stop its destructive steps?

From the *hotel of the federation* the mob proceeded to Doctor Priestley's Meeting-House, which they very nearly destroyed in a little time. Had they stopped here, all would yet have been well. The destruction of this temple of sedition and infidelity would have been of no great consequence; but, unhappily for them and the town of Birmingham, they could not be separated, before they had destroyed the houses and property of many members of the club. Some of these houses, among which was Doctor Priestley's, were situated at the distance of some miles from town; the mob were in force to defy all the efforts of the civil power, and, unluckily, none of the military could be brought to the place, 'til some days after the 14th of July. In the meantime, many spacious and elegant houses were burnt, and much valuable property destroyed; but it is certainly worthy [of] remark, that during the whole of these unlawful proceedings, not a single person was killed or wounded, either wilfully or by accident, except some of the rioters themselves. At the end of four or five days, this riot, which seemed to threaten more serious consequences, was happily terminated by the arrival of a detachment of dragoons; and tranquillity was restored to the distressed town of Birmingham.

The magistrates used every exertion in their power to quell this riot in its very earliest stage, and continued so to do to the last.[7] The Earl of Plymouth condescended to attend, and act as a justice of the peace; several clergymen of the church of England also attended in the same capacity, and all were indefatigable in their endeavours to put a stop to the depredations, and to re-establish order.

Everyone knows, that in such cases, it is difficult to discriminate, and that it is neither necessary nor just, if it be possible, to imprison, try, and execute the whole of a mob. Eleven of these rioters were, however, indicted; seven of them were acquitted, four found guilty, and of these four, two suffered death. These unfortunate men were, according to the law, prosecuted on the part of the king; and it has been allowed by the Doctor's own partizans, that the prosecution was carried on with every possible enforcement, and even rigour, by the judges and counsellors. The pretended lenity was laid to the charge of the jury! What a contradiction! They accuse the government of screening the rioters from the penalty due to their crimes, and at the same time accuse the jury of their acquittal! It is the misfortune of Doctor Priestley and all his adherents, ever to be inconsistent with themselves.[8]

After this general review of the riots, in which the doctor was unlawfully despoiled of his property, let us return to the merits of his particular case, and his complaint; and here let it be recollected, that it is not of the rioters alone that he complains, but of the laws and government of his country also. Upon an examination of particulars, we shall find, that so far from his having just cause of complaint, the laws have rendered him strict justice, if not something more; and that if any party has reason to complain of their execution, it is the town of Birmingham, and not Doctor Priestley.

Some time after the riots, the Doctor and the other Revolutionists who had property destroyed, brought their actions, for damages against the town of Birmingham, or rather against the hundred of which that town makes a part.[9] The doctor laid his damages at £.4122.11.9. *sterling*; of which sum, £.420.15.0. was for works in manuscript, which he said, had been consumed in the flames. The trial of this cause took up nine hours: the jury gave a verdict in his favour; but curtailed the damages to £.2502.18.0. It was rightly considered that the imaginary value of the manuscript works ought not to have been included in the damages; because the Doctor, being the author of them, he in fact possessed them still, and the loss could be little more than a few sheets of dirty paper. Besides, if they were to be estimated by those he had published for some years before, their destruction was a benefit instead of a loss both to himself and his country. This sum, then, of £.420.15.0. being deducted, the damages stood at £.3701.16.9; and it should not be forgotten, that even a great part of this sum was charged for an apparatus of philosophical instruments, which, in spite of the most unpardonable gasconade of the Philosopher,[2] can be looked upon as a thing of imaginary value only;

---

[2] "You have destroyed the most truly valuable and useful apparatus of philosophical instruments that perhaps any individual, in this or any country, was ever possessed of, in my use of which, I annually spent large sums, with no pecuniary view whatever, but only in the advancement of science, *for the benefit of my country and of mankind.*"—*Letter to the Inhabitants of Birmingham.*

and ought not to be estimated at its *cost* any more than a collection of shells or insects, or any other of the *frivola* of a virtuoso.

Now, it is notorious, that actions for damages are always brought for much higher sums than are ever expected to be recovered. Sometimes they are brought for three times the amount of the real damage sustained; sometimes for double, and sometimes for only a third more than the real damage. If we view, then, the Doctor's estimate in the most favourable light, if we supposed that he made but the addition of one third to his real damages, the sum he ought to have received would be no more than £.2467.17.10; whereas, he actually received £.2502.18.0; which was £.35.0.2 more than he had a right to expect. And yet he complains that he has not found protection from the laws and government of his country! If he had been the very best subject in England, in place of one of the very worst, what could the laws have done more for him? Nothing certainly can be a stronger proof of the independence of the courts of justice, and of the impartial execution of the laws of England, than the circumstances and result of this cause. A man who had for many years been the avowed and open enemy of the government and constitution, had his property destroyed by a mob, who declared themselves the friends of both, and who rose on him because he was not. This mob were pursued by the government, whose cause they thought they were defending; some of them suffered death, and the inhabitants of the place where they assembled, were obliged to indemnify the man whose property they had destroyed. It would be curious to know, what sort of protection this *reverend* Doctor, this "friend of humanity," wanted. Would nothing satisfy him but the blood of the whole mob? Did he wish to see the town of Birmingham, like that of Lyons, razed, and all its industrious and loyal inhabitants butchered, because some of them had been carried to commit unlawful excesses from their detestation of his wicked projects? BIRMINGHAM HAS COMBATTED AGAINST PRIESTLEY. BIRMINGHAM IS NO MORE.[10] This I suppose would have satisfied the charitable modern Philosopher, who pretended, and who the Democratic Society say, did "return to his enemies blessings for curses." Woe to the wretch that is exposed to the benedictions of a modern Philosopher. His "*dextre vengresse*" is ten thousand times more to be feared than the bloody poignard of the assassin: the latter is drawn on individuals only, the other is pointed at the human race. Happily for the people of Birmingham, these blessings had no effect; there was no National Convention, Revolutionary tribunal, or Guillotine, in England.

As I have already observed, if the Doctor had been the best and most peaceable subject in the kingdom, the government and laws could not have yielded him more perfect protection; his complaint would, therefore, be groundless, if he had given no provocation to the people, if he had in no-wise contributed to the riots. If, then, he has received ample justice, considered as an innocent man, and a good subject, what shall we think of his complaint, when we find that he was himself the principal cause of these riots; and that the rioters did nothing that was not perfectly consonant to the principles he had for many years been labouring to infuse into their minds?

That he and his club were the cause of the riots will not be disputed; for, had they not given an insulting notice of their intention to celebrate the horrors of the fourteenth of July, accompanied with an inflammatory hand-bill, intended to excite an insurrection against the government,[3] no riot would ever have taken place, and consequently, its disastrous effects would have been avoided.[11] But, it has been said, that there was nothing offensive in this inflammatory hand-bill; because, forsooth, "the matter of it (however indecent and untrue) was not *more virulent* than Paine's Rights of Man, Mackintosh's answer to Burke, Remarks on the constitution of England, &c.&c. which had been lately published without incurring the *censure of government*." So; an inflammatory performance, acknowledged to be *indecent* and *untrue*, is not offensive, because it is not *more virulent* than some other performances, which have escaped the censure of government! If this is not a new manner of arguing, it is at least an odd one. But this hand-bill had something *more malicious* in it, if not *more virulent*, than even the inflammatory works above mentioned. *They* were more difficult to come at; to have *them*, they must be bought. *They* contained something like reasoning, the fallacy of which, the government was very sure would be detected, by the good sense of those who took the pains to read them. A hand-bill was a more commodious instrument of sedition: It was calculated to have immediate effect. Besides, if there had been nothing offensive in it, why did the club think proper to disown it in so ceremonious a manner? They disowned it with the most solemn asseverations, offered a reward for apprehending the author, and afterwards justified it as an inoffensive thing. Here is a palpable inconsistency. The fact is, they perceived that this precious

---

[3] This hand-bill was disowned by the club, and they offered a reward for apprehending the author; but they took care to send him to France before their advertisement appeared.

morsel of eloquence, in place of raising a mob for them, was like to raise one against them: they saw the storm gathering, and in the moment of fear, disowned the writing. After the danger was over, seeing they could not exculpate themselves from the charge of having published it, they defended it as an inoffensive performance.

The Doctor, in his justificatory letter to the people of Birmingham,[12] says, that the company were assembled on this occasion "to celebrate the emancipation of a neighbouring nation from tyranny, without intimating a desire of *anything more than an improvement of their own constitution.*" Excessive modesty! *Nothing but an improvement?* A LA FRANÇOISE of course? However, with respect to the church, as it was a point of conscience, the club do not seem [to] have been altogether so moderate in their designs. "Believe me," says the doctor, in the same letter, "the church of England, which you think you are supporting, has received a greater *blow* by this conduct of yours than *I* and *all my friends* have ever *aimed at it.*" They had then it seems aimed *a blow* at the established church, and were forming a plan for *improving* the constitution; and yet the Doctor, in the same letter, twice expresses his astonishment at their being treated as the enemies of church and state. In a letter to the students of the college of Hackney, he says, a "Hierarchy, equally the *bane of christianity and rational liberty,* now confesses its weakness; and be assured, that you will see its complete reformation or *its fall.*"[13] And yet he has the assurance to tell the people of Birmingham, that their superiors have deceived them in representing him and his sect as the enemies of church and state.

But, say they, we certainly exercised the right of freemen in assembling together; and even if our meeting had been unlawful, cognizance should have been taken of it by the magistracy: there can be no liberty where a ferocious mob is suffered to supersede the law. Very true. This is what the Doctor has been told a thousand times, but he never would believe it. He still continued to bawl out, "The sunshine of reason will assuredly chase away and dissipate the mists of darkness and error; and when the majesty of the people *is insulted,* or they feel themselves oppressed by *any set of men,* they have the power to redress the grievance." So the people of Birmingham, feeling their majesty insulted by *a set of men* (and a very impudent set of men too), who audaciously attempted to persuade them that they were "*all slaves and idolators,*" and to seduce them from their duty to god and their country, rose "*to redress the grievance.*" And yet he complains? Ah! says he, but, my good townsmen,

> "——you mistake the matter.
> For, in all scruples of this nature,
> No man includes *himself*, nor turns
> The point upon his own concerns." [14]

And therefore he says to the people of Birmingham, "You have been misled." But had they suffered themselves to be misled by himself into an insurrection against the government; had they burnt the churches, cut the throats of the clergy, and hung the magistrates, military officers and nobility to the lamp-posts, would he not have said that they exercised a sacred right? Nay, was not the very festival, which was the immediate cause of the riots, held expressly to celebrate scenes like these? to celebrate the inglorious triumphs of a mob? The fourteenth of July was a day marked with the blood of the innocent, and eventually the destruction of an empire. The events of that day must strike horror to every heart except that of a deistical Philosopher, and would brand with eternal infamy any other nation but France; which, thanks to the benign influence of the Rights of Man, has made such a progress in ferociousness, murder, sacrilege, and every species of infamy, that the horrors of the fourteenth of July are already forgotten.

What we celebrate, we must approve; and does not the man, who approved of the events of the fourteenth of July, blush to complain of the Birmingham riots? "Happily," says he to the people of Birmingham, "happily the minds of Englishmen have a horror for *murder*, and therefore you did not, I hope, think of that; though, by your clamorous demanding me at the hotel, it is probable that, at that time, some of you intended me some personal injury." Yes, Sir, happily the minds of Englishmen have a horror for murder; but who will say that the minds of Englishmen, or English women, either [,] would have a horror for murder, if you had succeeded in overturning their religion and constitution, and introducing your Frenchified system of liberty? The French were acknowledged to be the most polite, gentle, compassionate and hospitable people in all Europe: what are they now? Let LaFayette, Brissot, Anacharsis Cloots, or Thomas Paine himself, answer this question.[15]

Let us see, a little, how mobs have acted under the famous government that the Doctor so much admires.

I shall not attempt a detail of the horrors committed by the cut-throat Jourdan and his associates in Provence, Avignon, Languedoc, and Rousillon.[16] Towns and villages sacked, gentlemen's seats and castles burnt, and their inhabitants massacred; magistrates insulted, beat, and imprisoned, sometimes killed; prisoners set at liberty to cut the throats of those they had already robbed. The exploits of this band of *patriots* would fill whole volumes. They reduced a great part of the inhabitants of the finest and most fertile country in the whole world, to a degree of misery and ruin that would never have been forgotten, had it not been so far eclipsed since, by the operation of what is, in "that devoted country," called the law. The amount of the damages sustained in property, was perhaps a hundred thousand times as great as that sustained by the Revolutionists at Birmingham. When repeated accounts of these murderous scenes were laid before the National Assembly, what was the consequence? what the redress? "We had our fears," says Monsieur Gentil, "for the prisoners of Avignon, and for the lives and property of the inhabitants of that unhappy country; but these fears are now changed into a certainty: the prisoners are released; the country seats are burnt, and" —. Monsieur Gentil was called to order, and not suffered to proceed; after which these precious "Guardians of the Rights of Man" passed a censure on him, for having slandered the patriots.[17] It is notorious that the chief of these cut-throats, Jourdan, has since produced his butcheries in Avignon, as a proof of his *civism*, and that he is now a distinguished character among the real friends of the revolution.

Does the Doctor remember having heard anything about the glorious achievements of the 10th of August, 1792?[18] Has he ever made an estimate of the property destroyed in Paris on that and the following days? Let him compare the destruction that followed the steps of that mob, with the loss of his boasted apparatus; and when he has done this, let him tell us, if he can, where he would now be, if the government of England had treated him and friends, as the National Assembly did the sufferers in the riots of the 10th of August. But, perhaps, he looks upon the events of that day as a glorious victory, a new emancipation, and of course will say, that I degrade the *Heroes* in calling them a mob. I am not disputing with him about a name; he may call them the heroes of the 10th of August, if he will: "The Heroes of the 14th of July," has always been understood to mean, *a gang of blood-thirsty cannibals*, and I would, by no means, wish to withhold the title from those of the 10th of August. . . .

From scenes like these, the mind turns for relief and consolation to the riot at Birmingham. That riot considered comparitively [sic] with what Doctor Priestley and his friends wished and attempted to stir up, was peace, harmony and gentleness. Has this man any reason to complain? He will perhaps say, he did not approve of the French riots and massacres; to which I shall answer, that he did approve of them. His public celebration of them was a convincing proof of this; and if it were not, his sending his son to Paris, in the midst of them, to request the *honour* of becoming a French citizen, is a proof that certainly will not be disputed.[4] If, then, we take a view of the riots of which the Doctor is an admirer, and of those of which he expresses his detestation, we must fear that he is very far from being that "*friend of human happiness*," that the Democratic Society pretend to believe him. In short, in whatever light we view the Birmingham riots, we can see no object that excites our compassion, except the inhabitants of the Hundred and the unfortunate Rioters themselves.

The charge that the Doctor brings against his country is, that it has not *afforded him protection*. It ought to be remarked here, that there is a material difference between a government that does not at all times afford *sufficient protection*, and one that is *oppressive*. However, in his answer to the New York addresses, he very politely acquiesces in the government and laws of England being oppressive also. Would he really prefer the proceedings of a *revolutionary Tribunal* to those of a court of justice in England? Does he envy the lot of his colleagues Manuel, Lacroix, Danton and Chabot?[19] How would he look before a tribunal like that of the Princess de Lambelle, for example?[20] When this much-lamented unfortunate lady was dragged before the villains that sat in a kind of mock judgement on her, they were drinking *eau de vie*, to the damnation of those that lay dead before them. Their shirt sleeves were tucked up to their elbows; their arms and hands, and even the goblets they were drinking out of, were besmeared with human blood! I much question if the assassin's stab, or even the last pang of death, with all its concomitant bitterness, was half so terrible as the blood-freezing fight of these hell-hounds. Yet this was a *court of justice*, under that constitution which "the friend of human happi-

---

[4] Another "hazarded assertion:" Let us hear the Doctor again. "My second Son, who was present both at the riot, and the assizes, felt more indignation still, and willingly listened to a proposal to settle in France; and there his reception was but too flattering." It is useless to ascertain the time of this flattering reception, in order to prove that it was in the midst of massacres; for the revolution has been one continued scene of murder and rapine; but, however, if the reader has an opportunity of examining the Paris papers, he will find that the ceremony took place within a very few days of the time when Jourdan filled the *Ice-house* at Avignon with mangled bodies.

ness" wanted to impose on his countrymen! Paine, in speaking of the English government, says exultingly, and as he fancies wittily, "they manage those things better in France."[21] I fancy, this boasting "representative of twenty four millions of freemen" would now be glad to exchange his post of deputy for that of under shoe-black to the meanest Lackey at the court of London! Would he not with joy exchange his *cachot* with the reversion of the guillotine into the bargain, for the darkest cell in that very Bastile, the destruction of which he has so triumphantly and heroically sung? His fate is a good hint to those who change countries every time they cross the sea. A man of all countries is a man of no country: and let all those citizens of the world remember, that he who has been a bad subject in his own country, though from some latent motive he may be well received in another, will never be either *trusted* or *respected*.[22]

The Doctor and his fellow labourers who have lately emigrated to Botany Bay, have been continually crying out, "a reform of Parliament." The same visionary delusion seems to have pervaded all reformers in all ages. They do not consider what *can* be done, but what they think ought to be done. They have no calculating principle to direct them to discover whether a reform will cost them more than it is worth or not. They do not sit down to count the cost; but the object being, as they think, desirable, the means are totally disregarded. If the French reformers had sit [sic] down to count the cost, I do not believe they were villains or idiots enough to have pursued their plan as they did. To have a tenth part of their income, they have given the whole, or rather it has been taken from them. To preserve the life of a person now and then unjustly condemned, they have drenched the country with the blood of the innocent. Even the Bastile, that terrible monument of tyranny, which has been painted in such frightful colours, contained but *two* state prisoners when it was forced by the mob; and the reformers, to deliver these two prisoners, and to guard others from a like fate, have erected Bastiles in every town and in every street. Before the Revolution, there were only *two* state prisoners; there are now above *two hundred thousand*. Do these people calculate? Certainly not. They will not take man as they find him, and govern him upon principles established by experience; they will have him to be "a faultless monster that the world ne'er saw," and wish to govern him according to a system that never was, or can be, brought into practice.[23]

These waking dreams would be of no more consequence than those of the night, were they not generally pursued with an unjustifiable degree of obstinacy and intrigue, and even villainy; and did they not, being always adapted to flatter and inflame the lower orders of people, often baffle every effort of legal power. Thus it happened in England in the reign of Charles the first; and thus has it happened in France. Some trifling innovation always paves the way to the subversion of a government. The axe in the forest humbly besought a little peace [sic] of wood to make it a handle: the forest, consisting of so many stately trees, could not, without manifest cruelty, refuse the "humble" request; but, the handle once granted, the before-contemptible tool began to lay about it with so much violence, that in a little time not a tree nor even shrub was standing. That a parliamentary reform was the handle by which the English revolutionists intended to effect the destruction of the constitution, needs not be insisted in; at least, if we believe their own repeated declarations. Paine and some others clearly expressed themselves on this head: the Doctor was more cautious while in England, but, safely arrived in his "asylum," he has been a little more undisguised: He says the troubles in Europe are the natural offspring of the *"forms of government"* that exist there; and that the abuses spring from the *"artificial distinctions in society."*—I must stop here a moment to remark on the impudence of this assertion. Is it not notorious that *changing* those forms of government, and *destroying* those distinctions in society, has introduced all the troubles in Europe? Had the form of government in France continued what it had been for twelve or thirteen hundred years, would those troubles ever have had an existence? To hazard an assertion like this, a man must be an idiot, or he must think his readers so. It was then the *form* of the English government, and those artificial distinctions; that is to say, of king, prince, bishop, &c. that he wanted to destroy, in order to produce that *"other system of liberty,"* which he had been so long dreaming about. In his answer to the address of "the republican natives of Great Britain and Ireland, resident at New York," he says, "the wisdom and happiness of republican governments, and the evils resulting from hereditary monarchical ones, cannot appear in a stronger light to you, than they do to me;" and yet this same man pretended an inviolable attachment to the *hereditary monarchical government* of Great Britain! Says he, by way of vindicating the principles of his club to the people of Birmingham, "the first toast that was drank, was, *"the king and constitution."* What! does he make a merit in England of having *toasted* that which he abominates in America? Alas! Philosophers are but mere men.

It is clear that a parliamentary reform was not the object:—an after-game was intended, which the vigilance of government, and the natural good sense of the people happily prevented; and the Doctor, disappointed and chagrined, is come here to discharge his heart of the venom it has been long collecting against his country. He tells the Democratic Society that he cannot promise to be a better subject of this government than he has been of that of Great-Britain. Let us hope that he intends us an agreeable disappointment, if not, the sooner he emigrates back again the better.

System mongers are an unreasonable species of mortals: time, place, climate, nature, itself, must give way. They must have the same government in every quarter of the globe; when perhaps there are not two countries which can possibly admit of the same form of government, at the same time. A thousand hidden causes, a thousand circumstances and unforeseen events, conspire to the forming of a government. It is always done by little and little. When compleated, it presents nothing like a *system*; nothing like a thing composed, and written in a book. It is curious to hear people cite the American government as the summit of human perfection while they decry the English; when it is absolutely nothing more than the government which the kings of England established here, with such little modifications as were necessary on account of the state of society and local circumstances. If, then, the Doctor is come here for a change of government and laws, he is the most disappointed of mortals. He will have the mortification to find in his "*asylum*" the same laws as those from which he has fled, the same upright manner of administering them, the same punishment of the oppressor and the same protection, of the oppressed. In the courts of justice he will every day see precedents quoted from the English lawbooks; and (which to him may appear wonderful) we may venture to predict, that it will be very long before they will be supplanted by the bloody records of the revolutionary tribunal. Let him compare the governments of these states, and the measures they have pursued, with what has passed under the boasted constitution that he wished to introduce into England, and see if he can find one single instance of the most distant resemblance. In the abolition of negro slavery for example, the governments of the United States have not rushed headlong into the mad plan of the National Convention.[24] With much more humane views; with a much more sincere desire of seeing all mankind free and happy, they have, in spite of clubs and societies, proceeded with caution and justice. In short, they have adopted, as nearly as possible, considering circumstances and situation, the same measures as have been taken by the government which he abhors. He will have the further mortification to find, that the government here is not, any more than in England, influenced by the vociferations of fish-women, or by the *toasts* and *resolutions* of popular societies. He will, however, have one consolation; here as well as there, he will find, that the truly great, virtuous and incorruptible man at the head of government, is branded for an *Aristocrat*, by those noisy gentry.[25]

Happiness being the end of all good government, that which produces the most is consequently the best; and comparison being the only method of determining the relative value of things, it is easy to see which is preferable, the tyranny which the French formerly enjoyed, or the liberty and equality they at present labour under. If the Doctor had come about a year sooner, he might have had the satisfaction of being not only an ear, but an eye witness also, of some of the blessed effects of this celebrated revolution. He might then have been regaled with that sight, so delectable to a modern Philosopher;— opulence reduced to misery.[26]

The stale pretence, that the league against the French has been the cause of their inhuman conduct to each other, cannot, by the most perverse sophistry, be applied to the Island of St. Domingo. That fine, rich colony was ruined, its superb capital and villas reduced to ashes, one-half of its inhabitants massacred, and the other half reduced to beggary, before an enemy ever appeared on the coast. No: it is that system of anarchy and blood that was celebrated at Birmingham, on the 14th of July, 1791, that has been the cause of all this murder and devastation.

Nor let the Doctor pretend that this could not be foreseen. It was foreseen and foretold too, from the very moment a part of the Deputies to the States General, were permitted to call themselves a national assembly. In proof of this, I could mention a dozen publications that came out under his own eye. . . .[27]

Either he foresaw the consequences of the French Revolution, or he did not foresee them: if he did not, he must confess that his penetration was far inferior to that of his antagonists, and even to that of the multitude of his countrymen; for they all foresaw them. If he did foresee them, he ought to blush at being called the "friend of human happiness;" for, to foresee such dreadful calamities and to form a deliberate plan for bringing them upon his country, he must have a disposition truly diabolical. If he did not foresee them, he must have an understanding little superior to that of an idiot; if he did, he must have the heart of a *Marat*.[28] Let him choose.

But it is pretty clear that he foresaw the consequences, or, at least, that he approves of them; for, as I have observed above, he sent his son into France, in the very midst of the massacres, to request the honor of becoming a French citizen; and in his answer to the addressers at New-York, he takes good care to express his disapprobation of the war pursued by his country (which he calls an infatuation) because its manifest tendency is to destroy that hydra, that system of anarchy which is the primary cause. Besides, is not his emigration itself a convincing proof, that his opinion still remains the same? If he found himself mistaken, he would confess his error; at least tacitly, by a change of conduct. Has he done this? No: the French revolution is his system, and sooner than not see it established, I much question, if he would not with pleasure, see the massacre of all the human race.

Even suppose his intended plan of improvement had been the best in the world instead of the worst, the people of England had certainly a right to reject it. He claims, as an indubitable right, the right of thinking for *others*, and yet he will not permit the people of England to think for *themselves*. Paine says, "what a whole nation *wills*, it has a right *to do*."[29] Consequently, what a whole nation does *not will*, it has a right *not to do*. Rousseau says, "the majority of a people has a right to *force* the rest to be *free*:"[30] but even the "insane Socrates of the national assembly," has never, in all his absurd reveries, had the folly to pretend, that a club of dissenting malcontents, has a right to *force* a whole nation to be *free*. If the English choose to remain slaves, bigots, and idolators, as the Doctor calls them, that was no business of his: he had nothing to do with them. He should have let them alone; and perhaps in due time, the abuses of their government would have come to that "*natural termination*," which he trusts "will guard against future abuses." But, no, said the Doctor, I will reform you,—I will enlighten you,—I will make you free. You shall not! say the people. But I will! says the Doctor. By ———, say the people, you shall not! . . .

I now beg the reader's company, in a slight review of the addresses, delivered to the Doctor by the several patriotic societies at New-York.[5]

---

[5]   I. An addres[sic] from "*the Democratic Society.*"
    II. From the "*Tammany Society.*"
    III. From the "*Associated Teachers.*"
    IV. From the "*Republican Natives of Great-Britain and Ireland.*"
These addresses, with the answers to them, having all appeared in the Gazettes, it will be useless to give them at length here.

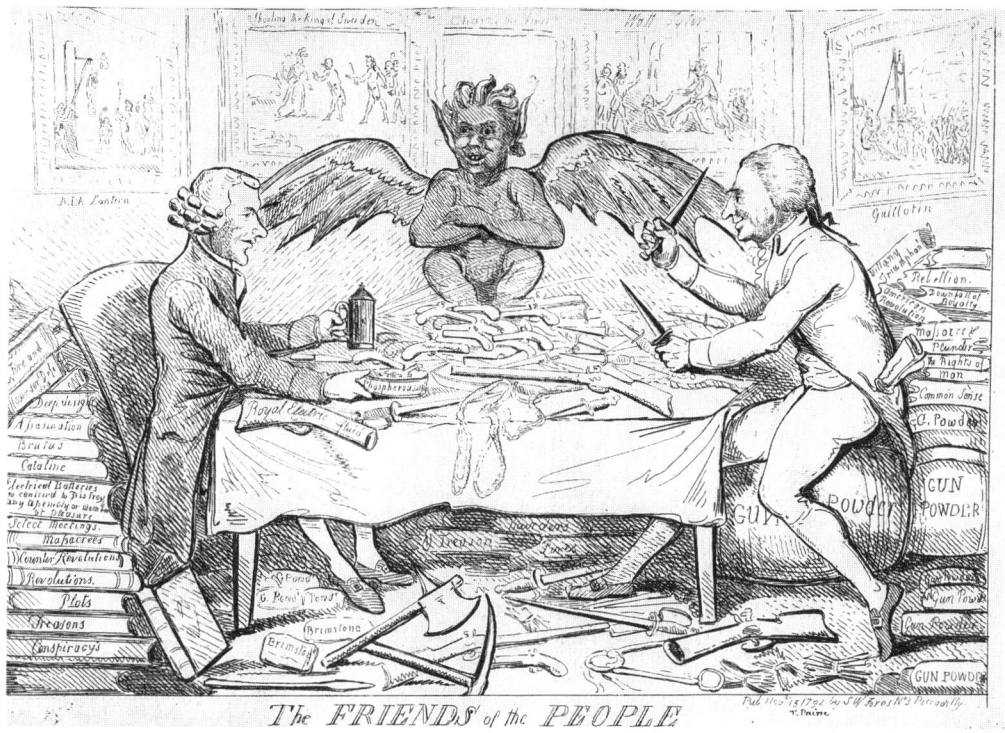

The Friends of the People: two of Cobbett's principal targets, Joseph Priestley (left) and Thomas Paine, as seen by the English cartoonist Isaac Cruikshank in 1792. The gunpowder is an allusion to Priestley's warning two years earlier that the clergy, by refusing to reform laws against dissenters, were "laying gunpowder, grain by grain, under the old building of error and superstition." Both men are surrounded by the words and weapons of treason, as they feast on the table of sedition. (Courtesy of the Trustees of the British Museum.)

It is no more than justice to say of these addresses, in the lump, that they are distinguished for a certain barrenness of thought and vulgarity of stile, which, were we not in possession of the Doctor's answer, might be thought inimitable. If the parties were less known, one might be tempted to think that the addressers were dull by concert; and that by way of retaliation, the Doctor was resolved to be as dull as they. At least, if this was their design, no-body will deny but they have succeeded to admiration.

"The governments of the old world," say the Democratic Society, "are most of them now basely combined to prevent the establishment of liberty in France, and to effect the total destruction of the rights of man."

What! The Rights of Man yet? I thought that *Liberty and Equality, the Rights of Man*, and all that kind of political cant, had long been discovered for the greatest Bore in nature. Are there people in this country, and people who pretend to possess a superior degree of sagacity too, who are dolts enough to talk about *French Liberty*, after what passes under their eyes every day? . . . Let us hear their own definition of this liberty. "Liberty," says Barrere, in his report to the National Convention, on the 3d of January 1794, "Liberty, my dear fellow citizens, is a privileged and general creditor; not only has she a right to our *property* and *persons*, but to our *talents* and *courage*, and even to our *thoughts!*"[31] Oh, Liberty! What a metamorphosis hast thou undergone in the hands of these political jugglers!

If this be liberty, may God in his mercy continue me the most abject slave. If this be liberty, who will say that the English did not do well in rejecting the Doctor's plan for making them free? The Democrats of New-York accuse the allies of being combined, to prevent the establishment of liberty in France, and to destroy the rights of man; when it is notorious, that the French themselves have banished the very idea of the thing from amongst them; that is to say, if they ever had an idea of it. Nay, the author of the *rights of man*, and the authoress of the *rights of women*, are at this moment starving in a dirty dungeon, not a hundred paces from the *sanctum sanctorum* of liberty and equality; and the poor unfortunate Goddess[6] herself is guillotined! So much for liberty and the rights of man.[32]

The Tammany society[33] comes forward in boasting of their "*venerable ancestors*," and, says the Doctor in his answer, "Happy would *our* venerable ancestors have been to have found, &c." What! Were they the Doctor's ancestors too? I suppose he means in a figurative sense. But certainly, gentlemen, you made a *faux pas* in talking about your ancestors at all. It is always a tender subject, and ought to be particularly avoided by a body of men "who disdain the shackles of tradition."

You say that, in the United States, "there exists a sentiment of free and candid enquiry, which disdains the shackles of tradition, prepar-

---

[6] Madame Hebert, who had the honor of representing this Deity, and who received, for a considerable time, the adorations and incense of the devout Parisians, was guillotined not long ago. It is impossible to say for what she was executed, as the court, by which she was tried, do not waste their precious time in committing their proceedings to writing.

ing a rich harvest of improvement and the glorious triumph of truth." Knowing the religious, or rather irreligious, principles of the person to whom this sentence was addressed, it is easy to divine its meaning. But, without flattery, your zeal surpasses that of the Doctor himself: he disdains *revelation only*; the authority of Moses, David, and a parcel of folks that no-body knows; but you disdain what your fathers have told you: which is the more surprising, as, at the same time, you boast of your "*venerable ancestors.*" People should always endeavour to be consistent, at least *when interest does not interfere*. However, suppose the shackles of revelation and tradition both completely shaken off, and the infidel Unitarian system established in their stead; what good would the country derive from it? This is certainly worth enquiry; because a thing that will do no good, can be good for nothing. The people of these states are, in general, industrious, sober, honest, humane, charitable and sincere; dutiful children and tender parents.[34] This is the character of the people, and who will pretend to say that the gospel, the belief of which has chiefly contributed to their acquiring of this amiable character, ought to be exchanged for the atheistical or deistical doctrines of a Monvel[7] or a Priestley? For my part, I can see nothing to induce us to try the experiment; no, not even "the rich harvest of improvement and the glorious triumph of truth," that, you say, it promises. We know *the truth* already; we want no improvement in religious knowledge; all we want is to practice, better, what we know; and it is not likely that our practice would be improved by disdaining the theory.

You allow, that a public and sincere spirit of toleration exists among us. What more is wanted? If you were to effect a general disdain of the shackles of tradition, perhaps the "rich harvest" would be a corruption of manners, discord, persecution and blood. The same causes generally produce the same effects: to see, and be terrified at those effects, we have only to turn our eyes to that distracted country, where it must be allowed even by yourselves, the shackles of tradition are sufficiently disdained.

---

[7] Upon the article of religion, *Monvel* says, "the world has seen three infamous imposters, Moses, Mahomet, and Jesus Christ; men have ever been divided into two classes, the deceivers and the deceived; they have always had false fears and vain hopes. These have introduced religions, that is to say, cheats and dupes; and in short, the soul of a man and that of a dog are just as precious, and as immortal the one as the other."

This *Monvel* was a player, and was chosen by the National Convention of France as a Priest of Atheism. The above sentiments, making part of a discourse delivered by him in the church of St. Roch, at Paris, were translated from the *Journal Republicain de Paris*.

Doctor Priestley professes to wish for nothing but toleration; liberty of conscience. But let us contrast these moderate and disinterested professions with what he has advanced in some of his latest publications. I have already taken notice of the assertion in his letters to the students of Hackney; "that the established church *must fall.*" In his address to the Jews (whom, by the bye, he seems to wish to form a coalition with) he says, "all the persecutions of the Jews have arisen from *trinitarian,* that is to say, *Idolatrous Christians.*"[35] Idolatrous Christians! It is the first time, I believe, these two words were ever joined together. Is this the language of a man who wanted only toleration, in a country where the established church, and most part of the dissenters also, are professedly *trinitarians?* He will, undoubtedly say, that the people of this country are *idolators* too, for there is not one out of a hundred at most, who does not firmly believe in the doctrine of the Trinity.

Such a man complains of persecution with a very ill grace. But suppose he had been persecuted for a mere matter of opinion; it would be only receiving the measure he has meted to others. Has he not approved of the unmerciful persecution of the unfortunate and worthy part of the French clergy; men as far surpassing him in piety and utility as in suffering? They did not want to coin a new religion; they wanted only to be permitted to enjoy, without interruption, the one they had been educated in, and that they had sworn, in the most solemn manner, to continue in to the end of their lives. The Doctor says, in his address to the Methodists, "you will judge whether I have not reason and scripture on my side. You will, at least be convinced, that *I have so persuaded myself*; and you cannot but respect a real lover of truth, and *desire to bring others into it,* even in the man who is unfortunately in an error."[36] Does not this man blush at approving of the base, cowardly and bloody persecutions that have been carried on against a set of men, who erred, if they did err at all, from an excess of conscientiousness? *He* talks of persecution, and puts on the mockery of woe: theirs has been persecution indeed.[37] Robbed, dragged from their homes, or obliged to hide from the sight of man, in continual expectation of the assassin's stab, some transported, like common felons, forever; and a much greater number butchered by those to whose happiness their lives had been devoted, and in that country that they loved too well to disgrace by their apostacy! How gladly would one of these unfortunate conscientious men have escaped to America, leaving fortune, friends and all behind him! And how different has been the fate of Doctor Priestley! Ah! Gentlemen! do not let us be deceived by false pretenders: the manner of his emigration is, of itself, a sufficient proof that the step was not necessary, to the enjoyment of "protection from violence."

You say, he has "long *disinterestedly* laboured for his country." 'Tis true he says so; but we must not believe him more disinterested than other reformers. If toleration had been all he wanted; if he had contented himself with the permission of spreading his doctrines, he would have found this in England, or in almost any other country, as well as here. The man that wants only to avoid persecution, does not make a noisy and fastidious display of his principles, or attack with unbridled indecency, the religion of the country in which he lives. He who avoids persecution is seldom persecuted. . . .

But the Doctor did not want to be remote from power or *profit* either; for, in his sermon on the test laws, he proposes "to set apart one church for the dissenters in every considerable town, and a certain allotment of *tithes* for their minister, proportioned to the number of dissenters in the district."[38] A very modest and disinterested request truly! Was this man seeking peace and toleration *only*? He thinks these facts are unknown in America. After all his clamour against tithes, and his rejoicing on account of their abolition in France, he had no objection to their continuing in England, provided he came in for a share. Astonishing disinterestedness!

In this country there is nothing to fear from the Doctor's disinterestedness; because there being no public revenue annexed to any worship whatever, there is nothing to wrangle for; but from the disseminating of his deistical doctrine there is much to fear. A celebrated deist in England, says, that there can be no such thing as an atheist; that it is impossible: for, says he, "every one must necessarily believe that some cause or other produced the Universe; he may call that cause what he pleases; *God, nature,* or even *chance*; still he believes in the efficacy of that cause, and therefore is no atheist."[39] And, indeed, we shall find that deism is but another name for atheism, whether we consider it in theory or in practice. That we should not be bettered by the introduction of deism or atheism, I think is a clear case. "The fear of the Lord is the beginning of wisdom." While this fear existed in France, there was some kind of manners, some kind of justice left; but ever since the deluded people have been taught that Jesus Christ was an infamous imposter; and the worship of him has been forbidden as "idolatrous," the whole infernal legion seems to be let loose amongst them; and the nation appears marked out for a dreadful example to mankind. Indeed, some such example was necessary to cure the world of the infidel philosophy of Voltaire, Rousseau, Gibbon, Priestley, and the rest of that enlightened tribe.[40]

We are continually exclaiming against prejudice, without attending to its effect on ourselves. I am afraid, prejudice in favor of the French Revolution, has led Americans to approve many things, which, a few years ago, they would have viewed with the utmost abhorrence; and that they would even now view with abhorrence, in any other nation. And here I cannot help taking notice of an article that appeared not many days ago in one of our public papers. The writer is giving a list of eminent persons who have "arisen on the democratic floor" which he concludes with *Marat, St. Paul,* and *Jesus Christ*.[41] Is it not a most horrid blasphemy to put the Son of God, the prince of peace, on a footing with the bloody author of the massacres at Paris and Versailles? I hope and believe, that such blasphemers are rare in the United States, and the only way to keep them so, is for the people to reject unanimously every attempt to debase christianity, in whatever shape, and under whatever disguise it may appear.

In the address of "the republican natives of Great-Britain and Ireland, resident at New-York," we find a very extraordinary passage indeed. But, before we say anything about this address, it will not be amiss to say a word or two about the addressers. I believe one might venture to say, that there are but few natives of Ireland among them; because the emigrants from that country, being generally engaged in agricultural pursuits from their first arrival here, have not the time to form themselves into political societies: and the words "Great-Britain" might probably have been supplied by *one word*. However, as the gentlemen have not thought this word worthy of a place in their address, I can by no means think of introducing it here. But let us see what they say of themselves: "After a *fruitless opposition* to a corrupt and tyrannical government, *many of us, like you,* sought freedom and protection in the United States of America. We look back on our native country with *pity* and *indignation,* at the outrages that humanity has sustained in the persons of the virtuous *Muir* and his patriotic associates." We may then fairly suppose, that these "republican natives of Great Britain and Ireland," can be no other than the members of that renowned convention of which the *"virtuous* Muir," who is now fortunately on his passage to Botany Bay, was president.[42]

The passage of their address, alluded to above, is as follows: "Participating in the many blessings, which the government is calculated to insure, we are happy in giving it this proof of our respectful attachment. We are only *grieved*, that a system of such beauty and excellence should be at all *tarnished* by the existence of *slavery in any form*; but, as friends to the equal rights of man, we must be permitted to say, that we wish these rights extended to every human being, *be his complexion what it may*. We however look forward with pleasing anticipation to *a yet more perfect state of society*; and from that love of liberty which forms so distinguished a trait in the American character, are taught to hope that this *last, this worst disgrace to a free government*, will finally and for ever be done away." So! These gentlemen are hardly landed in the United States, before they begin to cavil against the government, and to pant after a *more perfect state of Society*! If they have already discovered that the system is *tarnished* by *the last and worst disgrace of a free government*, what may we not reasonably expect from their future researches? If they, with their virtuous President, had been landed in the southern states, they might have lent a hand to finish the great work, so happily begun by citizens Santhonax [sic] and Polverel.[43] They have caught the *itch* of addressing, petitioning and remonstrating in their own country: let them scratch themselves into a cure; but let them not attempt spreading their disorder. They ought to remember, that they are come here "to seek freedom and protection" *for themselves*, and not *for others*. When the people of these states are ready for a total abolition of negro slavery, they will make a shift to see the propriety of adopting the measure without the assistance of these northern lights. In the mean time, as the convention cannot here enter on the legislative functions, they may amuse themselves with a fable written for their particular use.

The Pot-Shop, a Fable

In a pot-shop well stocked with ware of all sorts, a discontented ill formed pitcher unluckily bore the sway. One day, after the mortifying neglect of several customers, "gentlemen," said he, addressing himself to his brown brethren in general, "gentlemen, with your permission, we are a set of tame fools, without ambition, without courage: condemned to the vilest uses, we suffer all without murmuring. Let us dare to declare to ourselves, and we shall soon see the difference. That superb ewer, which, like us, is but earth; those gilded jars, vases, china, and, in short, all those elegant nonsenses, whose colours and beauty have neither weight nor solidity, must yield to our strength and give place to our superior merit."

This civic harangue was received with peals of applause, and the pitcher (chosen president) became the organ of the assembly. Some, however, more moderate than the rest, attempted to calm the minds of the multitude. But all those which are called jordans or chamber-pots, were become intractable. Eager to vie with the bowls and cups, they were impatient, almost to madness, to quit their obscure abodes, to shine upon the table, kiss the lip and ornament the cup-board.

In vain did a wise water jug (some say it was a platter) make them a long and serious discourse upon the peacefulness of their vocation. "Those," says he "who are destined to great employments are rarely the most happy. We are all of the same clay, 'tis true; but he who made us, formed us for different functions. One is for ornament, another for use. The posts the least important are often the most necessary. Our employments are extremely different, and so are our talents."

This had a wonderful effect; the most stupid began to open their ears: perhaps it would have succeeded, if a grease pot had not cried out with a decisive tone, You reason like an ass; "to the devil with you and your silly lessons."

Now, the scale was turned again: all the hord of jordans, pans and pitchers applauded the superior eloquence and reasoning of the grease pot. In short, they determined on the enterprize; but a dispute arose who should be chief: all would command, and none obey. It was then you might have heard a clutter: pots, pans and pitchers, mugs, jugs and jordans, all put themselves in motion at once; and so wisely and with so much vigour were their operations conducted, that the whole was soon changed—not into china, but *rubbish*.

Let us leave the application of this fable to those for whom it is intended, and come to the address of "the associated teachers in the city of New-York."

From the profession of these gentlemen, one would have wished not to find them among the Doctor's addressers; and it will be for those who employ the "associated Teachers" to judge, how far their approbation and praise of the writings of such a man, is a proof of their being calculated for "the arduous and *important* task of cultivating the human mind."[8] They very civilly invite the Doctor to assist them to *"form the man;"* and, in his answer, he seems to hint that he may possibly accept the invitation. All I can say on this matter, is, if he should embrace this profession, I hope he will be exactly as successful in forming the man, as he has been in reforming him.

In the answer to the "associated Teachers," the Doctor observes, that *classes* of men, as well "as *individuals*, are apt to form *too high* ideas of their *own importance*." Never was a juster observation than this, and never was this observation more fully verified than in the parties themselves. The Doctor's self-importance is sufficiently depicted in the quotation that I have given from his letter to the people of Birmingham; and as for the "associated Teachers," how familiarly soever they may talk of "the intrigueing politics and vitiating refinements of the European World," I must say, I think, they know but little of what passes in that world; or they never would have larded with such extravagant eulogiums, productions, which, in general, have been long exploded.

With respect to the Doctor's metaphysical reveries, or, in other words, his system of infidelity, I shall leave to himself the task of exposing that to the detestation of Americans, as it has long been to that of the English.[9] Of his scientific productions, I propose, in a little time, to give the public a short review;[10] meanwhile I refer the curious reader, to the publications of the Royal Society, of 1791 and 1792, and to Doctor Bewley's treatise on air. He will there see his system of chemistry and natural philosophy detected, exposed and defeated; and the "celebrated Philosopher" himself accused and convicted of plagiarism.[11] [44] He will there find the key to the following sentence: "The *patronage* to be met with, in monarchical governments, is ever *capricious*, and as often employed to bear down merit as to promote it, having for its object, not science, or anything useful to mankind, but

---

[8] I have been informed, that these *associated* brethren of the birch, complain of my attacking them in the dark; but let them lay their hands to their hearts, and say, if they can, that I fight more unfair than they do, when they discharge their ill humour on a poor little trembling wretch, whose pitiful look would soften the heart of a tiger. However, I cease the inglorious combat: I confess it is not fair to attack them with a pen. They know how to write with a rod only; and I dare say their answer to my observations on their address, is still legible on the back-sides of their unfortunate pupils.

[9] He has made a pretty good beginning already, as we shall see by and by.

[10] The Doctor has saved me the trouble of doing this.

[11] Have a little patience, reader, and you shall be satisfied of this.

the mere reputation of the patron, *who is seldom any judge of science.*"[12] This is the language of every soured neglected author, from a sorry ballad monger to a Doctor with half a dozen initials at the end of his name.

As to his talents as a writer, we have only to open our eyes to be convinced that they are far below mediocrity. His style is uncouth and superlatively diffuse. Always involved in *munitiae*, [sic] every sentence is a string of parenthesises, in finding the end of which, the reader is lucky if he does not lose the proposition they were meant to illustrate. In short, the whole of his phraseology is extremely disgusting; to which may be added, that even in point of grammar he is very often incorrect.

As a proof of what I have here asserted, I could give a thousand sentences from his writings; but I choose one or two from his answers to the addressers, as these pieces are in every body's hands; and, not to criticise unfairly, I shall take the first sentence I come at. It runs thus:

"Viewing with the deepest concern, as you do, the prospect that is now exhibited in Europe, those troubles which are the natural offspring of their forms of government, originating indeed in the spirit of liberty, but gradually degenerating into tyrannies, equally degrading to the rulers and the ruled, I rejoice in finding an asylum from persecution in a country in which those abuses have come to a natural termination, and produced another system of liberty, founded on such wise principles, as I trust, will guard against all future abuses; those artificial distinctions in society, from which they sprung, being completely eradicated, that protection from violence, which laws and government promise in all countries, but which I have not found in my own, I doubt not I shall find with you, though I cannot promise to be a better subject of this government, than my whole conduct will evince that I have been to that of Great Britain."

This is neither the *style periodique*, nor the *style coupé*, it is I presume the *style entortillé*: for one would certainly think that the author had racked his imagination to render what he had to say unintelligible. This sentence of monstrous length is cut asunder in the middle by a semicolon, which, except that it serves the weary reader by way of half way house, might be placed in any other part of the sentence, to, at

---

[12] This was addressed to the Philosophical Society at Philadelphia. We shall see all this unravelled by and by.

least, equal advantage. In fact, this is not a sentence; it is a rigmarole ramble, that has neither beginning nor ending, and conveys to us no idea of any thing but the author's incapacity.

"Viewing with the deepest concern as you do, the prospect that is now exhibited in Europe, those *troubles* which are the natural offspring of THEIR forms of government." What, in the name of goodness does this mean?—*Troubles* is the only antecedent that can be found to *their*, and the necessary conclusion is, *troubles have their forms of government*. . . .

I grant that there is great reason to believe, that the Doctor was resolved to be as dull as his addressers; but I assert, that it is impossible for a person accustomed to commit his thoughts to paper, with the smallest degree of taste or correctness, to fall into such gross solecisms, or to tack phrases together in such an awkward homespun manner. In short, he cannot be fit for even the post of *castigator*; and therefore it is to be hoped that the "associated Teachers" will not lessen their "importance" by admitting him amongst them; that is to say, except it be as a pupil.

There are many things that astonish us in the addresses, amongst which the *compassion* that the addressers express for that "*infatuated*" and "*devoted country*," Great-Britain, certainly is not the least.

The Democratic Society, with a hatred against tyranny, that would have become the worthy nephew of Damien,[13] [45] or the great Marat himself, say, "The multiplied oppressions which characterise that government, excite in us, the most painful sensations, and exhibit a spectacle as disgusting in itself as dishonorable to the British name."

And what a tender affectionate concern do the sons of Tammany express for the poor distressed unfortunate country of their "venerable ancestors." "A country," say they, "although now presenting a prospect frightful to the eye of humanity, yet *once* the nurse of sciences, of arts, of heroes, and of freemen, a country, which, although at present apparently *devoted to destruction*, we *fondly* hope, may yet *tread back the steps of infamy and ruin*, and *once more rise conspicuous among the free nations* of the earth."

But of all the addresses, none seem so zealous on this subject, as "the republican natives of Great Britain and Ireland." "While," say they "we look back on our native country with emotions of pity and indignation, at the outrages human nature has sustained, in the per-

---

[13] Robespierre.

sons of the virtuous *Muir* and his patriotic associates; and deeply lament the fatal apathy into which our *countrymen* have fallen; we desire to be thankful to the great author of our being, that we are in America, and that it had pleased him, in his wise providence, to make these United States an Asylum, not only from the immediate tyranny of the British government, but also from those impending calamities, which its increasing despotism, and multiplied iniquities, must infallibly bring down on a deluded and oppressed people." What an enthusiastic warmth is here! No solemn-league-and-covenant prayer, embellished with the nasal sweetness of the conventicle, was ever more affecting.

To all this, the Doctor very pitiously echoes back, "sigh for sigh, and groan for groan; and when the fountain of their eyes is dry, his supplies the place, and weeps for both."[46]

There is something so pathetic, so irresistably moving in all this, that a man must have a hard heart indeed, to read it, and not burst into laughter.

In speaking of Monarchies, it has often been lamented, that the sovereign seldom or never hears the truth; and much afraid I am, that this is equally applicable to democracies. What court sycophants are to a prince, demagogues are to a people; and the latter kind of parasites is by no means less dangerous than the former; perhaps more so, as being more ambitious and more numerous. God knows, there were too many of this description in America, before the arrival of Doctor Priestley: I can, therefore, see no reason for boastings and addressings on account of the acquisition.

Every one must observe, how the Doctor has fallen at once into the track of those, who were already in possession of the honourable post. Finding a popular prejudice prevailing against his country, and not possessing that *patriae caritas*,[47] which is the characteristic of his countrymen, he has not been ashamed to attempt making his court by flattering that prejudice. I grant, that a prejudice against this nation, is not only excusable, but almost commendable in *Americans*; but the misfortune is, it exposes them to deception, and makes them the sport of every intriguing adventurer. Suppose it be the interest of Americans, that Great-Britain should be ruined, and even annihilated, in the present contest; it can never be their interest, to believe that this desirable object, is already, nearly or quite accomplished, at a time when she is become more formidable than ever, in every quarter of the globe. And with respect to the internal situation of that country, we ought not to suffer ourselves to be deceived by "gleanings from morning chronicles, or Dublin gazettes:" for, if we insist, that newspaper report is the criterion by which we ought to judge of the governments, and the state of other countries, we must allow the same measure to foreigners with respect to our own country; and then what must the people of England think of the government of the United States, upon reading a page or two from the slovenly pen of *Agricola*.

"It is charitable," says this democrat,—"It is charitable to believe many who signed the constitution, never dreamed of the measures taking place, which alas! we now experience. By this double government, we are involved in unnecessary burdens, which *neither we nor our fathers* ever knew. Such a *monster of a government* has seldom ever been known on earth. We are obliged to maintain two governments, with their full number of officers from head to foot. Some of them receive such wages as never were heard of before in any government upon earth; and all this bestowed on *Aristocrats* for doing next to nothing. A blessed revolution! a blessed revolution indeed! but farmers, mechanics, and labourers have no share in it; we are the asses who must have the honor of paying them all, without any adequate service. Now, let the impartial judge, whether our government, taken collectively, answers the great end of *protecting our persons and property*! Or whether it is not rather calculated to drain us of our money, and give it to men who have not rendered adequate service for it. Had an inspired prophet told us the things which our eyes see, in the beginning of the revolution, he might have met Jeremiah's fate; or if we had believed him, *not one, in a thousand, would have resisted Great-Britain*. Indeed, my countrymen, we are so loaded by our new governments, that we can have little heart to attempt to move under all our burdens; we have this consolation, when things come to the worst, there must be a change, and *we may rest satisfied, that either the federal or state governments must fall*."

If "gleanings" like these were published in England, would not the people naturally exclaim,—What! the boasted government of America come to this already? The poor Americans are dreadfully tyrannized by the Aristocrats! There will certainly be a *revolution* in America soon! They would be just as much mistaken as the people in this country are, when they talk of a revolution in England.

Neither ought we to look upon the emigration of persons from England to this country as a proof of their being persecuted, and of the tyranny of the English government. It is paying America a very poor compliment, to suppose that nothing short of persecution, could bring settlers to its shores. This is, besides, the most unfortunate proof that could possibly be produced by the advocates of the French Revolution: for, if the emigration of a person to this country be a proof of a tyranny existing in that from which he comes, how superlatively tyrannical must the government in France be? But they say, those who emigrate from France are Aristocrats: they are not persecuted; they emigrate because they *hate a free country*. What! do they really come to *America* because they *hate a free country*? Did the governors of Martinico, &c. make a capitulation to be sent here, *to avoid going to a free country*? The Democratic Society will certainly oblige the world very much in explaining this enigma.

I am one of those who wish to believe that foreigners come to this country from choice, and not from necessity. America opens a wide field for enterprize; wages for all mechanics are better, and the means of subsistence proportionably cheaper than in Europe. This is what brings foreigners amongst us: they become citizens of America for the honest purposes of commerce, of turning their industry and talents to the best account, and of bettering their fortunes. By their exertions to enrich themselves, they enrich the state, lower the wages, and render the country less dependent upon others. The most numerous, as well as the most useful, are mechanics; perhaps a cobler [sic], with his hammer and awls, is a more valuable acquisition than a dozen philosophi-theologi-politi-cal empiricks with all their boasted apparatus.

Of all the English arrived in these States (since the war) no one was ever calculated to render them less service than Doctor Priestley; and what is more, perhaps no one (before or since, or even in the war) ever intended to render them less: his preference to the American government is all affectation: his emigration was not voluntary: he staid in England till he saw no hopes of recovering a lost reputation; and then, bursting with envy and resentment, he fled into what the Tammany society very justly call "banishment," with the universal detestation of his countrymen. . . .

Before I bid the Doctor adieu, I should be glad to ask him how he finds himself in his "*asylum.*" It is said, he has declared that the duplicity of our Land-Jobbers is more to be feared than the outrages of a Birmingham mob; and indeed, if all his complaints had had the same appearance of being well-founded, the public would never have been troubled with these observations; for, there is little doubt of his having been most cruelly fleeced. This honest profession, vulgarly called land-jobbing, a member of Congress very justly styled "swindling upon a broad scale;" it is, in fact, a South-Sea bubble upon *terra firma*, as hundreds and thousands of ruined foreigners, besides Doctor Priestley, can testify.[48]

It is to be hoped that the Doctor's anger against his country is by this time nearly assuaged: dear-bought experience has at last taught him, that an Utopia never existed any where but in a delirious brain. He thought, like too many others, to find America a Terrestrial Paradise; a land of Canaan, where he would have nothing to do, but to open his mouth to swallow the milk and honey: but, alas! he is now convinced, I believe, that those who cultivate the fertile Lesowes of Warwickshire,

"Where all around the gentlest breezes play,
Where gentle music melts on every spray,"

have little reason to envy him his rocks and his swamps, the music of his bull-frogs and the stings of his musquitoes.[49]

In the preface, so often mentioned, the Doctor expresses a desire of one day returning to "the land that gave him birth;" and, no offence to the New-York addressers, I think we ought to wish that this desire may be very soon accomplished. He is a bird of passage that has visited us, only to avoid the rigour of an inclement season: when the re-animating sunshine of revolution shall burst forth on his native clime, we may hope to see him prune his wings, and take his flight from the dreary banks of the Susquehannah to those of the Thames or the Avon.

The Short but Comprehensive Story of a Farmer's Bull.

A certain troublesome fellow, who turned his back upon the church, having occasion to pass through a large farm-yard in his way to a meeting house, met with a fine majestic venerable old Bull lying down at his ease, and basking in the sun-shine. This Bull was at times the tamest creature in the world; he would suffer the curs to yelp at him, the flies to tease him, and even some of the mischievous fellows to pull him by the horns. He was at this very moment in one of his gentlest humours; ruminating upon past and present scenes of delight; contemplating the neighbouring dairy and the farm-yard, where the milch cows had all their bags distended till they were nearly running over; the calves, and the pigs, and the poultry, were frisking, and grunting, and crowing on every dung-hill; the granaries were full, and the barns ready to burst, there were, besides, many a goodly rick of wheat, and barley, and oats, and pease, and beens, and hay, and rye-grass, and clover. The dairy was full of curds, and cream, and butter, and cheese of every kind. To be sure, there was plenty for the master and his family, and all the servants, and every body belonging to the farm. Nay, those that were poor and needy, and idle, and lazy, and sick, and proud, and saucy, and old, and infirm, and silly, were freely supplied: and even this troublesome fellow himself, notwithstanding he had long since quarrelled with the head-farmer and all his best friends, and an old grudge was still subsisting betwixt them, yet, upon making at any time a solemn promise to do no mischief, had free ingress, egress, and regress, in every part of the farm and the dairy, and was at liberty to help himself wherever he liked. In short, he was allowed to do any thing but *skim the cream* and set *his own mark upon the butter*.

Now, because the bull had happened to place himself across his favourite foot-path, although there was plenty of room to the right and to the left, nothing would satisfy this impudent fellow but he must kick *Old John*, for that was the Bull's name, out of his way: and all the world agrees that *John* suffered him to kick a long while, before he shewed the least inclination to rise and resent the affront. At last, however, he got upon his legs, and began to look round him, but still it was a look of contempt only, which the foolish fellow mistook for the marks of fear; and now, growing bolder, and bolder, and hallooing the curs, and calling all his comrades to prick and goad him in the tenderest parts of his body, the Bull began to threaten and roar;—this was on the 14th of July, one of the hottest days in the summer, when some body threw a fiery stick under his tail, at the very moment that a parcel of impudent half-witted fellows were trying to flourish a French flambeau (lighted and blazing at both ends) full in his face. No wonder that the Bull should set off with a vengeance in the street:— down went the gingerbread-stalls, and the hard-ware shops, the buckle menders and the razor-grinders, and the dagger-makers: he even got into private houses, and in one place threw down whole baskets full of bottles and chemical glasses, crucibles and gun-barrels;—

smash went all the jars of inflammable air, which instantly took fire, and spread all over the place; every thing went to rack and ruin; nothing was safe; even the religious houses themselves, where nothing had ever been heard but the most pious exhortations (like these of Doctor Vicessimus Knox),[50] to peace and harmony, and obedience to the governing powers. In short, nothing could pacify or put a stop to the fury of this poor enraged animal, till his honest master the farmer, as quiet and as good a kind of church-going man as ever lived in the world, father of a large family, hearing the rumpus, sent a number of his best and steadiest old servants to muzzle the beast, which had already tossed the fellow with the fiery stick over the tops of houses and gored him in fifty different places. It was next to a miracle that he escaped with his life; and every body thought he had reason to be thankful that he got off so well as he did; but no sooner did he find himself safe in a *Hackney*-coach, than, to the astonishment of all the world, he began to *preach* up his innocence, and to lodge a complaint against poor *Old John*, who, in the end, suffered a great deal more than himself. Some silly people pitied him; some laughed at him; others again were wicked enough to wish him at the devil:—even his best friends were ashamed of him; and although they, one and all, defended him as much as they could in public, there was a confounded deal of muttering and grumbling in private. "I thought what it would come to," said one; "a pretty method of driving a mad Bull through the church pales," said another.

But, to go on with my story; no sooner was the Bull fairly muzzled, and properly confined, than the friends and neighbours on both sides were called in, to enquire into the whole affair; but there were so many contradictory stories that it was impossible to come at the truth, how it happened, or who had first provoked him; but since it was plain to everybody that *Old John* did the mischief, and as he was proved to be the Town Bull, it was at last settled that the parish should pay all the damages, for not keeping him in better order.

And here again was fresh matter for discontent: some thought it hard to pay for all the inflammable air, which had done full as much mischief as the Bull. Others again objected to a monstrous out-of-the-way heavy demand for a large quantity (several reams) of fools-cap paper, which had been scribbled upon and spoiled long before the affair happened. Indeed, in the opinion of some sensible persons, it was fit for nothing but kindling the fire.

But the strangest part of the story remains to be told; for when this bustle was all over and settled, and every body thought the perverse fellow was going to take to his church, and get his living in an honest way, what did he do but set to work bottling up his own f-rts, and selling them for superfine inflammable air,[51] and what's still worse, had the impudence to want a patent for the *discovery*; and, indeed, a good many people were deceived for a long time; but, they say, two of a trade can never agree, and so it happened here; for a brother trade[r] one day catched him at his dirty tricks and exposed him to the whole parish. After this all the neighbours cried shame on him: the women laughed, the girls they tittered, even the little boys pointed at him, and made game of him as he went along the street. In short, one dark night when all the neighbourhood was quiet and every body fast asleep, up he got and sat off into the next parish, bag and baggage.

Here he trumped up a terrible story, pretended to be frightened to death, and swore and d——d his soul, if the Bull was not just at his heels. The good folks (who by the by, had a monstrous grudge against *Old John*) believed him at once; and now there was the devil to do again; the women screamed and fell into fits, out run the men and boys with broomsticks, and pitchforks, and scalping knives to kill the Bull: but it was all a sham, for poor *Old John* was quiet at home, grazing in the meadow, up to his eyes in clover, and bluebells, and daffodils, and cows-lips, and primroses, as contented as a lamb, and neither thinking nor caring any more about the fellow with the fiery stick than about one of the flies that he was brushing off with his tail.

But the worst of all is to come yet: for while these silly people were running about and making a hue and cry against *Old John*, their *own Bull* (a thirsty beast that they had penned up in a barren lot, without any pond or watering-place) broke loose, and did ten times more mischief than *John* had ever done. This made a fine laugh all round the country; every body said it served them just right; and to be sure it did, for they should have looked at home, and minded their own Bull, and not run bawling about after *Old John*.

[2]

A Bone to Gnaw, for the Democrats

THE OCCASION FOR THIS PAMPHLET WAS THE AMERICAN EDITION of *The Political Progress of Britain*, written by the Scottish "ideological immigrant" James Thomson Callender and originally published in Edinburgh. Callender had accused the British government of an "endless catalogue of massacres in Asia and America," and commented that "every other nation in the world must be entitled to wish that an earthquake or a volcano should first bury the whole British islands together in the centre of the globe." He had also condemned Britain's hereditary rulers for bleeding their own country dry and enriching themselves on the backs of the productive classes at home. Describing himself as "An Exile for writing this Pamphlet," Callender predicted that a revolution would occur in Scotland within the next ten years.

"A Bone to Gnaw, for the Democrats," published in January 1795, began as a counterattack on Callender's pamphlet, but soon broadened into a wide-ranging denunciation of democrats in America and culminated in a call for Anglo-American reconciliation. In the process, Cobbett poured scorn on the democratic "Crusade against Royalty" in the United States, with its attempt to revolutionize American theater, music, pictures, artwork, and language, and its intention to eradicate the remaining symbols of monarchy and the British connection in America.

Within this general attack on the democratic cultural revolution of the 1790s, Cobbett singled out specific examples of what he saw as democratic ingratitude, anarchism, and hypocrisy. The American democrats who welcomed the execution of Louis XVI, he argued, had conveniently forgotten that American independence had been made possible in the first place by Louis XVI's assistance and the Franco-American alliance of 1778; such patriots were nothing more than "ungrateful hell-hounds." The democrats who sympathized with or supported the Whiskey Rebels of 1794, Cobbett contended, were in fact hostile to all forms of government; the United States must be protected from men who thrived on chaos. And the democrats who mouthed the slogans of liberty, equality, and fraternity while refusing to renounce the right of holding slaves were an obvious target; one of the most effective parts of the pamphlet simply juxtaposed a report of a democratic feast in Philadelphia with an advertisement in the same newspaper for the sale of "two negro lads" and a "negro wench."

As well as providing further insights into the character of Cobbett's conservatism, "A Bone to Gnaw" presents a fascinating picture of the political culture of the American democratic movement—from Joel Barlow's revised version of "God Save the King" ("God Save the Guillotine"), through the adoption of Jacobin styles and symbols, to William Thornton's attempt to revolutionize the alphabet and replace it with the phonetics of liberty. The pamphlet was very popular; it went into three editions in three months, and Cobbett himself commented that "it was read in all companies, by the young and by the old."

A BONE TO GNAW, FOR THE DEMOCRATS; OR OBSERVATIONS ON A PAMPHLET, ENTITLED, "THE POLITICAL PROGRESS OF BRITAIN."

THE *THIRD* EDITION, REVISED.

> "Quand tu manges, donnes à manger
> Aux chiens, dussent-ils te mordre.
> *La Pompadour.*"

Preface

READER,

If you have a Shop to mind, or any other business to do, I advise you to go and do it, and let this book alone; for, I can assure you, it contains nothing of half so much importance to you, as the sale of a skein of thread or a yard of tape. By such a transaction you might possibly make a net profit of half a farthing, a thing, though seemingly of small value, much more worthy your attention than the treasures under the State House at Amsterdam, or all the mines of Peru. Half a farthing might lay the foundation of a brilliant fortune, and sooner than you should be deprived of it by this work, though it may be called my offspring, I would, like the worshippers of Moloch, commit it to the flames with my own hands.

If you are of that sex, vulgarly called the Fair, but which ought always to be called the Divine, let me beseech you, if you value your charms, to proceed no further. Politics *is a mixture of anger and deceit, and these are the mortal enemies of Beauty. The instant a lady turns politician, farewell the smiles, the dimples, the roses; the graces abandon her, and age sets his seal on her front. We never find* Hebe, *goddess ever fair and ever young, chattering politics at the table of the gods; and though* Venus *once interposed in behalf of her beloved* Paris, *the spear of* Diomede *taught her "to tremble at the name of arms." And, have we not a terrible example of recent, very recent, date? I mean that of the unfortunate* Mary Wolstoncraft.[1] *It is a well known fact, that, when that political lady began* The Rights of Women, *she had as fine black hair as you would wish to see, and that, before the second sheet of her work went to the press, it was turned as white, and a great deal whiter than her skin. You must needs think, I have the ambition common to every author; that is to say, to be read; but I declare, that, sooner than bleach one auburn ringlet, or even a single hair; sooner than rob the world of one heavenly smile, I would with pleasure see my pamphlet torn up to light the pipes of a Democratic club, or burnt, like the* Political Progress, *by the hands of a Scotch hangman, or even loaded with applauses by the* Philadelphia Gazette.

It is a little singular for an author to write a Preface to hinder his work from being read; but this is not my intention; all I wish to do, is to confine it within its proper sphere. I am aware that my sincerity in this respect may be called in question; and that malice may ascribe to me motives that never entered my thoughts: but of this I am totally regardless; my work answers to its title, and, consequently, nobody but the Democrats can have any thing to do with it. Nor does it court their approbation; I throw it in amongst them, as amongst a kennel of hounds: let them snarl and growl over it, and gnaw it and slaver it; the more they wear out their fangs this way the less dangerous will be their bite hereafter.

A Bone to Gnaw, for the Democrats

Though the good people of America cannot for their lives comprehend the views, from which they have been favoured with a publication of *The Political Progress of Britain*, we may suppose, that the fondness of the Author led him to see a possibility of its being read; and, as it is in the nature of reading to give rise to observations, he will not be surprised, that some of those, arising from the reading of his patriotic labours, have, by a very ordinary process, found their way into print. It is thus that books, more grateful than the children of men, never fail to yield assistance to those that have given them birth. Whenever neglect lays its icy hand on an unfortunate production, another flies to its aid; and, though it cannot cancel the irrevocable doom; it saves it, for a moment at least, from the jaws of the unclean monster, that is day and night gaping to receive it. Such being, at least in part, the charitable views of this pamphlet, it will undoubtedly meet with a hearty welcome from all the friends of *The Political Progress*, and particularly from its Author.

Let me then ask; what could induce him to come a' the wa' from Edinborough to Philadelphia to make an attack upon poor old England? And, if this be satisfactorily accounted for, upon principles of domestic philosophy, which teaches us, that froth and scum stopped in at one place will burst out at another, still I must be permitted to ask; what could induce him to imagine, that the citizens of the United States were, in any manner whatever, interested in the affair? What are his adventures in Scotland, and his "narrow escape," to us, who live on this side of the Atlantic? What do we care whether his associates, *Ridgway* and *Symons*, are still in Newgate, or whether they have been translated to Surgeon's Hall?[2] Is it any thing to us whether he prefers Charley to George, or George to Charley, any more than whether he used to eat his burgoo with his fingers or with a horn spoon?[3] What are his debts and his misery to us? Just as if we cared whether his posteriors were covered with a pair of breeches, or a kelt, or whether he was literally sans culotte?[4] In Great Britain, indeed, his barking might answer some purpose; there he was near the object of his fury; but here he is like a cur howling at the Moon.

Indeed, he himself seems to have been fully sensible of the ridiculousness of the situation in which this publication would place him, and therefore he has had the precaution to surround himself with company, to keep him in countenance. He says that *Mr. Jefferson*, late American Secretary of State, spoke of his work, on different occasions, in respectful terms; and that he declared, "it contained the most astonishing concentration of abuses, that he had ever heard of." He tells us besides, that *other gentlemen* have delivered their opinions to the same effect; and that their *encouragement* was one principal cause of the appearance of this American edition.

And did he in good earnest, imagine that mixture with such company would render his person sacred and invulnerable? He should have recollected, that, though one *scabby* sheep infects a whole stock, he does not thereby work his own cure.

As to *Mr. Jefferson*, I must suppose him entirely out of the Question; for, nobody that has the least knowledge of the talents, penetration and taste of that Gentleman, will ever believe, that he could find any thing worthy of *respect* in a production, evidently intended to seduce the rabble of North Britain. Besides, upon looking a second time over the words attributed to *Mr. Jefferson*, I think, it is easy to discover, that the quotation is erroneous: the word *abuses*, I am pretty confident, should be, *abuse*; and thus, by leaving out an *s*, the sentence expresses exactly what one would expect from such a person as *Mr. Jefferson*: "that the work contained the most astonishing concentration of *abuse*, that he had ever heard of."

With respect to those *other gentlemen* whose encouragement has thrusted the Author forward, it is not difficult to guess to what *clan* they belong; but, let them be who they may, and let their situation be what it may (and if I am right in my guess, it is at this time aukward enough), I think they would not exchange it for the one they have placed him in. He vainly imagines himself the hero of the farce, when he is nothing but the buffoon. Indeed he has described the part he is acting better than I, or any one else can do it. He says that Authors of revolutionary pamphlets form a kind of "forlorn hope on the skirts of battle." Every one knows, that the forlorn hope, or *enfans perdus*, was, amongst the ancient Gauls, composed of the outcasts of society; wretches whose lives were already forfeited (and who had not had the good luck, like our Author, to "escape") who were set in the front of battle, not for their *courage*, but their *crimes*. The comparison he has pilfered from Dean Swift; it is therefore just to return it to its owner; but as to the application of it to himself, I am certain, nobody can have the least objection.

However, I can hardly imagine, that the *encouragement* of these *gentlemen* would, alone, have dragged him into so dangerous a service. I think, his conduct may be, in part, accounted for upon physical principles. We are told, that there is, or ought to be, about every human body, a certain part called the *crumena*, upon which depends the whole œconomy of the intestines. When the *crumena* is full, the intestines are in a correspondent state; and then the body is inclined to repose, and the mind to peace and good neighbourhood: but when the *crumena*[1] becomes empty, the sympathetic intestines are immediately contrac-

[1] The Purse.

ted, and the whole internal state of the patient is thrown into insurrection and uproar, which, communicating itself to the brain, produces what a learned state physician calls, the *mania reformatio*; and if this malady is not stopped at once, by the help of an hempen necklace, or some other remedy equally efficacious, it never fails to break out into Atheism, Robbery, Unitarianism, Swindling, Jacobinism, Massacres, Civic Feasts and Insurrections. Now, it appears to me, that our unfortunate Author must be afflicted with this dreadful malady, and if so, I will appeal to any man of feeling, whether his friends would not have shewn their humanity, in relieving him by other means than those they have *encouraged* him to employ; which, besides being unproductive, have exposed both him and them to the birch of public opinion. . . .

What then is this blessed performance? what does it contain, that such uncommon, such unnatural efforts should be made to drag it into day? Why, *The Political Progress*, or *Sawney's Complaint*[5] (for this title would become it much better than the one it has assumed),[2] paints in as odious a light as black and white will admit of, those kings of England who have inflicted severities on the Scotch; it abuses all the most celebrated Whigs of the United Kingdoms, and in general, every body who was disposed to the cause of the *Pretender*; it contains the most sophistical and ill-digested account of the national debt, the wars, taxes, and expences of government in Great Britain, that has ever yet appeared; in short, the piece altogether, forms one of the most complete Whisky-boy Billingsgate libels, or, as *Mr. Jefferson* emphatically expressed it, "the most astonishing concentration of abuse," that ever was seen, or heard of.

Yes, reader, look at it again, and tell me what you can find here, that can merit the attention of an *American*. If you want to know the characters of the kings of England, you will find them recorded in history; you will there find the good with the bad: you will find, that they have

---

[2] I cannot leave the reader to imagine for a moment, that I am here at the Scotch *in general*. They are *a nation* I respect above any other, except my own. For prudence, perseverence, integrity, courage and learning, they are above all praise. And as to loyalty, by no means the least of virtues, the great body of the nation are far more loyal than their neighbours in the South. Witness the *American War*: it was the Scotch bore the brunt of it. They were, in fact, the Alpha and Omega of that war. But the merits and fidelity of *a nation* can never justify the apostacy of individuals, after having confessed candidly my admiration and respect for the one, I must be allowed to express as candidly my abhorrence of the other.

all had their faults, and most of them their virtues. If you find that some of them were wolves, you will never find that their subjects or their neighbours were lambs. From the same source you will learn, that, ever since the abdication of James II the embers of discontent have been kept alive in Scotland, by the means of ambitious demagogues: you will find that their influence is daily decreasing, but that, like the Antifederalists in America, they seize every opportunity to exert it, in reviling the government, representing every tax as an oppression, and exciting the ignorant to insurrection.[3] You will observe (and undoubtedly with a great deal of pleasure) that exertions of such a horrid tendency have not, latterly, had the same effects there, that they have here; but you must nevertheless agree, that it was as prudent and as justifiable in the government of Great Britain, to prosecute those who were endeavouring to kindle the flames of civil war in Scotland, as it is in the government of the United States to prosecute the men, who, for a similar crime, are now in Philadelphia jail, waiting their trials. As to the taxes in Great Britain, they are heavy, and I believe in my soul it is in their very nature to be heavy, as much as it is in the nature of lead; for, the people complain of their weight not only there, but here, and every where else. You will, perhaps, like many other compassionate people, feel a good deal of anxiety about the *national debt* of Great Britain, and may possibly have your fears of *a general bankruptcy*: but, suffer me to caution you against an excess of sensibility; for, though compassion is, in itself, amiable, it degenerates into weakness, when lavished on an unworthy object: nay, it even looks meddling, if not childish, to be eternally expressing a solicitude for people who do not seem at all sensible of your kindness. . . .

In defence of the conduct of the *gentlemen encouragers* of *The Political Progress of Britain*, it has been roundly asserted, that there exists a Monarchy Party in the United States, and that every thing tending to

---

[3] I wish we could say, that a change of air had produced a change of conduct in some of them. The comrades of *Muir* and *Palmer* were no sooner landed at New York last year, than they began to pick a hole in the coat of the *American Government*. They openly declared, that it was "*tarnished by the last and worst disgrace of a free government*" and said, that they looked forward to "*a more perfect state of Society*" (see their address to the *Unatarian* [sic] *Doctor*.[)] I do not say that they had any immediate hand in the western affair [the Whiskey Rebellion]: but when rebels from all quarters of the world are received with open arms, as persecuted patriots, it is no wonder that rebellion should be looked upon as patriotism.

render it odious is necessary and laudable; and that, consequently, it was no more than fair play to borrow, or hire, the pen of a needy foreigner to lampoon the government and constitution of his own country. But, whoever will give themselves the trouble to open their eyes, or make use of a very little recollection, will be convinced, I fancy, that there is no reason for alarm on this account.

Our democrats are continually crying shame on the satellites of Royalty, for carrying on a Crusade against Liberty; when the fact is, the sattelites [sic] of Liberty[4] are carrying on a Crusade against Royalty. . . .

Their first object of attack was the Stage. Every Royal or Noble character was to be driven into everlasting exile, or, at least, none such was ever to be introduced except by way of degradation. The words your majesty, My Lord, and the like, were held to be as offensive to the chaste ears of Republicans, as silks, gold lace, painted cheeks and powdered periwigs to their eyes. In short, the highest and lowest titles were to be *citizen* and *citess*, and the dresses were all to be *à la mode de Paris*.

That the Theatre might not suffer for want of pieces adapted to the reformed taste, the reformers had the goodness to propose *William Tell* and several others equally amusing. —— *William* was to be modernized: in place of shooting the Governor with a bow and arrow, he was to stab him in the guts with a dagger, cut off his head, and carry it round the Stage upon a *pike*, while the music was to play the *Murderer's Hymn* and *Ha, ça ira*. . . .[6]

To make the reader amends for *William Tell*, I am going [to] treat him with a delicate morsel indeed; and, which adds to its merit, it is not in every body's hands, the publication, from which I have extracted it, being, thank God, but very little known.

"A new Song called the *Guilliotine*, Sung at the celebration of the *fourth of July*, by a number of French and *American* citizens at Hamburg. Written by the celebrated Mr. *Barlow*, who was then at that place.[7]

---

[4] Take care, reader, how you confound terms here. *Liberty*, according to the Democratic Dictionary, does not mean *freedom from oppression*; it is a very comprehensive term, signifying, among other things, *slavery, robbery, murder*, and *blasphemy*. Citizen David, painter to the Propagande, has represented *Liberty* under the form of a *Dragon*; it is, I suppose, for this reason that our democrats cry out against St. George as "the most dangerous of Liberticides."

> God save the Guilliotine,
> 'Till *England's King* and *Queen*,
>   Her power shall prove:
> 'Till each anointed knob
> Affords a clipping job,
> Let no vile halter rob,
>   The Guilliotine.
>
> Fame, let thy trumpet sound,
> Tell all the world around,
>   How *Capet* fell:
> And when great *George's* poll
> Shall in the basket roll,
> Let mercy then controul
>   The Guilliotine.
>
> When *all* the *sceptred crew*
> Have paid their homage, due
>   The Guilliotine,
> Let freedom's flag advance,
> 'Till all the world like France,
> O'er tyrants graves shall dance
>   And peace begin".

With respect to this tender madrigal, we are at a loss which to admire most; the style and sentiments of the "celebrated Author,"[5] the delicacy of the Editor, or the taste of his readers. I say *his* readers, for I should be sorry to think it was the taste of the inhabitants, in general, of Philadelphia. . . .

That there should be found amongst us men so vindictive as to pray for the murder of the King and Queen of England, people who had offended us, is not so very astonishing; unfortunately there are men of that stamp in all countries, and consequently, we must expect to find some of that description amongst those who live by entertaining the public. It is not therefore more wonderful that such a sentiment

---

[5] It would be worth the reader's while to enquire whether this *celebrated author* has never employed his poetic talent in making an addition to Doctor Watt's version of the Psalms? If this should appear to be the case, it must be allowed he is in a fair way to become an universal genius, and an honor to his country.

should find its way into a Newspaper than that it should be conceived. But that there should be found a *number of Americans*, or even *one*, capable of rejoicing and laughing at the tragic fall of the unfortunate Louis XVI, is a fact of such a horrid nature, that we wish not to believe our eyes and ears.

Who is not sensible of the efforts, the mighty, the successful efforts, made by that Monarch in favour of these States? Who is not sensible, that to those efforts America owes her Independence? Every one is sensible of it; and it is for this reason, that all parties join in celebrating the 6th. of February, the anniversary of the conclusion of the Treaty of Alliance between Louis XVI and the United States.[6] Recollect, reader, that the song above quoted, was sung on the *fourth of July*; on the anniversary of that Independence we boast of as a sovereign good. Recollect that a number of Americans, assembled to rejoice on Account of this blessing, called to the universe at the same time, to witness their joy at the murder of him who conferred it! This was all that was wanted to the humiliation of the house of Bourbon and to the revenge of its Rival. Poor Louis might deserve something of this kind in the eyes of Englishmen; by them he might expect his memory would be execrated. Could he now look from the grave, what would be his astonishment to see them among the first to defend it, and some of us among the first, among the very first, to tear it to pieces? Could this innocent, this virtuous, this injured Prince, now behold the ungrateful hell-hounds, that, from all quarters of the world, assail his reputation, would he not exclaim, like the Caesar when he saw the dagger of his beloved Brutus,——*and you too Americans?*

Let us leave these Bacchanalians, whose beverage is the blood of their benefactors, and return to our Crusaders; though I am afraid we shall gain but little by the change.

Their next attack was on all pictures, carved work, and stucco work. At the distance of a few miles from the Metropolis, a Tavern-Keeper, who, about a dozen years ago, hoisted the *Queen of France*, to attract

---

[6] I say Louis and the United States, for it was *he*, and he alone. There were no Fayettes; no Robespierres, no Barreres in those days: the king was absolute, and to him was the alliance owing and to nobody else. He was then as much, and more, an absolute Monarch than he was at the beginning of the French Revolution; yet none of us ever dreamed of calling him a *despot*, a *tyrant*, "an *ermined monster*." The Congress, the very Congress that declared us independent, declared him to be our *great* and *good* ally, our *deliverer*; and not a word about *despotism*. Whence come all these approbrious [*sic*] terms now? From the ungrateful hearts of those who make use of them.

custom to his house, found it necessary last summer, to sever her head from her body, and set the blood streaming down her garments.[7]

Who can have forgotten the card, sent to the Clergy and Vestry of Christ Church? This card begged, or rather demanded, of the persons to whom it was addressed, to remove the image and crown of George II and to be as quick as possible in doing it, for fear it should endanger the salvation of the citizens; "for," says the card, "that *mark of infamy* has a tendency to keep many *young and virtuous men* from attending public worship."

For my part, I look upon the destruction of this image and Crown as an event of about as much consequence to the citizens of Philadelphia as the destruction of the *Swiss*,[8] *at the door of their Library*, would be. The church is full as well without it, as with it. I have frequented Christ Church for near about thirty years, without ever observing that such a thing was on the walls of it; nor did I ever imagine that *my salvation could be endangered* by the form of a lump of stucco. . . .[8]

Of a piece with this heroic action was that of the Democrats, of *Charleston*, South Carolina, when they precipitated the statue of the late Lord Chatham from its pedestal, and bragged in the gazettes of having severed the head from the body. If one were to ask these wiseacres, what honor of profit they could promise themselves in this triumph over a piece of marble, I wonder what would be their answer. It was not the English that placed it there; it was themselves. It was an idol they had raised with their own hands. Did they expect to find it, like the man's wooden God, stuffed with gold and silver? Had this been the case, and had their expectation been well founded, the profit of the enterprise might have kept them in countenance: but, as it was, their sally of sans-culottism has produced them nothing but derision; has fixed them as a mark, "for the hand of scorn to point its slow and moving finger at." People compare them to the child who fights with his man of clay, and calls out to his playmates to admire his bravery. No wonder that the Jacobin Club at Paris should object to the adoption of ninnies like these.

---

[7] The reader will undoubtedly feel a considerable relief, when he hears that this complaisant creature was a *patriotic* Englishman. But who were his customers?

[8] This image has obtained the name of the *Swiss* for two reasons: First, because the citizens of Switzerland are generally employed by other nations in the capacity of *Porters*; and, secondly, because their motto is, "*Point d'argent, point de Swiss;*" in English, "*No pay, no Swiss.*" I leave the reader to determine whether the name be applicable or not to the image in question.

I will not fatigue the reader with any more of these feats of modern chivalry; what I have here related will, I think, be sufficient to prove, that the pictures of half a dozen old kings, painted with a Caledonian mop, were by no means necessary to frighten the people into Democratic principles.

I now come to an epoch of American sans-culottism, that ought not to be forgotten in haste. I mean the beginning of the Western Rebellion.[9] When the back-door Clubs[10] first received the news, they put a Janus's-face upon the matter: they pretended not to approve, altogether, of the *hostile* operations of *their* "Western Brethren"; but at the same time they took good care to declare, that they would *never cease to oppose the law which had given them umbrage.* The manoeuvres, that were employed to prevent the Militia of Pennsylvania from turning out, and the sarcasms that were thrown out on the Jersey Militia, only because they did turn out, are fresh in every one's memory. . . .

Nobody can doubt, that the scheme of the Democrats was, by means like these, to deaden the limbs of Government, and then seize the reins themselves. But success was dubious; they therefore proceeded with caution. Look at, and admire their conduct, from this time, 'till they saw a sufficient force ready to march against their "Western Brethren." You will find them lying on their arms, silent and snug, but the instant such a force appeared, adieu all *relationship*: the poor devils were in a moment transformed from "Western Brethren" into "Insurgents," and (Oh, monstrous transformation!) even into "Royalists"! If this be the way they treat their own flesh and blood, what have strangers to expect at their hands?[11]

Let this be a warning to you, all you understrappers of Democratic Clubs; leave off your bawling and your toasting, go home and sell your *sugar* and your *snuff*, and leave the care of "*Posterity*" to other heads; for, when the hour of discomfit arrives, your Jack Straws and your C. Foxes will leave you in the lurch.[12] When you get your carcases bastinadoed, or, which is far worse, penned up within the walls of a jail, they will scoff at you, as the devil ever does at a baffled sinner. This is an article of their creed. Do you want a proof of it? Look at their conduct towards their venerable founder, Citizen Genet: no sooner had the poor citizen made his political exit, than they began to "dance on his grave," as their brother Barlow did on that of Louis XVI. However, all their ungrateful efforts, all their unnatural malice has not been able to injure their immortal Sire. Though baffled and persecuted on this side the Styx, he has bribed old Charon to ferry him over into the Island of Bliss, where he may, uninterrupted by tormenting Aristocrats, sip the live long day, and the live long night too, at the lovely stream, flowing from the pure fountain of the purest democracy.[13]

But to return; our democrats had another view in stigmatizing their "western brethren" for Royalists, besides that of disowning them. They saw a good opportunity of throwing the blame on the shoulders of Great Britain, at the same time they shifted it from their own. Thus, by a stroke of address peculiar to themselves, they turned misfortune to advantage: this was making the best of a bad market with a vengeance! Hence all the grave alarming accounts of people's crying out, "King George for ever;" and of billets being "stuck upon trees with, *British freedom will never oppress you*." . . .[14]

I must be excused also, if I do not give full credit to what the Governor of Pennsylvania asserted on this subject, when he was harranguing the militia officers to persuade them to assemble their quotas, for the purpose of marching against the "Western Brethren." "Listen," said he, "to the language of the *Insurgents*, and your spirit will rise with indignation.⁹ They not only assert that certain laws shall be repealed, let the sense of the majority be what it may, but they threaten us with the establishment of an independent government, or *a return to the allegiance of Great Britain*."

Most people thought this was a *bolt shot*; but they forgot, that he said, in the same harrangue, that, "from defects in the militia system, *or some other unfortunate cause* the attempts to obtain the quota of militia by regular drafts *had failed*." If they had recollected, that under such circumstances, the end of an harrangue was to "stir men's bloods," and not to be very nice in the statement of facts, they would not have been surprised, that our Solomon (I can have no intention to hint, that the wise Governor has ever had *three hundred concubines* at a time; human nature cannot stand that, now a days) they would not, I say, have been surprised, that our Solomon should choose Great Britain as a spur.

Reader, when you were a little boy, did you never carry on a secret correspondence with the pies and tarts; and, when by the rattling of the plates, or some other accident, you were like to be caught at it, did you never raise a hue and cry against the poor dogs and cats? Those

---

⁹ Ah, Sir! ought the Officers and Soldiers of the State *of Pennsylvania* to feel *indignation* against nobody but the *deluded* "Western Brethren?"

who look upon the conduct of our Democrats as unnatural, forget their own little roguish tricks.

I will venture to say, that there are not five persons in the United States, possessing a degree of understanding superior to that of the brute creation, who believe that the Rebels have ever had, from first to last, the least idea of seeking protection from the British. From whence comes the probability? *All* their partizans *in this quarter* were to be found among the *revilers* of Great Britain. Read their resolves, and see if you can find any thing that leaves them a possibility of fraternizing with the British. Besides, can any body suppose, that the British would have accepted of them? Unless, indeed, they had had them in Europe, where they might have employed them as a "forlorn hope;" as the Democrats have the poor Author of the *Political Progress*. I fancy, if they, with *all* their partizans, and *Tom* the Tinker and his *prevaricating* Coadjutor at their head, had went and offered themselves, bodies and souls, to Old foxy Dorchester, he would have said, as Louis XI. did to the Genoese: "*Vous vous donnez de moi, et moi, je vous donne au Diable.*"10 [15]

I ask any reasonable man, what they could possibly expect to do among the British? The British have so many of this stamp already, that they are sending off ship loads to Botany Bay every month. Could a fellow, for instance, imagine, that having been the *secretary of a back door club*, would recommend him to the post of secretary in Canada? Prudence would prevent the employment of one whose *only talent* is, *blowing hot and cold with the same mouth*; because such a person might become *the tool of every intriguing foreigner*, and, by his *prevarication*, might embroil the whole government. Would any one (except one *like himself*) put such a man in a post of confidence? I put this question to every thinking American, and particularly to every Pennsylvanian.

And with respect to *Tom* the Tinker himself (for he is, on every account, entitled to the preeminence), what could he expect among the British? If he were to play any of his drunken tinker-like tricks amongst them, it would not be begging pardon, that would bring him off. If he were to tell them that his "hammer was up, and his ladle hot, and that he would not *travel the country for nothing*", I am mistaken if they would not pay him off with a good five hundred lashes, well counted; for the British are punctual in paying their debts. They would teach him how to set people together by the ears another time.

---

10 "You give yourselves to me, and I give you to the devil."

Could a sot like *Tom* imagine that the Canadian ladies would have fallen in love with him, because his scull had often been decorated with a liberty Cap, to testify his attachment to the nation from which they are descended? No; the ladies, all the world over, are, from long experience, too well convinced of the truth of Goldsmith's maxim: "A man who is eternally vociferating liberty! liberty! is generally, *in his own family*, a most cruel and *inhuman tyrant.*"[16]

The truth is, those among us who have made the most noise, and have expressed the most rancour against Great Britain, seem to have done it only to cover their enmity to the Federal Government, and consequently to their country, if we may with propriety call it *their* country. Let any man take a review of their conduct since the beginning of the present European war, and see if this observation is not uniformly true. It was they who raised such a clamour against the President's wise Proclamation of Neutrality; it was they who encouraged an insolent and intriguing foreigner to set the laws of the Union at defiance, and to treat the Supreme Executive Authority as if he had been a Talien or a Barrere,[17] or the President of nothing but a Democratic or Jacobin Club; it was they who brought the vexations and depredations on the commerce, and then Guillotined in effigy the Embassador extraordinary, the Angel of Peace,[18] who went to repair their fault; finally, it was they who fanned the embers of Rebellion in the West into a flame, and caused fourteen or fifteen thousand men to be taken from their homes, to undergo a most fatiguing campaign, at the expence of a million and a half of Dollars to the United States. The same perverse clan that heroically hurled down the Statue of Lord Chatham, and manfully made war upon an Image and a Crown, endeavoured to introduce a law to prevent the President of the United States from being re-elected, and openly declared (by the usual vehicle of their manifestos, a gazette) that it was improper to send the Chief Judge as Embassador Extraordinary to England, because they might want him here to—try the President!¹¹

It is rather an awkward circumstance, I must confess, that the meddling enemies of the British Government and of that of the United States should be the same. . . . Nobody will deny, that a hatred of the

---

¹¹ Will not the reader be surprised to hear that the following toast was a favorite with them? "May national gratitude ever distinguish Americans." This is a pretty clear proof, I think, that they did not look upon themselves as Americans; or, at least, that, in their capacity of Democrats, they looked upon themselves as exempted from all those moral obligations that bind the rest of mankind.

British Government and of that of the United States go hand in hand. Nor is the reason of this at all mysterious; it is not because of their resemblance to each other in form, nor, as the Democrats have ingeniously observed, because "there is some dangerous connection between Great Britain and our public affairs;" it is because they are both pursuing the same line of conduct with respect to clubs and conspirations; it is because they have both the same radical defect, a power to suppress anarchy; it is, to say all in one word, because they are *governments*. Great Britain has a government of some sort (nobody will deny that, I suppose), and this is sufficient to merit their execration. It is not the form of a government, it is not the manner of its administration; it is the thing itself, they are at war with, and that they must be eternally at war with; for, government implies order, and order and anarchy can never agree. The Carmagnole system (if there can be any system in annihilation) is exactly adapted to their taste and interest; a system that has made "rich men look sad and ruffians dance and sing."[19] If this were not the true reason, why such an eternal larum about the British Government? What have we or our Democrats to do with it? If the people of that country like it, why need it pester us? That pious and patriotic Scotchman, the Author of *the Political Progress*, tells us "to wish that on [sic] Earthquake or a Volcano may bury the whole British Islands[12] together in the centre of the globe; that a single, but decisive exertion of Almighty vengeance may terminate the *progress*[13] and the remembrance of their crimes." Yea, be it even as thou sayest, thou mighty Cyclop; but let us leave them then to the vengeance of the Almighty; let us not usurp the place of the Thunderer.

Understand me, reader; I would by no means insinuate, that a man cannot be a firm friend of the Federal Government, and at the same time wish all manner of success to the French, in their present struggle for what their vanity and our complaisance have termed Liberty; on the contrary, I think it very natural for an American, who has no other idea of Liberty than that which is conveyed to him by his senses; who is not refined enough to taste that metaphysical kind of Liberty, that can exist only in a brain afflicted with the *mania reformatio*; who in short, has no notion that Liberty consists in yielding up the crop he has laboured all the year to raise, and in receiving three or four

---

[12] And the Isle of Sky, that "terrestrial Paradise," among the rest?

[13] If some such exertion had terminated another *progress*, it might have spared somebody a good many fits of the gripes.

ounces of black bread a day in lieu of it: it is natural, and even laudable for such a man to be zealous in the cause of the French, who, as he is told, are fighting for Liberty; but even he ought to keep his zeal within the bounds of decency: when it breaks out into Civic-Feasts, Cockades *à la tricolor,* and such like buffoonery, it exposes him to ridicule, and makes him one of the rabble. "Let the French wear their garlands of straw; let them dress up their strumpets in leaves of oak, and nickname their calendar; let them play those pranks at home, and we shall be but merry spectators." These are the words of a gentleman, who seems to have been, on this occasion, and, indeed, on most other occasions, rather unfriendly to our allies. I am for carrying our complaisance further; I am for not only letting them play their pranks at home, but here also, if they please. If there be something, the seeing of which may turn to our amusement or profit, I see no reason why we should shut our eyes? Did not the wise Lacedemonians make their slaves drunk, and turn them loose, once a year, to inspire their youth with a horror for that beastly vice? In short, I am for hearing them, looking at them, laughing at them or any thing but imitating them. Imitation here is ridiculous. When Shakespear [sic] wrote the character of an *Iago* or a *Caliban,* or Moliere that of a *Tartuffe,* they certainly never meant to excite imitation. Thousands of mob crowd to see one of their friends hanged, but not one of them ever dreams of participating in the ceremony....

Among the many shining talents of our Democrats, there is none for which they are more justly deserving admiration than their adroitness in transferring their attachment from one object to another. It is beyond the power of figures or words to express the hugs and kisses that were lavished on Citizen Genet. The poor citizen had like to have shared the fate of the image of Abel on the church of our Lady of Loretto, which, we are told, is almost worn away by the ardent kisses of the Pilgrims: for, our Pilgrims who went to meet the Citizen, were by no means less eager to give this mark of their affection to the darling of the great Alma Mater of Anarchy. Such was their eagerness to obtain precedence on this joyful occasion, that very few parts, if any, of the Citizen's body, escaped a salute; and before he arrives safe at the "*Capitol*" of some places, he was licked as clean as a bear at three hours after being whelped.

For a long time *Lafayette* was their god;[14] but it was found just and

---

[14] *Payne* dedicated his second part of *The Rights of Man* to *Lafayette,* and, in less than a year afterward, assisted in passing an act of condemnation against him; and another

fit to exchange him for the "virtuous Egalite." *Egalite* was supplanted by *Danton*; "the great and dreadful *Danton*, who comes thundering on the Aristocrats, like *Neptune* from *Olympus*."[15] But the Olympian thunder of this Neptune was obliged to give place to the "*morals and religion of Robespierre.*"[20] After his pious report on the subject of religion, which the Unitarian Doctor (Priestley) read "with pleasure, and even enthusiasm," it is thought, that our Democrats really began to believe there was a God; and there is no telling what a favourable change of conduct this might have produced, if the news of the unfortunate catastrophe of the 18th of July had not come to set their affection afloat again.[21] Alas! it is now wandering on the sea of uncertainty; nor can we ever expect to see it cast anchor, 'till we know who has the secure possession of the Guilliotine.

Yet (for, though I hate the very name of Democrat, I would scorn to detract from their merit) there is one character to whom they have ever conserved an unshaken attachment. How grateful must it be to thee, injured shade of the gentle *Marat*! whether thou wanderest on the flowry banks of the Stygian Pool, or bathest thy pure limbs in the delightful liquid of Tartarus, or walkest hand in hand with *Jesus Christ* in that Literary Elysium, the *Philadelphia Gazette*,[16]—how grateful must it be to thee, though thou makest Hell more hideous and frightenest the very furies into fits, to be yet adored by the Democrats of the city *of brotherly love*!

The American Union presents, at this moment, a spectacle that startles the eye of reason. We see a kind of political land-mark, on one

---

act, by which his innocent wife and children were left without bread to eat! Poor Lafayette! to make use of a parody on your words, "May your fate serve as a lesson to demagogues, and as an example to governments."

[15] See the *General Advertiser*.

[16] In this print, for the month of July last [actually June 20, 1794], is a list of Democrats, *the great benefactors of mankind*; among them are *Marat* and *Jesus Christ*.

I hope, reader, you are sensible of the benefits *Jesus Christ* has conferred on the world; but perhaps you may not know what has entitled *Marat* to an equality with him. Know then, that *Marat* was the principal author of the *massacres* of the 2d and 3d September, 1792, in which upwards of two thousand five hundred innocent persons were inhumanly butchered; and that, after this, he openly declared in the National Convention, and published repeatedly, that another two hundred & fifty thousand heads were necessary to the establishment of the Liberty of the French.

Doctor Moore (who was far from being an enemy to revolutionary principles) speaks of *Marat* in the following terms[:] "*Marat* is a little man of a cadaverous complexion, and a countenance exceedingly expressive of his disposition; to a painter of massacres, *Marat* is said to love carnage like a vulture, and to delight in human sacrifices like Moloch, God of the Ammonites." Here, reader, you see the man that the *Philadelphia Gazette* (whose end is the "public good") puts upon a level with the *Blessed Jesus*!!

side of which, Order walks hand in hand with the most perfect Liberty; and, on the other, Anarchy revels, surrounded with its den of slaves. We see, that those who are most accustomed to the exercise of tyranny, are the first to oppose every measure for the curbing of licentiousness, or, in other words, we see, that anarchy and despotism are the same.

If there could be found a person in this country who has a doubt of this, I think, the following authentic pieces would operate his conviction. We ought not to speak ill of our neighbours, but if people will speak ill of themselves, believing them ought not to be termed malice. Let us hear then what our Democrats say of themselves.

Toasts drunk on the 6th of Feb. 1794. by the French and American Citizens.

"1. The Democratic Societies throughout the world——may they ever be the watchful guardians of Liberty."

"2. Citizen *Maddison* and the *Republican party* in Congress."

"3. The firm patriot, and *true Republican*, Citizen Genet.[17]——a salute from the French Sloop of War."

"4. The Guilliotine to all Tyrants, Plunderers, and *funding* Speculators."

"5. May the flags of France and America ever be united against regal tyranny."

"6. The 6th of February, 1778, *the day which secured liberty to America,*[18] and sowed its seeds in the soil of France."

"7. Gratitude. The first of National as well as individual virtues."[19]

"8. May laws and *not proclamations*,[20] be the instruments by which free men shall be regulated."

"9. The persecuted Citizen Genet; may his country reward his honest zeal, and the shafts of *calumny* levelled against him, recoil upon the Archers."[21]

---

[17] This was candid indeed. The Democrats might have left us to believe, that the *"republican party"* in Congress meant the real friends of this country; but they have taken care to avoid leading us into this error, by calling Citizen Genet a *true republican.*

[18] Here they confess then, that the treaty with Louis XVI. *secured liberty to America.*

[19] Do you doubt of their gratitude? Hear them sing.
"Fame let thy trumpet sound,
Tell all the world around
How *Capet* fell; &c."

[20] The reader hardly wants to be told, that the President's Proclamation of Neutrality is meant here.

[21] The President of the United States was the Archer that brought the Citizen from his lofty perch.

Reader, is it not rather surprising that Thomas Mifflin, Governor of the State of Pennsylvania, should assist at the drinking of these two toasts?

"10. May all men who aspire *to the supreme power* be brought below the level of their fellow citizens."

"11. The courageous and virtuous mountain, may it crush the moderates, the traitors, the *federalists* and all aristocrats, *under whatever denomination* they may be disguised."

"12. Success to the brave Republicans of *Louisiana*."[22]

"13. Destruction to the enemies of the French Republic, both by Sea and Land."

"14. Henry Grattan, and the Opposition of Ireland."

"15. Citizens Fox and Stanhope, and the Opposition in England."

"16. Liberty, Equality, and Fraternity——may they pervade the Universe. Three cheers, and a salute of three guns."

To these extracts I shall take the liberty of adding two others; both from the same Newspaper. One of them is an elegant account of the close of a Civic-feast, and the other, though not absolutely on the same subject as the first, certainly adds to its beauty. The first is the precious jewel, and the last the foil; I shall therefore place them as near as possible to each other.

"After this the Cap of Liberty was placed on the head of the President, then on each member. The marsellois hymn and other similar songs were sung by different French citizen members. Thus chearfully glided the hours away of this feast, made by congenial souls to commemorate the happy day, when the sons of Frenchmen joined the sons of America to overthrow tyranny in this happy land."

"*For Sale*,
Two negro lads one about twelve and the other about fifteen years old—both remarkably healthy;—the youngest is near four feet nine inches high, and the oldest above five feet.——Also a negro wench for sale, coming eighteen years old, and far advanced with child——but very strong and capable of any kind of work."!!!!

Leaving this without comment, I shall add an extract or two from a debate of Congress, which I shall also leave without comment: such things scorn the aid of declamation.

The subject of the debate I allude to was, an amendment to a bill of Naturalization. A member from *Virginia* had proposed, that a clause should be inserted to exclude foreign noblemen from becoming citizens of the United States of America, unless they would first make a solemn *renunciation of their Titles*. A member from New England proposed, as an amendment to this, that such noblemen should also

---

[22] These Republicans were a gang of brigands, committing robberies in the Spanish territories, and who were proscribed by proclamation.

renounce the right of *holding slaves*. On this amendment a member from *Carolina* said: "That the gentleman *durst not* come forward, and tell the house, that men who *possessed slaves* were unfit for holding an office under a *Republican* government.—He desired the gentleman to consider what might be the consequence of this motion, at this time, considering what has happened in the West Indies.—His amendment would irritate the minds of thousands of *good citizens* in the *southern* States, as it affects the *property* which they have acquired by their *industry*.—He thought that the amendment partook more of *monarchical principles* than any thing which he had seen for some time."[23]

A member from *Virginia* said on the same occasion, that "he held *property sacred*, and never could consent to prohibit the emigrant nobility *from having slaves* any more than other people. But as for *titles of nobility* they were *quite a different thing*."[24] [22]

Oh! happy Carolina! happy, thrice Virginia! No tyrannical Aristocrat dares to lord it over the free born swains who cultivate the delicious weed, that adorns, first thy lovely fields and then the lovlier chops of the drivling drunkard! After having spent the day in singing hymns to the Goddess of Liberty, the virtuous Democrat gets him home to his peaceful dwelling, and sleeps, with his *property* secure beneath his roof, yea, sometimes in his very *arms*; and when his "*industry*" has enhanced its value, it bears to a new owner the proofs of his Democratic Delicacy! . . .

This I must confess is a gloomy subject, and therefore we will, if you please, reader, return once again to the *Political Progress of Britain*; for change, they say, even of calamities, is chearful.

Though the *encouragers* of this work might think it a means of deceiving the ignorant, and adding to the prejudice against Great Britain, yet they seem to have had another view, which perhaps the

---

[23] It is not amiss to hear *Republicans* declare, that *monarchical principles* tend to *discountenance Slavery*. A doctrine like this would surprise the partizans of Citizens Stanhope and Fox.

[24] This gentleman's motion against titled foreigners has excited some curiosity, and still appears inexplicable to many, feeling that it was totally unnecessary: but, if we reflect, we shall find it is no more than natural. It is in the heart of man, reader, you must search for an explication of motions like this. When you go to take an airing in a chair, do you not find, that every Drayman and Clodpole, you meet or overtake thwarts you in your road as much as he can? Does he not force creatures, much more humane and polite than himself, to stifle you with dust or cover you with mire? Is it, not a luxury to him, if he can overset your carriage and break your limbs? You stare, and wonder what you have done to the malicious Boor. Alas! you have done nothing to him: all your fault is, having a chair while he has none.

cudden of an author knew nothing of. The *Political Progress* professes to show "*the ruinous consequences of taxation.*" And, indeed, this is the burden of the song; almost every paragraph closes with melancholy reflections on the consequence of *taxation*. The author even goes so far, in one place, as to declare, that "*the highest* and *most necessary taxes, are very destructive.*" This it was that recommended the piece to the gentlemen who *encouraged* the author to publish it in America: it was so apropos too; so just the very thing.

With respect to the expediency of taxation in general, it is not to my present purpose to say any thing about it; every one that is not already upon four legs, knows that he soon must be so without something of this kind:[25] what I wish to direct the reader's attention to, is, the real object of the publication in question. If then he will take the trouble to compare the above doctrine on taxation, with that held forth by the "Western Brethren," and their relations in every quarter of the Union; and if he will please to take notice of the time when the *Political Progress* was preparing for press (the month of August last) he will, I fancy be of opinion, with me that the *encouragers* had the United States in their eye, much more than Great Britain. As if they had said: *look here, Americans, see what taxation has done in another country; and, if you do not put a stop to it, if you do not resist it with all your might, it will certainly do the same in your own.* The national debt, taxes, &c. of Great Britain were all adapted to their purpose; they knew, by themselves, that the bulk of readers were incapable of going into calculations of this kind; of making just comparisons between this country and that: it was like reading the history of a giant to a pigmy.

Nobody can doubt, particularly if *country* be taken into the consideration, that the grinders and retailers of *Mundungus* were among the author's *encouragers*.[23] I remember hearing a speaker of this honourable body, holding a talk to his brothers, in the month of May last, from the window of a certain State House. I shall not easily forget his saying, among many other things equally modest and unassuming, that *he* had told the *Secretary of the Treasury*, that if the *Mundungus* was taxed, "he would be *damn'd* if ever *he forgave him*, while he had an existence." His speech, though from the sample here given, it may be supposed to surpass in ribaldry those of *Tom* the Tinker or even *Tom* the Devil,[24] had an amazing effect upon the loons below, who were

---

[25] May not this be the reason why our Democrats are continually crying out against taxes? I must confess, I think they would not look amiss upon all fours.

all watching with their jaws distended to catch, not the oracular, but the anarchical belches. When the resolve was put, it would have done your heart good to see and hear. What a forest of rusty hats and dirty paws were poked up into the air in token of approbation of *"no excise!"*

> "Jack Straw at London—Stone with all his rout
> Struck not the City with so loud a shout."[25]

But this had no effect; and now they run about, stunning us

> "With many a deadly grunt and doleful squeak,
> Poor swine, as if their pretty hearts would break."[26]

It is certainly worthy of remark, that, among the speechifiers at this talk, there was but *one American*, and that, among the hollow boys, perhaps there were not twenty. How kind is this of foreigners, to come and put us in the right road, when we are going wrong!

Compare the principles of the supporters of this talk, and those of their "Western Brethren," with the principles inculcated in *The Political Progress of Britain*, and see if they do not exactly tally; if they do not all point to the same object; that is to say, to the undermining of all government, and to the destruction of the social system. Is it not fair then to conclude that *The Political Progress* was employed as an auxiliary in this laudable enterprize?

If this was not its object, what was its object? I would ask the lovers of their country, if such there are among the *encouragers* of this author, what good they could intend to render it by such a step? I think they would be puzzled for an answer. Did they imagine, could they imagine, that his having narrowly escaped transportation in his own country, was a sufficient security for his being a most excellent citizen in this? Because his book had been burnt by the hands of the common hangman in Scotland, did they imagine that it was calculated for the edification of the people of the United States? That the author believed this to be the case is clear, otherwise he would not have introduced himself by exposing that, which he certainly would have kept out of sight, if he had been appealing to virtue or reason, instead of prejudice.

To what a pitch must this unmeaning, this fruitless ill-nature against a foreign country be carried, if to be declared infamous there, is become a recommendation here! If a fellow, to usher himself into favour, must cry out: *I have had a narrow escape! Look ye, good folks, here's the mark of the halter about my neck yet*! If this be the case we may as well adopt at once that famous decree of the Jacobin Club at Paris, which requires as an essential qualification in each member, that he shall, previous to his admission, have committed some crime worthy of the gibbet! A regulation like this was very proper, and even necessary in a democratic club; and, for that very reason, unnecessary and improper every where else.

The Political Progress is in politics, what mad Tom's *Age of Reason* is in religion, and they have both met with encouragement from some people here, from nearly the same motive. Had not the last mentioned piece been suppressed in England, there is every reason to believe, that it would never have rivaled the Bible among us, in so many families as it does. What a preposterous thing! People, who detest blasphemous publications, will tolerate, will read them, and put them into the hands of their children, because other people have declared them blasphemous! *Pope* would have said;

> "Thus Infidels the true Believers quit,
> And are but damn'd for having too much wit."[27]

To what deceptions, to what insulting quackery of all sorts has not this prejudice exposed us? A projector (and I think, like the Author of the *Political Progress*, of the Caledonian race) proposed, some time ago, to change the language of the country.[28] He even went so far as to have his scheme and proposals printed. As to the scheme itself, it consisted in the introduction of several new characters into the Alphabet, and in changing the shape, or manner of writing, of some of the old ones. To give the reader as good an idea, as he can possibly have, of the merits of this scheme, it will be sufficient to tell him, that the *i* was to be turned upside down, and the point placed under the line, thus ¡. Ridiculous as this may seem, and much as the Author may, in some people's opinion, appear to merit a cap and bells, yet we must suppose, he knew whom he was making the proposal to. There is hardly any thing too gross for an appetite whetted by revenge. The *preface* to this greasy dab was a sharpening sauce, well calculated to make it go down. It was printed in the "Amərɪpan Lanȝuaȝə" (I go as far as "barbarian" types will permit me); but, for the benefit of the unlearned, the Author had the complaisance to give a translation of it on the opposite page. This *preface* set forth, as near as I can recollect, that, the United States of America having, by a most successful and glorious war, shaken off the disgraceful yoke of British Bondage, they ought to endeavour by every possible means to obliterate the memory of having ever borne it; and that, nothing could be more conducive to the attainment of this desirable object than the disuse of a *barbarous* language, imposed on them by tyrants, and fit only for slaves, &c. &c.——I would advise the Author never to read this preface in a stable; the horses would certainly kick his brains out.

Some readers may imagine, perhaps, that this is all a joke; but I certainly saw the thing, as I have described it, and in the hands of several persons too. It was in the month of October, 1793, that I saw it; it was in a small octavo volume, printed at Philadelphia, and the Author's name, if I am not mistaken, *Thornton*.

After this, who would wonder if some one were to tell us, that it is beneath Republicans to eat, and that we ought to establish a system of French starvation, only because the English live by eating?

There is nothing that might not be received without surprise after the project of this Linguist, and therefore we may remember with less astonishment the notable project of that Democrat Brissot, for curing the *consumption*. He tells us,[26] that our women are more subject to the consumption than men, "because they want (as they do in England) *a will or a civil existence*: the submission which women are habituated to, causes *obstructions*! deadens the vital principle and impedes circulation." As a remedy for this, he produces us, quack like, his infallible nostrum, *Liberty and Equality*! Gracious Heavens! Liberty and Equality to cure the consumption!

Yes, let him persuade us, if he can that our wives and daughters die of the consumption, because they do not, like his execrably patriotic *concitoyennes*, change gallants as often as they do their *chemises*. If he could even convince us of the efficacy of his remedy, we should certainly reject it, as ten thousand million times worse than the disease. And you, ye Fair Americans, are you ashamed to follow the bright example of your Mothers? Would you accept of Mr. Brissot's nostrum? No; you are too mild, too lovely, to become the tribune of a Democratic Club: your lilly hands were never made to wield a dagger: you want no rights, no power but what you possess: your empire is much better guarded by a bosom of snow, than it would be by the

---

[26] See the 28th letter of his Travels in America.

rusty battered [sic] breast plates, worn by those terrible termagants, the "heroines of Paris."

When I said that *we* should certainly reject Mr. Brissot's remedy, I by no means meant to include the members of Democratic Societies and others of that stamp: because they are so diametrically opposite in their tastes, to the rest of mankind, that I question much whether they do not look upon a pair of antlers as an honourable mark of distinction. Nor is it impossible that many of them may really be decorated to their heart's content; for, certain it is that the ladies do not bear them a very great affection. They imagine, and with reason, that the Democrats, in their rage for equality, may, one of these days, attempt to reduce them to a level with their sable "*property.*" Besides, if they stood ever so fair in the opinion of the ladies, must not their gander-frolicks, and their squeezing, and hugging, and kissing one another, be expected to cause a good deal of pouting and jealousy? And then, at the back of all this, comes their intriguing with that outlandish Goddess of Liberty! this alone must inevitably wean them from their lawful connexions: for, it is morally impossible, that one, who is admitted to clandestine familiarities with a Deity, should not disdain a poor thing in petticoats. La Fontaine has a verse which says, that a man can never bend his knees too often before his God and his Mistress; but our Democrats have laid aside both God and Mistress, and have taken up with a strumpet of a Goddess, who receives the homage due to both.[29]

Being upon this subject, it is hardly fair to omit mentioning a great and mighty democrat, who is universally allowed to be a perfect platonist both in politics and love, and yet has the unconscionable ambition to set up for a man of *gallantry*.[30] He has taken it into his head to run dangling from one Boarding School to another, in order to acquire by the art of speechifying, a reputation for which nature seems to have disqualified him. My imagination cannot form to itself any thing more perfectly comic than to see a diminutive superannuated bachelor, cocked up upon a stool, and spouting out compliments to an assembly of young Misses. Ah! dear Plato! take my word for it, if your reputation had been no higher among the Democrats than among the ladies, your name would never have found a place on their list. "Phillis the fair, in the bloom of fifteen," feels no more emotion at your fine speeches, than she would at the quavers of an Italian Singer: for, though they are both equally soft and smooth, there is a certain concatenation of ideas (do you understand me?) that whispers her heart, that all you have said, and all you can say, is not worth one broken sigh from blooming twenty two. Hear what a brother democrat says:[27]

> "Fut-il sorti de l'Epire, eut-il servi les Dieux,
> Fut-il né du Trident, il languit s'il est vieux!"[31]

This is a sorrowful truth; but, take heart, citizen: all men are not made for all things; if a man does not know how to play at cards, it is kind of him to hold the candle; he that has not teeth, cannot crack nuts; but that does not hinder him from preparing them for those who can.

Now, reader, suffer me to return, for the last time, to *The Political Progress [of] Britain*; though I must confess it has acted only the part of an usher, it ought certainly to appear at the breaking up of the ball.

The Political Progress contains, among many other religiously patriotic things too numerous to mention, a *prophecy*,—not of the destruction of the Whore of Babylon and the "*personal reign* of Jesus over the Unitarians,"[28] but of the destruction of the empire of Great Britain! This is certainly a most desirable event, and so absolutely necessary to *our* happiness, that every thing which has been said on the subject merits our attention. The Unitarian Doctor tells us, and in a sermon too, that his country must soon undergo a "purification," or, as he calls it in another place, "the destruction of them that have destroyed the earth." This opinion is a good deal strengthened by a volume of *dreams and predictions*, published at Philadelphia by a bookseller from North Britain, and the whole appears to be fully confirmed by this plain unqualified prophecy of the author of *The Political Progress*: "A Revolution will take place in Scotland before the lapse of *ten years* at farthest."

If we want to know what sort of Revolution is here meant, we have only to look at the toasts drunk by the *republican* Britons at New York:—"A revolution in Great Britain and Ireland, *upon sans culotte principles*—three cheers."—But the long term of *ten years*, mentioned in the Prophecy of the Author of the *Political Progress*, has given a good deal of uneasiness to some of his zealous friends in this country. Ten years! 'tis an eternity! they thought the Woe-Trumpet had already sounded, and that the kingdom of Priestley's sans culotte Heav-

---

[27] Observe, that he was no democrat when he wrote these lines, or he never would have written them.
[28] See Priestley's Sermons.

en was at hand. As a proof that I do not advance this upon slight surmise, I beg leave to remind the reader of what was said on the subject, in Congress, the other day, by that "true republican, Citizen Madison."[29] "If a Revolution," said he, "was to take place in Britain, which for my part I expect and believe will be the case, the Peerage of that country will be thronging to the United States. I shall be ready to receive them with all that hospitality, respect and *tenderness* to which misfortune is entitled. I shall *sympathize* with them, and be as ready to afford them whatever friendly offices lie in my power, as any man." 'Tis a pity poor devils are not apprised of all this. It would certainly be an act of humanity in our good Citizen to let them know what blessings he has in *store* for them: they seem attached to their Coronets and Coach-and-sixes at present; but were they informed that they can have as much homony and fat pork as they can gobble down (once every day of their lives,) liberty to chew tobacco and smoke all the week, and to ride out on the meeting-going mare on Sundays, it might tempt them to quit their baubles and their poor bit of an Island without a struggle, and fly to the free State of Virginia.

And do you really imagine, Sir, that you will see the Peerage of Great Britain come thronging, round your habitation? Do you really promise yourself the extatic delight of seeing them stand in need of your "sympathy, tenderness, hospitality and good offices?" It is well enough for Dreamers and Fortune-tellers, for a baffled Unitarian from Birmingham, or a second-sighted Mumper from the Isle of Skye to entertain us with such visions; but for you, Sir, whom the populace calls "a damn'd Clever Fellow," to become their dupe, is something amazing. If I am not mistaken, you observed the other day, that it was improper for Congress to meddle with the affairs of the Democratic Societies: and, is it not full as proper for one of its members to turn Soothsayer concerning the affairs of other nations? And as for *Sympathy* and *tenderness*, Sir; these things, though amiable in themselves, may sometimes appear ungraceful. Certain Legislators have very wisely observed, that liberty is not a bird of every climate; nor is *tenderness* Sir: and though I do not absolutely aver, that a Jamaica

---

[29] This is the same citizen who amused the Legislature last year with a string of Resolutions, as long as my arm, about commercial restrictions with respect to Great Britain. They are now and were then, called by way of excellence; "Madison's Resolutions;" but, though they caught like touchwood, touchwood like, they lay smouldering upon the table for nearly two months, without ever producing either light or heat. All the good they did, was to cost the Union about 20 or 30 thousand dollars in debates. O! rare Patriotism!

Slave-Dealer cannot possess one grain of humanity, yet I confess, if he were to talk to me of his *tenderness*, I should hardly forbear laughing.

Laying aside dreaming and soothsaying, what indications do we perceive of an approaching dissolution of the Empire of Britain? Has she lost an inch of territory, or has the enemy set a foot on any of her extensive dominions since the beginning of the war? Is she not in possession of almost the whole Western Archipelago? Are not her possessions increased to an amazing extent in the East-Indies? Has she not more men and more cannon afloat than the whole world besides; and is she not the undisputed Mistress of the Ocean? For my part, the English are no favourites of mine; I care very little if their Island were swallowed up by an Earthquake, as the Author of the *Political Progress* says; but truth is truth, and let the Devil deny, if he can, that this is the truth.

Are these indications of weakness and distress? Are these indications of approaching dissolution? . . .

But we are told that there *must* be a Revolution in England; for, that the people are all ripe for revolt. Where is the proof of this? Not in the conduct of their land or sea forces. At the beginning of the war, the Convention decreed, that the crew, of every vessel captured from the English, should share in the prize. What good did this base satanic democratic decree produce? What good did the fraternizing speech of the Carmagnole Admiral do? I do not believe he even found time to pronounce it. How did the crew of the *Ship Grange* behave to Citizen Bompard, when he told them they were to share in the prize, and that they were not his prisoners, but his *brothers*? "No," said they, "you French B——r, we are none of your brothers." Alas! I see nothing here that affords, the least glimps of hope.——But the people are discontented, and complain of their taxes:——where? in England? or here?—But they have insurrections every year:—and every day too, if we believe our Newspapers; it appears however, that there has been only one in England, of late years; and that was *for* the government, instead of against it. A troop of horse put an end to that insurrection; while fifteen thousand men were obliged to march to put an end to ours. But they have a dozen prisoners going to be tried for High Treason:——and have not we more than two dozen, going to be tried for the same offence?——O! but they have their Carmagnole Clubs, and their Stanhopes, and Foxes, and Sheridans:—yes, and, God confound them! so have we, to our sorrow; and have them we shall, 'till we take the same method with them that the English have been taking with theirs, for some time past. Suppose Bradford, the Wat Tyler of the West,[32] were to get over to London, and write a *Political Progress of America*, foretelling the dissolution of the Union; would he not deserve a horse-whip in place of *encouragement*? When the militia was called out and cannon were planted opposite the State House, last May, to keep off a gang of insolent Sailors, were we apprehensive of a Revolution? No; but if our Democrats were to hear of such an event taking place in the neighbourhood of the British Parliament, I question but it might produce a Civic-Feast.

Even suppose, that that accursed thing, called a Revolution, were to take place among the British; what good would it do us? Would it weaken their power? that cannot be, because we say, it has rendered the French stronger than ever. Would it destroy their credit, and starve them? No; for our gazettes all assure us upon their words and honours, that the French treasury is running over, and that the people's bellies are ready to burst. Would it make them turn athiests [sic] and cannibals? Yes, but then, it is a good thing to cast off superstition and punish Aristocrats. In short, which ever way I turn the matter, we are, according to my simple judgement, upon a wrong scent. We are wishing for a Revolution in England! and for what, I would be glad to know? to give the English a share of all the goody goodies, eh? No, no; they are the exclusive property of our dear allies, and, in the name of God, let them keep them all to themselves. To be sure they have just given *us* a taste, but then, I hope, we shall have too much sense to run about crying roast meat.

Let us open our eyes; it is pretty near time, if we do not wish to be led blindfolded to the end of the farce, and even after it is over.— How can it be our interest to give way to this moody temper towards a nation, with which, after all, our connexions are nearly as close as those of Man and Wife? (I avoid the comparison of Mother and Child, for fear of affecting the nerves of some delicate constitutions.) Because a war once existed between the two countries, is that a reason that they should now hate one another? They had their battle out; let them follow the good old custom, drink and shake hands, and not suffer themselves to be set together by the ears by a parcel of outlandish butchers. If the animosity were on the side of the British, they would have some excuse; it is almost impossible for the vanquished party not to retain some tincture of revenge; but for him who boasts of his victory to brood over his ill-nature, is, to say the best of it, very unamiable. That maxim in war: "a foe vanquished, is a foe no more," ought ever to operate with him who calls himself the vanquisher, and, I believe, we should be very loath to surrender that title.

The depredation on the commerce is now pleaded as the cause of all this ill-blood; but every man of candour will acknowledge that this is not the cause. The Newspapers teemed with abuse, the most unprovoked, unheard-of, infamous abuse against Great Britain, before a single American Vessel had been stopped by the British. Do we find any thing of this kind in the English papers? Do the English publish to the world that they wish to see our Constitution subverted? Have they a *Marat* to mark out *our beloved President and his Lady* for the Guilliotine?[30] Do their Governors, Magistrates, Military Officers, &c. assemble with cannon firing, drums beating, and bells ringing to celebrate every little advantage gained over our troops by the Indians? Do they hoist the colours of our enemy, and trample our own under their feet, and *even burn them*?[31]

But, say we, have we not a right to do as we please? Have we not a right to hate them? Yes; but do we expect them to love us for this? Do we imagine that revenge can find a place no where but in the breasts of Americans? Do we, because a set of fawning foreigners tell us we are the only virtuous people upon the face of the earth, possess the exclusive privilege of being systematically vindictive? Forgiveness of injuries is what we have right to expect at the hands of all men; but love in return for hatred is what no mortal ought to expect from another; it is an effort beyond the power of human nature.

The publication of sentiments like these undoubtedly require an apology on the part of the Publisher; but I think, it is easily found. Many devout and sanctified christian Booksellers, indeed all of the trade in the United States, have assisted in distributing the AGE OF REASON; and not one of them has yet expressed the least remorse of conscience for so doing. Now, though it may be, and certainly is, a terrible thing to publish the name of Britain unconnected with execration, yet it is not much worse, at most, than publishing a libel against God.

As for myself, reader, I most humbly beseech you to have the Goodness to think of me—JUST WHAT YOU PLEASE.

---

[30] For, you must know, reader, *Marat* published what *Doctor Moore* calls "*the bloody Journal.*" The Editor of the *Philadelphia Gazette* will certainly think himself honoured by being compared to a person whom he has compared to *Jesus Christ*.

[31] Perhaps the reader did not see the British Flag committed to the flames to appease the manes of the heroes of the *Vengeur*; I did, and should hope to see the manly democratic scene repeated, if the Carmagnole Fleet would but take another Cruize.

[3]

A Kick for a Bite

As Cobbett's popularity grew, his writings increasingly attracted the attention of the reviewers, including Samuel Harrison Smith of the newly launched *American Monthly Review*. Although he praised Cobbett's "magical pen" and his satirical skills, Smith also criticized Cobbett's grammar and commented on the "tyranny" of the British government—hitting two very sensitive nerves. Cobbett, identifying himself for the first time as "Peter Porcupine," decided to get even.

He began "A Kick for a Bite" by attacking Smith's literary style; the idea was to demonstrate that the reviewer was "totally unqualified" to evaluate other people's writing. This is a classic example of the way Cobbett judged the moral worth and intelligence of his opponents by the quality—or lack of quality—of their grammar. And his observations about effective writing also illustrate Cobbett's emphasis on the plain style, clarity of expression, and the effective use of metaphor. As he remarked in the *English Grammar*, which he wrote in 1818, "he who writes badly thinks badly."

To show Smith how a review ought to be written, Cobbett decided to dissect the writings of Susanna Rowson, the English-born playwright, novelist and actress who was based in Philadelphia's New Theatre. Cobbett's critique is a useful source on the origins of American feminism; we learn, for example, about Rowson's views on the equality of the sexes, and the efforts of reformers to remove the word "obey" from the marriage service. His attack on Rowson in particular and women's rights in general was countered by the Philadelphia radical and pioneer of female education, John Swanwick. Cobbett's reply to Swanwick, which appeared in the preface of "A Bone to Gnaw, Part II," is included in this chapter.

A KICK FOR A BITE; OR, REVIEW UPON REVIEW; WITH A CRITICAL ESSAY, ON THE WORKS OF MRS. S. ROWSON; IN A LETTER TO THE EDITOR, OR EDITORS, OF THE AMERICAN MONTHLY REVIEW.

BY PETER PORCUPINE,

Author of the Bone to Gnaw, for the Democrats.

"Autant de traits que d'ennemis."

To the Editor, or Editors, of the American Monthly Review.

IN ADDRESSING MYSELF TO YOU, ON THE PRESENT OCCASION, I FEEL A considerable embarrassment on account of your number. I do not mean the number of your shop, but the number of your person. From certain circumstances, which shall here be nameless, I was led to suppose you of the singular; but your Review for February seems to contradict this supposition. However, whether you are one, and have only made use of the plural pronoun *we*, and its correspondent *our*, in imitation of the style royal; or whether, like Legion, you are really many, I hope, no charge of impoliteness will be brought against me for addressing you as an individual; since it may be fairly presumed, that no more than one person can have been employed in the composition of one page, and since it is very clear, that there is but one page of original composition in all your Review.

Having settled this point of ceremony, I shall proceed to business, without delay.

After the appearance of your first number, I did not imagine that the work would ever contain any thing, with which an inhabitant of these regions could have the least concern; but, it seems, the *Bone to Gnaw, for the Democrats,* has awakened in you the dormant powers of criticism; you have, at last, entered on the exercise of your censorian function, and the offending production has been summoned to your bar.

Of your opinion, or rather sentence, on this pamphlet it is not my intention to say a single word; the object of my letter is, to prove to you, yourself, that you are totally unqualified for judging of that, or any other literary performance; and, if I succeed in this, a justification of the one in question will, of course, become unnecessary.

After stating what you imagine to be my motives in writing the *Bone to Gnaw,* you say:

"Now, reader, what, think you, are *the means* which our author uses for compassing his ends? Not a profound view of his subject, in the developement of which he displays the logical accuracy of the expert politician——Not *by pouring* on you a flood of important information, raised by laborious study.—No—no—these are the common *methods* of producing coincidence of thought between writer and reader. This circumstance, therefore, is a sufficient reason with him for spurning such *instruments* of conviction. He is no ordinary character—he will, therefore, have nothing to do with any thing that is ordinary (unless it be with the Democratic Societies and the author of the Political Progress) Well, but what *are* the *means?*——Simple *laughter.*"

Now, Sir, before you go any further, examine your own work here, paying particular attention to the words that I have distinguished by italicks.——What? you can perceive no fault? all is right, is it? Well, now listen to me then, if you please.

You ask what are the *means* that the author uses, and then you say "Not a profound view of his subject—Not *by pouring* on you," &c. The first of these sentences has nothing in it that offends against the rules of grammar; but surely the same cannot be said of the second. *Pouring,* like every other gerund, may, sometimes, be looked upon as a substantive, but never, when immediately preceded by *by.* The first sentence indicates a *mean*, proper to be made use of for compassing his ends: viz. "A profound view of his subject." But, "*by pouring* on you, &c." indicates a *manner* in which he might have proceeded, and not a *mean* that he might have employed. Had you put the question thus: "How does the author compass his ends?" It would have been proper to answer: "Not *by pouring*, &c." but, having heard you ask about the *means* for compassing his ends, nobody expected to hear your answer contain the *manner* of compassing them.

We shall see this fault in its proper light, if we divest the sentences of all their adjuncts, and bring the accusatives close to their verb: thus: "Our author uses a profound view of his subject: our author uses by pouring on you a flood, &c." Is this sense? or is it nonsense?

You proceed: "These are the common *methods* of producing coincidence of thought between writer and reader." And then again, you say: "This is a sufficient reason with him for spurning such *instruments* of conviction." How is this, Sir? First you indicate the *means*; then those *means* become *methods*; and, by-and-by, those *methods* become *instruments*. You talk of my magical pen, but, without flattery, Sir, I think yours leaves it far, very far, behind. One may, with a very moderate share of ingenuity, place in a ridiculous light, things which have the essential of ridicule within themselves; but to turn *means* into *methods*, and then to turn those *methods* into *instruments*, is, to say the least of it, a sort of literary legerdemain approaching very near to the supernatural.

It is easy to conceive that the *means*, made use of for compassing one's ends, may, by a very easy step towards figurative language, become *instruments*; but neither *means* nor *instruments* can, except by an effort of the hocus-pocus, ever become *methods*. An *instrument* or a *mean*, is the thing made use of; a *method* is the *manner* of making use of it. For instance, a right angle is formed by raising a perpendicular upon a right line: this is the *method* of forming a right angle; but the *instruments* made use of in the operation, are, the dividers, the ruler, and the pencil. "His *means*" (says Hume, in speaking of Henry the Eighth) "his *means* were sufficient, but his *method* was defective."

To almost any other person I should think it necessary to apologize for having said so much to explain a distinction, which, in fact, is self-evident; but, for one who has confounded the *means* of compassing a thing with the *method* of doing it, it is much to be feared that any explanation will prove too short. However, hoping the best, I shall come to the next sentence.

"He is no ordinary character—he will, therefore, have nothing to do with any thing that is ordinary (unless it be with the Democratic Societies and the author of the Political Progress)—"

In all the books you ever have read, Sir (and, I presume, they are very numerous), did you ever see a parenthesis at the end of a period? I am inclined to think you never did; but, whether you did or not, permit me to tell you, it is extremely ungrammatical. And it is the more unpardonable in the present instance, as there was no occasion for a parenthesis at all: the exception, contained in it, is by no means extraneous; it is a complete number of the period, and, in my opinion, a very necessary one too.

But, though I find great fault with this parenthesis, I cannot help commending the motive that induced you to employ it. You were anxious to get us back to your subject at a single jump; and, upon my soul, it was high time; for you had led us a confounded jack-in-a-lantern dance. You had set out with asking what were the means the author employed for compassing his ends; but, in place of going right on, you had wandered away quite through the author's own character, and were entering into that of his opponents; when your good genius twitched you by the elbow, and brought you back to where you first set out, with a, "Well, but what are the means?" And, I wish I could say, that your answer to this question was as correct, as the question itself was pertinent.

"Well, but what *are* the *means*?—Simple *laughter*." And nothing else, Sir? Nothing but simple laughter? *Are* the *means* simple *laughter*? Why then, simple *laughter are* the *means*; and if it be good english to say, that simple *laughter are* the *means*, so is it to say, that a simple *Review are* the *books*.

You seem, my dear Sir, to be very anxious to scrape acquaintance with me; observe then; if you should see a person with one ear hanging down upon his cheek, like the ear of an old sow, that is PETER PORCUPINE, at your service.—For, you must know, when I was a little boy at school, this very self same phrase, "simple *laughter are* the *means*," happened to come blundering into my translation; for which the enraged brutal pedagogue (not Mr. Andrew Brown),[1] after having loaded me with half a score dunces and numskulls, seized me by the unfortunate ear, and swinging me in the air, as huntsmen do young hounds, to see if they are of the right breed, left me in the condition above described.

From the indignation that I cannot help expressing at this treatment, you may easily imagine, Mr. Reviewer, that I cannot wish to see the same happen to you.

Hitherto I have taken notice of grammatical errors only; I am now to speak of one of another sort.

You could not content yourself, Sir, with plain language; you must embellish this sample of your style with rhetorical figures; but, in doing this, you have not observed that scrupulous exactness, so very requisite in one who is a critic by profession, or rather by trade. You say: "Not by *pouring* upon you a *flood* of important information, *raised* by laborious study." I have often heard of *pouring* a *flood*, but of *raising* one I never did. We *raise* houses; storms may be *raised*; I can even conceive it possible to *raise* ghosts and devils; but as to the *raising* of *floods*, I must beg to be excused. The water *rises*; but who ever *raises* it, except it be from the bottom of a well? At a first reading of the sentence, this idea forces itself upon one in such an irresistible manner, that for some time, it is impossible to get rid of it; nor am I, even now, certain, that it is not the one you meant to convey. In this case, the figure is not so much amiss; but it is not supported quite so well as it might have been. By changing the word *laborious* for *windlass of*, the figure is rendered complete. Observe now.

"Not by *pouring* upon you a *flood* of important information, *raised* by the *windlass* of study."

Here, you see, the figure is supported: all is of a piece.

It may be further remarked upon this figure, that, as it appears by the context, you were pointing out the method of producing conviction in the reader, pouring a flood of information on him is by no means a good one. Pouring a flood of information on an opponent may be a good method of overwhelming him; but we endeavour to enlighten the gentle reader, and not to overwhelm him with a deluge.

Indeed, the word *flood* is every way an improper one on this occasion, and its place may be so naturally supplied by the word *mass*, that, were it not for the unlucky *pouring* which precedes it, one would be almost tempted to believe it a fault of the Printer. How much more natural does the figure appear, when amended thus: "Not by placing before you a *mass* of important information, raised by laborious study."

Upon this subject, Sir, I beg leave to observe to you, that, though tropes and figures are very useful things, when they fall into skillful hands, they are very dangerous, when they fall into those of a contrary description. When I see you flourishing with a metaphor, I feel as much anxiety as I do when I see a child playing with a razor.

Perhaps it would be better for you, to forego altogether the use of what are usually called bold figures. I am aware, that this would be an act of self-denial; but, I think, I can promise you, that it would be fully compensated by the approbation of your readers. *Verecunda debet esse translatio*, was the precept of one who understood the use of figurative language better than you and I, Sir; and he might have applied this precept to all other figures, as well as to the one here mentioned.[2] Bold figures are sometimes graceful and every way becoming; but in a cool *critique* none ought to be attempted, except such as tend to illustration; such as light, without dazzling. The figure that has taken up so much of our time, is so far from being of this description, that it absolutely throws an obscurity over the whole passage.

We will now descend to where you say: "but sometimes his *mirthful laughter* is sublimated into a ferocious grin." *Mirthful laughter*, Sir, is, in point of propriety, equal to *sweet sugar* or *sour vinegar*. It is easy to perceive, that this expletive has been thrown in, to balance against *ferocious*, as I observe, it is a rule with you, constantly to make one part of the sentence a counterpoise to the other. This is, by some, called the see-saw, and by others, the up-and-down, style and it is said, that the ladies, particularly the young ones, are remarkably fond of it. But, though pleasing the fair sex ought to be a capital consideration with every one who puts pen to paper, yet it is certainly unseemly in a grave Reviewer, to affect the silly lisping style of a writer of love-letters. A downy chin covers a multitude of sins, which a grey beard serves only to expose.

One more fault and I have done; not for want of matter, but for want of time.

"With due submission to the author of the Bone to Gnaw, for the Democrats, we do not think he ought to chastise so severely those gentlemen, since in some respects, we trace a strong resemblance between him and his opponents. Fellow-feeling should have whispered, the policy of exercising some mercy, to HIM, who, if he does not think like a democrat, certainly writes very much like one."

Now, Sir, may I ask, to *whom* this mercy was to be exercised? You say, to *him*; but who is this *him*? The author? How is it possible that he should stand in need of mercy from the Democrats, when you complain that he has chastised those gentlemen too severely? And yet, this must be your meaning; for, common charity forbids me to suppose, that you thought it necessary to advise the author to have compassion on himself.

I have heard it suggested, that you might possibly mean to say, that fellow-feeling should have whispered *to him* the policy of exercising some mercy towards the Democrats; but, though this observation would have been very natural, after what had gone before, yet I cannot think that this was your meaning; because, in that case, a different collocation would have been so necessary, and at the same time so easy, that you would not, you could not, have left the sentence in the questionable form it now wears. However, if this were your meaning, the transposing of two words, and the changing of another, would render the sentence not only perspicuous but even elegant; thus:

"*To him* fellow-feeling should have whispered some mercy; for, if he does not think like a democrat, he certainly writes very much like one."

How clear is this, Sir? Here is nothing obscure, nothing dubious; while the sentence, as you left it, is, in spite of the typographical aid of commas and capitals, so completely equivocal, that, I declare to heaven, I do not now, after the most attentive consideration, know precisely the sense in which you meant it should be taken.

Of all the faults a Reviewer can fall into with respect to style, this is most assuredly the greatest; you write to convey your opinion to others, and, if the words you make use of for that purpose, are so ill-chosen, or so illy arranged, as to leave the reader in doubt with regard to that opinion, you may as well save yourself the trouble of writing and the expence of printing, and present the public with pages filled with pot-hooks and hangers. Indeed, perspicuity is so essential a quality in every writer, that hardly anything can make up for the want of it. I know but of one profession in which this equivocal round-about style can be cultivated and practised to advantage; and, to confess a truth, I could hardly persuade myself, when I got to the end of the second paragraph of your *critique*, that I was not reading a declaration, drawn up against me by some second hand limb of the law, for an assault and battery on the bodies of citizen Callender and his friends of the Democratic Club. Had this really been the case, I must have pleaded; but as to your literary court, I deny its authority. And, though I have no very high opinion of your sagacity, I cannot help believing, that you must, by this time, have discovered your incapacity as a judge.

Now comes the agreeable part of my task.—How pleasant is it to pass from censure to commendation! It is like turning from the frowns of surly Winter, to behold the smiling Spring come dancing o'er the daisied lawn, crowned with garlands and surrounded with melody. Yes, Sir, I cannot deny that there is one thing in your *critique* that has my entire approbation; I mean its brevity. You seem to have been penetrated with the truth of that good old proverb: "Least said is soonest mended." We often say, that we cannot have too much of a good thing, but with much more truth may it be said, that we cannot have too little of a bad one; and, upon this maxim, I must have more than the malice of the devil, not to approve of the brevity of the original composition contained in your Review....

But, after all, allowing your Review to be a necessary, and consequently a laudable, undertaking, what excuse have you for having ommitted to take notice of the voluminous productions of the celebrated *Mrs. Rowson?*[3] Sins of ommission are ever inexpiable when a lady is in the case; the fair do generally, in the long run, pardon sins of commission, but those of ommission they never do. Indeed, Sir, it was giving them but a pitiful idea of your galantry, to slip by without casting a single glance at our American Sappho. At your age, when a lady tunes her lyre, he must be a sniveling devil of a critic whose bow remains unstrung. You had here the fairest opportunity in the world of ingratiating yourself with the whole tribe of female scribblers and politicians; this opportunity you have neglected, and now, like poor silly Sir Andrew Ague Cheek, you are sailed into the north of their opinion, where you might hang for ever, like an icicle upon a Dutchman's beard, if I had no more compassion for you, than you have shown for me.[4]

You will readily allow, that you have no reason to expect, that I should release you from frozen durance; but I like, now and then, to do good for evil, if it be only for novelty's sake; and therefore, I have determined to thaw you into favour, by a *critique* on *Mrs. Rowson's* works which I hereby permit you to insert in your next Number, as you[r] own. As this is all between ourselves, it will be your own fault, if the truth be ever discovered; and, at any rate, the piece will be as much yours, as any thing you have hitherto published.

Review on the roman-drama-poë-tic works of Mrs. S. Rowson, of the New Theatre, Philadelphia.

This lady some where mentions "the unbounded marks of approbation," with which her works have been received in this country. Whether this observation from the authoress was dictated by an extreme modesty, or by the overflowings of a grateful heart, is a matter of indifference; the fact, I believe, will not be disputed, and therefore I cannot withold my congratulations on the subject, either from the lady or my countrymen. It is hard to tell which is entitled to most praise on this occasion, she for the possession and exertion of such transcendent abilities, or they for having so judiciously bestowed "their unbounded marks of approbation."

It is the singular good fortune of these States, to be the receptacle of all that is excellent of other nations: they sow and plant, while we gather fruit. But, as the following elegant lines, on Mrs. Whitelock's last year's benefit, express my sentiments on this subject, much better than it can possibly be done in prose, I shall avail myself of their aid.[5]

"From Albion's Isle when *genius* takes *her* flight
'Tis ever sure on these blest shores to light;
Whether by party or by *fancy driven*,
Here sure *it* finds an ever fostering heav'n,
Here first *it* breathes invigorating air,
And learns to do whatever *man* should dare;
Here among freemen lifts its *manly* voice
And dreads no ills where all the world rejoice,
Here *Priestley* finds the rest he sought in vain
And *Whitelock* meets applauding *crowds* again.[1]
In these *blest shades* no Lords or Despots sway,
But sons of freedom their own laws obey,
Distress of course is to the land unknown,
And guardian *Science marks it for her own.*"

Yes; and these lines are a proof of it. What charming ideas! Genius *driven* by Fancy, all the way from some barn (dubbed with the name of

---

[1] A writer's thus coupling the Reverend Doctor with a Play Actress, may, to some folks, appear as absurd as it would be for a sportsman to couple a crusty old lurcher with a striking spaniel; but it will be found upon reflection, that there is a much nearer affinity between their professions, than one would, at first sight, imagine.

Play-House) to the Land's end in Cornwall; and then taking its flight, like one of Mother Carey's chickens, over the Atlantic Ocean, to America, where it finds a *fostering heaven*. And how artfully has the author (or authoress) managed the personification of *genius*! First it is *her*, then an *it*, and by-and-by it acts like a *man*, and raises its *manly* voice. An author of ordinary merit would have confined himself to one gender only, or would, at most, have made an hermaphrodite of *genius*; but in a land that "guardian science has marked for her own," that *genius* is not worth a curse, that is not masculine, feminine and neuter, all at once.

If I were to indulge myself in a detail of all the particular beauties, in this little piece, I should never have done; suffice it to say, that it yields to nothing of the kind extant; except perhaps, to some parts of Mrs. Rowson's incomparable Epilogue to that unparalleled play, the *Slaves in Algiers*.[6]

I hope the reader will excuse this digression: in a labyrinth of sweets, it is almost impossible not to lose one's way.

"The necessary conciseness of this article" forbids me to enter into a distinct analysis of each of this lady's performances; I shall, therefore, content myself (and the reader too, I hope) with an extract or two from the *Slaves in Algiers*; which, I think, may be looked upon as a criterion of her style and manner.

The lady asserts the superiority of her sex in the following spirited-manner.

"But some few months since, my father (who sends out many corsairs) brought home a *female captive*,[2] to whom I became greatly attached; it was she who nourished in my mind the love of liberty, and taught me, woman was never formed to be the abject slave of man. Nature made us equal with them, and gave us the power to render ourselves superior."

This is at once an assertion and a proof. The authoress insists upon the superiority of her sex, and in so doing, she takes care to express herself in such a correct, nervous, and elegant style, as puts her own superiority, at least, out of all manner of doubt. Nor does she confine her ideas to a superiority in the *belles lettres* only, as will appear by the following lines from her epilogue.

"Women were born for universal sway,
Men to adore, *be silent*, and *obey*."

[2] Commonly called *a Woman*.

Sentiments like these could not be otherwise than well received in a country, where the authority of the wife is so unequivocally acknowledged, that the *reformers* of the *reformed church*, have been obliged (for fear of losing all their custom) to raze the odious word *obey* from their marriage service. I almost wonder they had not imposed it upon the husband; or rather, I wonder they had not dispensed with the ceremony altogether; for most of us know, that in this enlightened age, the work of generation goes hummingly on, whether people are married or not.

I do not know how it is, but I have strange misgivings hanging about my mind, that the whole moral as well as political world is going to experience a revolution. Who knows but our present house of Representatives, for instance, may be succeeded by members of the other sex? What information might not the Democrats and grog-shop politicians expect from their communicative loquacity! I'll engage there would be no secrets then. If the speaker should happen to be with child that would be nothing to us, who have so long been accustomed to the sight; and if she should even lie in, during the sessions, her place might be supplied by her aunt or grandmother.

I return from this digression to quote a sentence or two, in which our authoress speaks highly in praise of our alacrity in paying down the ransom for our unfortunate countrymen in Algiers.

"But there are souls to whom the aflicted never cry in vain, who, to dry the widow's tear, or free the captive, would share their last possession.—*Blest spirits of philanthropy*, who inhabit my native land, never will I doubt your friendship, for sure I am, you never will neglect the wretched."

This, you must know, gentle reader, is a figure of speech, that rhetoricians call a *strong hyperbole*, and that plain folks call a *d——d lie*: We will therefore leave it, and come to her verification.

This is an art, in which the lady may be called passing excellent, as I flatter myself the following verses will prove. They are extracted from her Epilogue; where, after having rattled on for some time, with that air folâtre, so natural to her profession, she stops short with,

> "But pray forgive this flippancy——indeed,
> Of all your clemency I stand in need.
> *To own the truth*, the scenes this night display'd,
> Are only *fictions*——drawn by *fancy's* aid.
> 'Tis what I wish——But we have cause to fear,

> No ray of comfort, the sad *bosoms* cheer,
> Of many *a christian*, shut from *light* and *day*,
> In *bondage*, languishing *their lives* away."

This is a little parterre of beauties.

It was kind of the authoress to tell her gentle audience, that her play was a *fiction*; otherwise they might have gone home in the full belief, that the American prisoners in Algiers had actually conquered the whole country, and taken the Dey prisoner. I confess there was reason to fear that an audience, who had bestowed "unbounded marks of approbation" on such a piece, might fall into this error.

It was not enough to tell them, that the subject of her play was a *fiction*, but she must tell them too, that it was a *fiction* drawn by *fancy's* aid. This was necessary again; for *they* might have thought it was a *fiction*, drawn by the aid of *truth*.

"'*Tis what I wish.*"——What do you wish for, my dear lady? Do you wish *that your scenes may be fictions drawn by fancy's aid*? Your words have no other meaning than this; and if you may have another, you have not told us what it is.

Being shut from *light* is the same thing as being shut from *day*, and being shut from day is being *in bondage*; either of these, then, would have been enough, if addressed to an audience of a common capacity.

Many a christian's having a plurality of *bosoms* and *lives*, is an idea, that most assuredly bears in it all the true marks of originality.—The lady tells us somewhere, that she has never read the ancients: so much the better for us; for if she had, she might have met with, "*Prima solaecismi faeditas absit,*"[7] and then we had inevitably missed the charming idea, which is here the object of our admiration.³

I would now, reader, indulge you with an extract or two from this amiable authoress's romances; but, as I am rather in haste,⁴ I hope it will be sufficient to observe, that they are, in no respect, inferior to her poetic and "dramatic efforts."

Among the many treasures that the easterly winds have wafted us

---

³ May we not, Mr. Reviewer, ascribe several of the beauties, to be found in your composition, to the same cause.

Memorandum. This note is not to come into print. Take care about this, for heaven's sake.

⁴ The last Review was kept back nearly three weeks; but, it is hoped, the subscribers will find the great quantity of original matter contained in it (almost a whole page) a sufficient compensation for the want of punctuality.

over, since our political emancipation, I cannot hesitate to declare this lady the most valuable. The inestimable works that she has showered (not to say *poured*, you know) upon us, mend not only our hearts, but, if properly administered, our constitutions also: at least, I can speak for myself. They are my *Materia Medica*, in a literal sense. A liquorish page from the *Fille de Chambre* serves me by way of a philtre, the *Inquisitor* is my opium, and I have ever found the *Slaves in Algiers* a most excellent emetic. As to *Mentoria* and *Charlotte*, it is hardly necessary to say what use they are put to in the chamber of a valetudinarian.[8]

Before we were so happy as to have *a Rowson* amongst us, we were, or seemed to be, ignorant of our real consequence as a nation. We were modest enough to be content with thinking ourselves the only enlightened, virtuous, and happy, people upon earth, without having any pretension to universal dominion; but she, like a second Juno, fires our souls with ambition, shows us our high destiny, bids us "soar aloft, and wave our *acknowledged* standard *o'er the world*."

After this, it is not astonishing that she should be called the poetess laureate of the Sovereign People of the United States; it is more astonishing that there should be no salary attached to the title; for, I am confident, her dramatic works merit it much more than all the birth-day and new-year odes, ever addressed to her quondam king.

Notwithstanding all this, there are (and I am sorry to say it), some people, who doubt of her sincerity, and who pretend that her sudden conversion to republicanism, ought to make us look upon all her praises as ironical. But these uncandid people do not, or rather will not, recollect, what the miraculous air of America is capable of.[9] I have heard whole cargoes of imported Irish say (and swear too), that, when they came within a few leagues of the coast, they began to feel a sort of regenerative spirit working within them, something like that which is supposed to work in the good honest methodist, when he imagines himself called from the lapstone to go and hammer the pulpit. However, whether our air do really possess this amazing virtue or not, there are certainly other causes sufficient to work a conversion in any heart, not entirely petrified by the frowns of despotism. Is not the sound of *Liberty*, glorious *Liberty*! heard to ring from one end of the continent to the other? Who dares print a book or news-paper, without bespangling every page with this dear word in STARING CHARACTERS? Have not our sign-post daubers put it into the mouths of all the birds in the air and all the beasts of the field? What else is heard in the senate, the pulpit, the jail, the parlour, the kitchen, the cradle? Do not our children squall out *Liberty*, as naturally as kittens mew; and do not their careful, tender, patriotic parents deck them out in national cockades, and learn them to sing "*dansons la carmagnole*," long before they learn them their A.B.C? In short, is there any thing to be seen, heard, or felt, but *Liberty*? Is it not through it we live, and move, and have our being? What great wonder is it then, that she, whose feelings are so "exquisitely fine," whose soul is like tinder, should catch the "heavenly flame that gilds the life of man?"

Let us reject the ungenerous insinuations of envy and malice; let us not damp a genius that promises such ample encouragement to our infant manufactories of ink and paper. That old cynic, Mr. Peachum,[10] has said, that women bring custom to nobody but the hangman and the surgeon; and this might, in some measure, be true, if confined to that vile country, England; but when stretched across to us, it becomes absolutely false. Here, as Mrs. R. very elegantly observes, "virtue, heavenly virtue, in *either sex*, is the only mark of superiority." Under our virgin constellation frailty is unknown, lovers' vows are like the laws of the Medes and Persians, every marriage ring is equal to the *anneau* of Hans Carval,[11] and even the Green Room, so long known for the temple of Venus, is here consecrated to the Goddess of the Silver Bow.

Long may the Theatre thus continue the school of politeness, innocence, and every virtue. Long may "the Eagle suffer little birds to sing," and may their melodious caroling never be rendered discordant by the voice of the ominous cuckoo. . . .

With this, Sir, I take my leave, hoping that nothing that I have said, will tend to cool that zeal which you have shown for the advancement of anti-britannick literature. Write, write away, for the love of fun, 'till there is not a sheet of blank paper left in the whole State; recollect only, that, though patriots are permitted to talk nonsense with impunity in all other republics, they have not, nor ever will have, any such privilege in the Republic of Letters.

I am,
    With an unspeakable degree of respect,
        Yours, &c.

                                              P. P.

March 6th, 1795.

[From the Preface of *A Bone to Gnaw, Part II*]

Perhaps the reader may expect from me, on this occasion, an answer to citizen *Scrub*; but in this, I must forewarn him that he will be disappointed.[12] I hate controversy more, if possible, than I do sansculottism. The parties concerned in a paper war, usually bear an infinite resemblance to a gang of sharpers: a couple of authors knock up a sham fight to draw the public about them, while the booksellers pick their pockets. However, there is one passage in master Scrub's epistle that I cannot pass over in silence. He accuses me of rudeness and malice towards Mrs. Rowson, of the new theatre! this is amazingly cruel. To accuse me of malice towards an authoress, when I am the only person who has ever condescended to take the least notice of her works, and when my only motive in so doing was to deliver her unfortunate play, "the slaves in Algiers," from its dismal obscurity! I must confess, that I have been severe on the romances that bear this ladies [sic] name; but then, it must be remembered that any censure passed on them, ought to be understood as dividing itself among all the writers from whom she has thought proper to borrow (mind, I only say *borrow*) and, consequently, that a very small portion of it will fall to her share.

"I do not surmise," says brother Scrub, "but I proclaim absolutely, that you are as base a poltroon as ever trembled." And for what? "Because you have sallied forth in the *dark* and attacked the literary character of a woman." But, be a little reasonable Brother Scrub. This lady, whom you say I have attacked in the *dark*, tells us, that "nature made women equal to men, and gave them the power to render themselves superior;" and you, my dear Scrub, tell us, that she herself possesses abilities far superior to mine; that she has, besides, a husband, before whom I should "stand no more chance than an insect under a discharge of thunderbolts;" and that even you, "her heroic Scrub," have ever stood ready to interpose your shield in her defence. Now, I will appeal to the candid reader, whether attacking a literary Amazone like this, and thus defended, be not a proof of bravery in place of cowardice. As to the attack's being made in the *dark*, Brother Scrub knows no more of the fair sex than he does of me, if he does not perceive that that circumstance was to her advantage. But he is all unreasonableness, all inconsistency. One minute he says, the lady despises me from her soul, and the very next, he hints that I have drawn tears from her "tearful eyes." If she has been seen to shed tears lately, I presume it was for the untimely fate of that last offspring of her miawling muse, called "The Volunteers," and not on account of any thing that could flow from my pen. It would have been preposterous to scatter about those precious "pellucid drops" for a person whom "she despised."

I should be very sorry to regulate my conduct by that of Master Scrub; but he certainly steps forward with a very bad grace, to complain of my want of respect to Mrs. Rowson of the New Theatre, while he has not been ashamed to abuse, in the most outrageous manner, in language that would become a scolding queen of the suds or a drunken Drury-Lane bully, several ladies, who, independent of their being allied to men of the first talents, and most elevated situations, are objects of universal admiration and respect.[13] I suppose, that he, as a democrat, looks upon a play-actress as something better than the wife of a member of Congress; but for me, who cannot raise my ideas to the sublime "morality of the sans culottes," I must be excused for thinking otherwise. I shall still believe myself at liberty to speak without the least reserve, of the performances of those whom I pay for diverting me, while I shall be extremely careful not to "*damn*" like Brother Scrub, those whom fortune and merit have placed above me.

If Scrub can be believed, Mrs. Rowson intends to "indulge her audience with an epilogue at her next benefit," in which my quills are to be roasted. This, it seems, is to procure her a clap from "her heroic Scrub," and much good may it do her!

This male virago, not content with accusing me of rudeness to Mrs. Rowson, hints that I am a hater of all woman kind. This is the most slanderous insinuation that ever dropt from the pen of malice. Is it not evident that I want the ladies to continue women, and not turn men? Scrub asks me: "can you prove that a male education would not qualify a *woman* for *all* the *duties of a man*?" If he means a man like himself, I will undertake to prove no such thing; for I have no doubt but any *scrubbing* old washerwoman would perform *all* the functions of a man every bit as well as he: but if he means a man *indeed*, I say that * * * * and I appeal to Mrs. Rowson, or any other lady, for the truth of my assertion.

[4]

The Bloody Buoy

WRITTEN IN MARCH 1796, THIS WORK IS A BLISTERING ATTACK on the principles and practice of the French Revolution, and a warning to Americans that the terror could happen in their own country unless Jacobin ideas and actions were stamped out. Drawing on French counterrevolutionary sources, Cobbett spent over 150 pages recounting in lurid detail the atrocities of the September Massacres, the Parisian Terror, the dechristianization movement, and the mass murders at Nantes. This extract includes only a few typical examples of Cobbett's material; the reader quickly gets the general idea.

Central to Cobbett's interpretation of these events is his notion of the wide gap between the language of liberty, equality and republicanism and the reality of "insurrection, robbery, and murder." Rejecting the view that revolutionary violence was the product of wartime emergencies, Cobbett traced the roots of totalitarianism to the "licentious politicians" of 1789 and the "infidel philosophers" of the ancien régime. Thinking in conspiratorial terms, he argued that the leaders of the National Assembly in 1789 were motivated by hatred and envy of the rich, and that they used the mask of liberty and equality to conceal their own self-interested ambition. To break down the barriers of respect for authority, Cobbett continued, they set out to destroy traditional morality and religious teachings that had emphasized humility, peace, and obedience. There was, he noted, a kind of "fanaticism in irreligion, that leads the profligate atheist to seek for proselytes with a zeal that would do honour to a good cause, but which, employed in a bad one, becomes the scourge of society." And the flames of irreligion and intolerance were fanned by the popular press, "which was made free for the worst of purposes." The conclusion was clear: unbridled ambition, revolutionary fanaticism, and irreligion had reduced France to blood and ashes.

Having torn the veil from French notions of liberty and equality, Cobbett attempted to sever the ties of sentiment that attached many Americans to the "sister republic" across the Atlantic. The word "republic" was, in itself, meaningless, Cobbett argued; what mattered were the realities that lay behind the word. "What more stupid doltish bigotry can there be," he asked, "than to make the sound of a word the standard of good or bad government?" Americans should "look to the characters and actions of men, and not to their professions; let us attach ourselves to things, and not to words; to sense, and not to sound."

He also warned Americans against an it-can't-happen-here attitude. After all, the United States was sheltering "political projectors from every corner of Europe" and had its own native Jacobins who compared Marat to Jesus Christ, toasted the guillotine, and attacked the character of George Washington as vehemently as the French had attacked Louis XVI before executing him. If ever these people got into power, Cobbett wrote, they would "render the annals of America as disgraceful as those of the French revolution." All men of sense, all the friends of order and virtue, must unite and employ the same kind of energy against the Jacobins that the Jacobins had shown against them. Only then, he argued, would America be safe from democracy.

"The Bloody Buoy" was one of Cobbett's most popular works in the 1790s. It ran into many editions, was translated into German, was reprinted in England, and was republished in Pennsylvania right up to 1823.

THE BLOODY BUOY,

THROWN OUT AS A

Warning to the political Pilots of all Nations:

OR, A FAITHFUL RELATION OF A MULTITUDE OF ACTS OF HORRID BARBARITY,

SUCH AS THE EYE NEVER WITNESSED, THE TONGUE EXPRESSED, OR THE IMAGINATION CONCEIVED,

UNTIL THE COMMENCEMENT OF THE

FRENCH REVOLUTION

TO WHICH IS ADDED AN INSTRUCTIVE ESSAY,

Tracing these dreadful Effects to their real Causes.

"You will plunge your country into an abyss of eternal detestation and infamy; and the annals of your boasted revolution will serve as a BLOODY BUOY, warning the nations of the earth to keep aloof from the mighty ruin."

Abbé Maury's Speech to the National Assembly.

Introduction

THE OBJECT OF THE FOLLOWING WORK IS TO GIVE THE PEOPLE OF AMERIca a striking and experimental proof of the horrible effects of anarchy and infidelity.

The necessity of such an undertaking, at this time, would have been, in a great measure, precluded, had our public prints been conducted with that impartiality and undaunted adherence to truth, which the interests of the community and of suffering humanity demanded from them. But, so far from this, the greater part of those vehicles of information have most industriously concealed, or glossed over, the actions, as well as the motives of the ruling powers in France; they have extenuated all their unheard-of acts of tyranny, on the false, but specious pretence, that they were conducive to the establishment of a free government; and one of their editors has not blushed to declare, that "it would be *an easy matter to apologize for all the massacres that have taken place in that country.*"[1]

We have seen, indeed, some exceptions; some few prints that have not dishonoured themselves by going this length: but even these have observed a timid silence, and have avoided speaking of the shocking barbarities of the French, with as much caution as if we were to partake in the disgrace, and as if it were in our power to hide them from the world, and from posterity. If they have now and then given way to a just indignation, this has been done in such a manner, and has been so timid, as to do them but little honour. They have acted the part of the tyrannized people of Paris: they have huzza'd every succeeding tyrant while on the theatre of power, and, the instant he was transferred to a scaffold, they have covered him with reproach. They have attributed to factions, to individuals, what was the work of the national representatives, and of the nation itself. They have, in short, inveighed against the murderers of the fallen assassins, while they have, in the same breath, applauded the principles on which they acted, and on which their survivors and their partisans do still act.

Thus has the liberty of the press, a liberty of which we so justly boast, been not only useless to us during this terrible convulsion of the civilized world, but has been so perverted as to lead us into errors, which had well nigh plunged us into the situation of our distracted allies. Nor are we yet secure. Disorganizing and blasphemous principles have been disseminated among us with but too much success; and, unless we profit from the awful example before us, we may yet

The Times: A Political Portrait. This anonymous cartoon, from 1798, illustrates the Federalist fear that the antigovernment activities of American Republicans were opening the way for a French invasion of the United States. George Washington, back in command of the American army, is obstructed by his political enemies. Benjamin Bache, the editor of the radical *Aurora* newspaper, is being trampled underfoot by the soldiers: James Madison is trying to block Washington's carriage with his pen; Albert Gallatin, the Swiss-born Republican, attempts to "stop de wheels of de gouvernement"; Thomas Jefferson tries to assist him. Meanwhile, in the background, the French "cannibals" are approaching; the reference is to Cobbett's *The Cannibals' Progress* (1798), which described French atrocities in Europe, just as "The Bloody Buoy" described the terror within France itself. (Collection of the New-York Historical Society, New York, New York, negative number 2737.)

experience all the calamities that Heaven and earth now call on us to deplore.

Fully impressed with this persuasion, the author of these sheets has ventured to undeceive the misguided; to tear aside the veil, and show to a yet happy people the dangers they have to fear. With this object in view, he has too much confidence in the good sense and piety of the major part of his countrymen, not to be assured, that his efforts will be seconded by their zeal in the cause of order and religion.

The materials for the work have been collected from different publications, *all written by Frenchmen*, and all, except one, from which only a few extracts were made, *printed at Paris.*

Well aware that persons of a certain description will leave nothing untried to discredit a performance of this nature, the author has taken particular care to mention the work, and even the page, from which each fact is extracted.

He foresees that the cant of *modern patriotism* will be poured forth against him on this occasion. He knows that he shall be represented as an enemy of the French nation, and of the cause of liberty. To this he will answer beforehand, with the frankness of a man who thinks no freedom equal to that of speaking the truth. As to the individuals composing this formerly amiable nation, many of them, and he hopes very many, are still entitled to his love and esteem. He has, from his infancy, been an admirer of their sprightly wit; he owes a thousand obligations to their officious hospitality, and has long boasted of their friendship. But with respect to the *regenerated* French, he would blush to be thought their friend, after what he has recorded in this volume. And, as to the cause of liberty, if that cause is to be maintained by falsehood, blasphemy, robbery, violation, and murder, he is, and trusts he ever shall be, its avowed and mortal enemy.

The
Bloody Buoy &c. &c.

It will be recollected by the greater part of my readers, that soon after the beginning of the French revolution, the National Assembly conceived the plan of destroying the religion of their forefathers. In order to effect this, they separated the Gallican church from that of Rome, and imposed an oath on the clergy, which they could not take without becoming apostates in the fullest sense of that word. All the worthy and conscientious part of that body refused of course, and this refusal was made a pretext to drive them from their livings, and fill the vacancies with such as had more pliant consciences, principles better adapted to the impious system which the leaders in the Assembly had prepared for their too credulous countrymen.

The Bloody Buoy

The ejectment of the priesthood was attended with numberless acts of most atrocious and wanton cruelty: these have been recorded by the Abbé Barruel, in a work entitled, *The History of the French Clergy*; and though what is here to be found will dwindle into nothing, when compared to what I have extracted from other works, yet it could not be wholly omitted, without showing a degree of insensibility for the sufferings of these men, that I am persuaded the reader would not have excused. I shall therefore begin the relation with some extracts from that work. . . .

> *Page 210.*—Several priests were conducted to Lagrave, where they were told that they must take the oath,[1] or suffer death. Among them was [a] Sulpician, of 98 years of age, and a young Abbé of the name of Novi. The whole chose death, the venerable Sulpician leading the way. The trial of Mr. Novi was particularly severe. The ruffians brought his father to the spot, and told him, if he could persuade his son to swear, he should live. The tender old man, wavering, hesitating between the feelings of nature and the duties of religion, at last yields to parental fondness, throws his arms round his child's neck, buries his face in his bosom, and with tears and sobs presses his compliance. "O! my child, my child, spare the life of your father!"— "My dearest father! my dearest father," returned the Abbé, "I will do more. I will die worthy of you and my God. You educated me a Catholic: I am a priest, a servant of the Lord. It will be a greater comfort to you in your gray hairs, to have your son a martyr than an apostate."—The villains tear them asunder, and, amidst the cries and lamentations of the father, extend the son before him a bleeding corpse.
>
> *Page 211.*—In the same town, and on the same day, the axe was suspended above the head of Mr. Teron, when the revolutionists bethought them that he had a son. This son was about ten years of age, and, in order to enjoy the father's torments and the child's tears both at a time, he was brought to the place of execution. His tears and cries gave a relish to the ferocious banquet. After tiring themselves with the spectacle, they put the father to death before the eyes of the child, whom they besmeared with his blood. . . .
>
> *Page 327.*—A great fire was made in the Place Dauphine, at which

---

[1] This oath amounted to neither more nor less than direct perjury: since, by taking it, they must break the oath they had made when they entered the priesthood.

many, both men and women, were roasted. The Countess of Perignan, with her three daughters, were dragged thither. They were stripped, rubbed over with oil, and then put to the fire. The eldest of the daughters, who was fifteen, begged them to put an end to her torments, and a young fellow shot her through the head. The cannibals, who were shouting and dancing round the fire, enraged to see themselves thus deprived of the pleasure of hearing her cries, seized the too merciful murderer, and threw him into the flames.

When the Countess was dead, they brought six priests, and cutting off some of the roasted flesh, presented them each with a piece to eat. They shut their eyes, and made no answer. The oldest of the priests was then stripped and tied opposite the fire. The mob told the others, that perhaps they might prefer the relish of a priest's flesh to that of a Countess; but they suddenly rushed into the flames. The barbarians tore them out, to prolong their torments; not, however, before they were dead, and beyond the reach even of Parisian cruelty....

Facts selected from the *Trial of the Members of the Revolutionary Committee at Nantz, of the Representative Carrier*....

Vol i. *Page* 68—Old men, women with child, and children, were drowned without distinction. They were put on board of lighters, which were railed round to keep the prisoners from jumping overboard if they should happen to disengage themselves. There were plugs made in the bottom, or sides, which being pulled out, the lighter sunk, and all in it were drowned. These expeditions were first carried on by night, but the sun soon beheld the murderous work. At first the prisoners were drowned in their clothes; this, however, appeared too merciful; to expose the two sexes naked before each other was a pleasure that the ruffians could not forego.

I must now, says the witness, speak of a new sort of cruelty. The young men and women were picked out from among the mass of the sufferers, stripped naked, and tied together face to face. After being kept in this situation about an hour, they were put into an open lighter; and after receiving several blows on the skull with the but of a musket, thrown into the water. These were called *republican marriages*....

After having led the reader through such rivers of blood, it seems indispensably necessary to insert a few facts, showing by whose authority that blood was spilt; for it could answer no good purpose to excite this detestation, without directing it towards the proper object. . . . [It must be explained] how so great a part of the nation were led to butcher each other; how they were brought to that pitch of brutal sanguinary ferocity, which we have seen so amply displayed in the previous chapters. This is what, with the reader's indulgence, I shall now, agreeably to my promise endeavour to explain.

An Instructive Essay,

Tracing all the Horrors of the French Revolution to their real Causes, the licentious Politics and infidel Philosophy of the present Age.

. . . The first National Assembly had hardly assumed that title, when they discovered an intention of overturning the Government, which had been called together, and which their constituents had enjoined them to support, and of levelling all ranks and distinctions among the different orders in the community. To this they were not led, as it has been so falsely pretended, by their love of liberty and desire of seeing their country happy; but by envy, cursed envy, that will never let the fiery demagogue sleep in peace, while he sees a greater or richer than himself. . . .

This task of destruction was, however, an arduous one. To tear the complicated work of fourteen centuries to pieces at once, to render honours dishonourable, and turn reverential awe into contempt and mockery, was not to be accomplished but by extraordinary means. It was evident that property must change hands, that the best blood of the nation must flow in torrents, or the project must fail. The Assembly, to arm the multitude on their side, broached the popular doctrine of *equality*. It was a necessary part of the plan of these reformers to seduce the people to their support; and such was the credulity of the unfortunate French, that they soon began to look on them as the oracles of virtue and wisdom, and believed themselves raised, by one short sentence issued by these ambitious imposters, from the state of *subjects* to that of *sovereigns*. . . .

Hardly had the word *equality* been pronounced, when the whole kingdom became a scene of anarchy and confusion. The name of liberty (I say the *name*, for the regenerated French have known nothing but the name), the name of liberty had already half turned the heads of the people, and that of equality finished the work. From the moment it sounded in their ears, all that had formerly inspired respect, all that they had reverenced and adored, even began to excite contempt and fury. Birth, beauty, old age, all became the victims of a destructive equality, erected into a law by an Assembly of ambitious tyrants, who were ready to destroy every thing that crossed their way to absolute dominion. . . .

Let this, Americans, be a lesson to you; throw from you the doctrine of equality as you would the poisoned chalice. Wherever this detestable principle gains ground to any extent, ruin must inevitably ensue. Would you stifle the noble flame of emulation, and encourage ignorance and idleness? Would you inculcate defiance of the laws? Would you teach servants to be disobedient to their masters, and children to their parents? Would you sow the seeds of envy, hatred, robbery, and murder? Would you break all the bands of society asunder, and turn a civilized people into a horde of savages? This is all done by the comprehensive word *equality*. But they tell us we are not to take it in the unqualified sense. In what sense are we to take it then? Either it means something more than liberty, or it means nothing at all. The misconstruction of the word *liberty* had done mischief enough in the world; to add to it a word of still more dangerous extent, was to kindle a flame that never can be extinguished but by the total debasement, if not destruction, of the society who are silly or wicked enough to adopt its use. We are told, that every government receives with its existence the latent disease that is one day to accomplish its death; but the government that is attacked with this political apoplexy is annihilated in the twinkling of an eye.

The civil disorganization of the state was but the forerunner of those curses which the Assembly had in store for their devoted country. They plainly perceived that they never should be able to brutify the people to their wishes without removing the formidable barriers of religion and morality. Their heads were turned, but it was necessary to corrupt their hearts.

Besides this, the leaders in the Assembly were professed modern philosophers; that is to say, atheists or deists. . . . It was not to be wondered at, that the vanity of such men should be flattered in the hope of changing the most Christian country into the most infidel upon the face of the earth; for there is a sort of fanaticism in irreligion, that leads the profligate atheist to seek for proselytes with a zeal that would do honour to a good cause, but which, employed in a bad one, becomes the scourge of society.

The zeal of these philosophers for extirpating the truth was as great at least as that shown by the primitive Christians for its propagation. But they proceeded in a very different manner. At first, some circumspection was necessary. The more effectually to destroy the Christian religion altogether, they began by sapping the foundation of the Catholic faith, the only one that the people had been taught to revere. They formed a schism with the Church of Rome, well knowing that the opinions of the vulgar, once set afloat, were as likely to fix on atheism as on any other system: and more so, as being less opposed to their levelling principles than the rigid though simple morality of the Gospel. A religion that teaches obedience to the higher powers, inculcates humility and peace, strictly forbids robbery and murder, and, in short, enjoins on men to do as they would be done unto, could by no means suit the armed ruffians who were to accomplish the views of the French Assembly.

The press, which was made free for the worst of purposes, lent most powerful aid to these destructive reformers. While the Catholic religion was ridiculed and abused, no other Christian system was proposed in its stead; on the contrary, the profligate wretches who conducted the public prints, among whom were Mirabeau, Marat, Condorcet, and Hebert, filled one half of their impious sheets with whatever could be thought of to degrade all religion in general.[2] The ministers of divine worship, of every sect and denomination, were represented as cheats, and as the avowed enemies of the sublime and sentimental something which the Assembly had in store for the regeneration of the world. . . .

Let the reader now look back, and he will easily trace all the horrors of the French revolution to the decrees of the Constituent Assembly. It was they that rent the Government to pieces; it was they that first broached the destructive doctrine of equality; it was they that destroyed all ideas of private property; and finally, it was they that rendered the people hardened, by effacing from their minds every principle of the only religion capable of keeping mankind within the bounds of justice and humanity. Look also at their particular actions, and you will see them breaking their oaths to their constituents and to their King; you will see their agents driving people from their estates, beating and killing them; you will see them surrounded with a set of hireling writers and assassins, employed to degrade and murder peaceful people attached to the religion of their forefathers; and you will see them not only pardoning murderers, in spite of their poor humiliated Monarch, but even receiving the assassins at their bar, covering them with applauses, and instituting festivals in their honour. What have the members of the Convention and their agents done more than this? They have murdered in great numbers. True; but what have numbers to do with the matter? The principle on which those murders were committed was ever the same: it was more or less active as occasion required. The wants of the Convention were more pressing than those of the Constituent Assembly. The Assembly were not driven to the expedient of *requisitions*, nor was the hour yet arrived for the promulgation of the Paganish Calendar.[3] Consequently they met with less opposition, and therefore fewer murders were necessary; but, had they continued their sittings to this day, the devastation of every kind would have been the same that it has been.

The whole history of the revolution presents us with nothing but a regular progress in robbery and murder. The first Assembly, for instance, begin by flattering the mob, wheedling their King out of his title and his power; they then set him at defiance, proscribe or put to death his friends; and then shut him up in his palace, as a wild beast in a cage. The second Assembly send a gang of ruffians to insult and revile him, and then they hurl him from his throne. The third Assembly cut his throat. What is there in all this but a regular and natural progression from bad to worse? And so with the rest of their abominable actions.

To throw the blame on the successors of the first despotic Assembly is such a perversion of reason, such an abandonment of truth, that no man, who has a single grain of sense, can hear of with patience. As well might we ascribe all the murders committed at Nantz to the under-cut-throats, by whom they were perpetrated, and not to the Convention, by whose order, and under whose protection, these cut-throats acted. The Constituent Assembly knew the consequences of their decrees, as well as Foucault knew the consequence of his order for throwing forty women from the cliff Pierre Moine into the sea;[4] and it is full as ridiculous to hear them pretend that they did not wish those consequences to follow, as it would be to hear Foucault pretend that he did not wish forty women should be drowned. True, the Convention are guilty of every crime under heaven; assassins and blasphemers must ever merit detestation and abhorrence, from whatever motive they may act, or by whomsoever taught and instigated; but still the pre-eminence in infamy is due to their teachers and instigators: the Convention is, in relation to the Constituent Assembly, what the ignorant desperate bravo is in relation to his crafty and sculking employer.

Before I conclude, it may not be improper, as I have hitherto spoken of the Constituent Assembly in a general way, to make some distinctions with respect to the persons who composed it. I am very far from holding them all up as objects of abhorrence, or even of censure. There were many, very many, men of great wisdom and virtue, who were elected to the States-General, and even who joined the Assembly, after it assumed the epithet *National*. It would be the height of injustice to reproach these men with the consequences of measures, which they opposed with such uncommon eloquence and courage. History will make honourable mention of their names, when the epitome I have here attempted will be lost and forgotten. Suffice it to say, that the weight of our censure, of the censure of all just and good men, ought to fall on those licentious politicians and infidel philosophers alone, who sanctioned the decree for the annihilation of property and religion.

Here, too, we ought to divest ourselves of every thing of a personal or party nature, and direct our abhorrence to principles alone. As to the actors, they have, in general, already expiated their wickedness, or folly by the loss of their lives. We have seen the atheist Condorcet obliged to fly in disguise from the capital, the inhabitants of which he had corrupted, and by whom he had been adored as the great luminary of the age: we have seen him assume the garb and the supplicating tone of a common beggar, lurking in the lanes and woods, like a houseless thief, and, at last, literally dying in a ditch, leaving his carcass a prey to the fowls of the air, and his memory as a lesson to future apostles of anarchy and blasphemy.[5] Scores, not to say hundreds, of his coadjutors have shared a fate little different from his own; and those who have not, can have little reason to congratulate themselves on their escape. The tornado they have raised for the destruction of others, has swept them from the seat of their tyranny, and scattered them over every corner of the earth. Those haughty usurpers, who refused the precedence to the successors of Charlemagne, are now obliged to yield it to a peasant or a porter. Those who decreed that the "folding-doors of the Louvre should fly open at their approach," are now glad to lift the latch of the wicket, and bend their heads beneath the thatch of a cabin. And what language can express the vexation, the anguish, the cutting reflections, that must be the companions of their obscurity! When they look back on their distracted country, when they behold the widows, the orphans, the thousands and hundreds of thousands of murdered victims, that it presents; when they behold the frantic people, carrying the dagger to the hearts of their parents, nay, digging their forefathers from their graves, and throwing their ashes to the winds; when they behold all this, and reflect that it is the work of their own hands, well might they call on the hills to hide them. The torments of such an existence, who can bear? Next to the wrath of Heaven, the malediction of one's country is surely the most tremendous and insupportable.

Now, what is the advantage we ought to derive from the awful example before us? It ought to produce in us a watchfulness, and a steady resolution to oppose the advances of disorganizing and infidel principles. I am aware that it will be said by some, that all fear of the progress of these principles is imaginary; but constant observation assures me that it is but too well founded. Let any man examine the change in political and religious opinions since the establishment of the general government, and particularly the change crept in along with our silly admiration of the French revolution, and see if the result of his inquiries does not justify a fear of our falling under the scourge that has brought a happy and gallant people on their knees, and left them bleeding at every pore.

Unfortunately for America, Great Britain has thrown from her the principles of the French revolutionists with indignation and abhorrence. This, which one would imagine should have had little or no influence on us, has served, in some measure, as a guide to our opinions, and has been one of the principal motives for our actions. A combination of circumstances, such as, perhaps, never before met together, has so soured the minds of the great mass of the people in this country, has worked up their hatred against Great Britain to such a pitch, that the instant that nation is named, they lose not only their temper, but their reason also. The dictates of nature and the exercise of judgment are thrown aside: whatever the British adopt must be rejected, and whatever they reject must be adopted. Hence it is, that all the execrable acts of the French legislators, not forgetting their murders and their blasphemy, have met with the most unqualified applauses, merely because they were execrated in the island of Britain.

The word *Republic* has also done a great deal. France is a *republic*, and the decrees of the Legislators were necessary to maintain it a republic. This *word* outweighs, in the estimation of some persons (I wish I could say they were few in number), all the horrors that have been and that can be committed in that country. One of these modern republicans will tell you that he does not deny that hundreds of thousands of innocent persons have been murdered in France; that the people have neither religion nor morals; that all the ties of nature are rent asunder; that the rising generation will be a race of cut-throats; that poverty and famine stalk forth at large; that the nation is half depopulated; that its riches, along with millions of the best of the people, are gone to enrich and aggrandize its enemies; that its commerce, its manufactures, its sciences, its arts, and its honour, are no more; but at the end of all this, he will tell you that it must be happy, because it is a *republic*. I have heard more than one of these republican zealots declare, that he would sooner see the last of the French exterminated, than see them adopt any other form of government. Such a sentiment is characteristic of a mind locked up in a savage ignorance; and I would no more trust my throat within the reach of such a republican, than I would within that of a Louvet, a Gregoire, or any of their colleagues.[6]

Our enlightened philosophers run on in a fine canting strain about the bigotry and ignorance of their ancestors; but I would ask them, what more stupid doltish bigotry can there be, than to make the sound of a word the standard of good or bad government? What is there in the combination of the letters which make up the word *Republic*? What is there in the sound they produce, that the bellowing of it forth should compensate for the want of every virtue, and even for common sense and common honesty? It is synonymous with liberty.— Fatal error! In the mouth of a turbulent demagogue it is synonymous with liberty, and with every thing else, that will please its hearers, but, with the man of virtue and sense, [it] has no more than its literal value; that is, it means of itself neither good nor evil. If he calls our own Government that of a *republic*, and judge of the meaning of the word by the effects of that Government, it will admit of a most amiable interpretation; but if we are to judge of it by what it has produced in France, it means all that is ruinous, tyrannical, blasphemous, and bloody. Last winter, one of these republican heroes in Congress, accused a gentleman from New-England of having adopted *anti-republican* principles, because he proposed something that seemed to militate *against negro-slavery*!—Thus, then, republicanism did not mean liberty. In short, it means any thing: it is the watch-word of faction; and if ever our happy and excellently constituted republic should be overturned, it will be done under the mask of republicanism.

Let us then, be upon our guard; let us look to the characters and actions of men, and not to their professions; let us attach ourselves to things, and not to words; to sense, and not to sound. Should the day of *requisition* and *murder* arrive, our tyrants calling themselves republicans, will be but a poor consolation to us. The loss of property, the pressure of want and beggary, will not be less real because flowing from republican decrees. Hunger pinches the republican, the cold blast cramps his joints as well as those of other men. This word does not soften the pangs of death. The keen knife will not produce a delectable sensation, because drawn across the throat by a republican; nor will the word *republican* parry a bullet, or render a flaming fire a bed of down. When Monsieur Berthier had the ghastly head of his father pressed against his lips, when his own heart was afterwards torn from his living body, and placed, all reeking and palpitating, on a table before a committee of magistrates, the agonies of his mind, and of his mangled carcass, were not assuaged by the shouts of his republican murderers.[7]

Shall we say that these things never can take place among us? Because we have hitherto preserved the character of a pacific humane people, shall we set danger at defiance? Though we are not Frenchmen, we are men as well as they; and consequently are liable to be misled, and even to be sunk to the lowest degree of brutality, as they have been. They, too, had an amiable character: what character have they now? The same principles brought into action among us would produce the same degradation. I repeat, we are not what we were before the French revolution. Political projectors from every corner of Europe, troublers of society of every description, from the whining philosophical hypocrite to the daring rebel, and more daring blasphemer, have taken shelter in these States. Will it be pretended that the principles and passions of these men have changed with the change of air? It would folly to suppose it.

Nor are men of the same stamp wanting among the native Americans. There is not a single action of the French revolutionists, but has been justified and applauded in our public papers, and many of them in our public assemblies. Anarchy has its open advocates. The divine Author of our religion has been put upon a level with the infamous Marat. We have seen a clergyman of the episcopal church publicly abused, because he had recommended to his congregation to beware of the atheistical principles of the French. Even their Calendar, the frivolous offspring of infidelity, is proposed for our imitation. Where persons whose livelihood depends on their daily publication are to be found, who are ever ready to publish articles of this nature, it were the grossest folly not to believe that there are hundreds and thousands to whom they give pleasure.[2] But we are not left to mere surmise here. How many numerous companies have issued, under the form of toasts, sentiments offensive to humanity, and disgraceful to our national character? We have seen the *guillotine* toasted to three times three cheers, and even under the discharge of cannon. If drunken men, as is usually the case, speak from the bottom of their hearts, what quarter should we have to expect from wretches like these? It must be allowed, too, that where the cannons were fired to give eclat to such a sentiment, the convives were not of the most despicable class. And what would the reader say, were I to tell him of a Member of Congress, who wished to see one of these murderous machines employed for lopping off the heads of the French, permanent in the State-house yard of the city of Philadelphia?

If these men of blood had succeeded in plunging us into a war; if they had once got the sword into their hands, they would have mowed us down like stubble. The word *Aristocrat* would have been employed to as good account here, as ever it had been in France. We might, ere this, have seen our places of worship turned into stables; we might have seen the banks of the Delaware, like those of the Loire, covered with human carcasses, and its waters tinged with blood: ere this we might have seen our parents butchered, and even the head of our admired and beloved President rolling on a scaffold.

I know the reader will start back with horror. His heart will tell him that it is impossible. But, once more, let him look at the example before us. The man who in 1788 should have predicted the fate of the last humane and truly patriotic Louis, would have been treated as a wretch or a madman. The attacks on the character and conduct of the aged *Washington*, have been as bold, if not bolder, than those which led to the downfal [sic] of the unfortunate French Monarch. His impu-

---

[2] It is a truth that no one will deny, that the newspapers of this country have become its scourge. I speak with a few exceptions. It is said that they enlighten the people; but their light is like the torch of an incendiary, and the one has the same destructive effect on the mind as the other has on matter. The whole study of the editors seems to be to deceive and confound. One would almost think they were hired by some malicious demon, to turn the brains and corrupt the hearts of their readers.

dent and ferocious enemies have represented him as cankered with every vice that marks a worthless tyrant: they have called him the betrayer of his country, and have even drawn up and published *articles of accusation* against him! Can it then be imagined, that, had they possessed the power, they wanted the will to dip their hands in his blood? I am fully assured that these wretches do not make a hundred thousandth part of the people of the Union: the name of *Washington* is as dear and dearer to all the moderate Whigs, than it ever was. But of what consequence is their affection to him, of what avail to themselves, if they suffer him to be thus treated, without making one single effort to defeat the project of his infamous traducers? It is not for me to dictate the methods of doing this: but sure I am, that had the friends of virtue and order shown only a hundredth part of the zeal in the cause of their own country, as the enemies of both have done in the cause of France, we should not now have to lament the existence of a hardened and impious faction, whose destructive principles, if not timely and firmly opposed, may one day render the annals of America as disgraceful as those of the French revolution.

[5]

The Life and Adventures of Peter Porcupine

THIS IS COBBETT'S AUTOBIOGRAPHY, WRITTEN WHEN HE WAS only thirty-three. It was occasioned by accusations that he was in the pay of the British government and that the Philadelphia bookseller Thomas Bradford had first "put a coat upon my back"—accusations that affronted Cobbett's sense of independence and his pride.

He began with a lyrical evocation of his upbringing in rural England, interspersed with satirical remarks about Benjamin Franklin's *Autobiography*. Cobbett described his years in the army, his thirst for knowledge, and his struggle to master English grammar. Significantly, given the context in which he was writing, he said nothing at all about corruption in the army, his attempt to court-martial four officers, or his authorship of *The Soldier's Friend*—although he did admit that he "had imbibed principles of republicanism," and "was ambitious to become a citizen of a free state." His account of his American career focused on his relationship with Thomas Bradford, on the discrepancies between the principle and practice of freedom of the press in the United States, and on his journalistic integrity and independence. "My writings, the first pamphlet excepted," he wrote, "have had no other object than that of keeping alive an attachment to the Constitution of the United States and the inestimable man who is at the head of the government, and to paint in their true colours those who are the enemies of both; to warn the people, of all ranks and descriptions, of the danger of admitting among them, the anarchical and blasphemous principles of the French revolutionists, principles as opposite to those of liberty as hell is to heaven."

In its romantic idealization of Old England and its nostalgic images of rural life, "Life and Adventures" anticipates Cobbett's best-known English writings, sprinkled throughout the *Political Register* and *Rural Rides*. "Written in his most forthright and amiable style," commented Cobbett biographer George Spater, "it is something that can still be read for sheer enjoyment."

THE LIFE AND ADVENTURES OF PETER PORCUPINE, WITH A FULL AND FAIR ACCOUNT OF

All his Authoring Transactions;

BEING A SURE AND INFALLIBLE GUIDE FOR ALL

ENTERPRISING YOUNG MEN WHO WISH TO MAKE

A FORTUNE BY WRITING PAMPHLETS.

BY PETER PORCUPINE Himself

"Now, you lying Varlets, you shall see how a plain tale will put you down."
Shakespeare.

TO BE DESCENDED FROM AN ILLUSTRIOUS FAMILY CERTAINLY REFLECTS honour on any man, in spite of the sans-culotte principles of the present day. This is, however, an honour that I have no pretension to. All that I can boast of in my birth, is, that I was born in Old England; the country from whence came the men who explored and settled North America; the country of Penn, and of the father and mother of General Washington.

With respect to my ancestors, I shall go no further back than my grand-father, and for this plain reason, that I never heard talk of any prior to him. He was a day-labourer, and I have heard my father say, that he worked for one farmer from the day of his marriage to that of his death, upwards of forty years. He died before I was born, but I have often slept beneath the same roof that had sheltered him, and where his widow dwelt for several years after his death. It was a little thatched cottage with a garden before the door. It had but two windows; a damson tree shaded one, and a clump of filberts the other. Here I and my brothers went every Christmas and Whitsuntide, to spend a week or two, and torment the poor old woman with our noise and dilapidations. She used to give us milk and bread for breakfast, an apple pudding for our dinner, and a piece of bread and cheese for supper. Her fire was made of turf, cut from the neighbourhood heath, and her evening light was a rush dipped in grease.

How much better is it, thus to tell the naked truth, than to descend to such miserable shifts as Doctor Franklin has had recourse to, in order to persuade people, that his fore-fathers were men of wealth and consideration. Not being able to refer his reader to the herald's office for proofs of the same and antiquity of his family, he appeals to the etymology of his name, and points out a passage in an obsolete book, whence he has the conscience to insist on our concluding, that, in the Old English language, a *Franklin* meant a man of *good reputation and of consequence*. According to Doctor Johnson, a Franklin was what we now call a gentleman's steward or land-bailiff, a personage one degree above a bumbailiff, and that's all. [1]

Every one will, I hope, have the goodness to believe, that my grand-father was no philosopher. Indeed he was not. He never made a lightning rod nor bottled up a single quart of sun-shine in the whole course of his life. He was no almanac-maker, nor quack, nor chimney-doctor, nor soap-boiler, nor ambassador, nor printer's devil: neither was he a deist, and all his children were born in wedlock. The legacies he left, were, his scythe, his reaphook, and his flail; he bequeathed no old and irrecoverable debts to an hospital: he never *cheated the poor during his life*, nor *mocked them in his death*. He has, it is true, been suffered to sleep quietly beneath the green-sord; but, if his descendants cannot point to his statue over the door of the library, they have not the mortification to hear him daily accused of having been a whoremaster, a hypocrite and an infidel.

My father, when I was born, was a farmer. The reader will easily believe, from the poverty of his parents, that he had received no very brilliant education: he was, however, learned, for a man in his rank of life. When a little boy, he drove plough for two-pence a day, and these his earnings were appropriated to the expenses of an evening school. What a village school-master could be expected to teach, he had learnt, and had besides considerably improved himself in several branches of the mathematicks. He understood land surveying well, and was often chosen to draw the plans of disputed territory: in short, he had the reputation of possessing experience and understanding, which never fails, in England, to give a man in a country place, some little weight with his neighbours. He was honest, industrious, and frugal; it was not, therefore, wonderful, that he should be situated in a good farm, and happy in a wife of his own rank, like him, beloved and respected.

So much for my ancestors, from whom, if I derive no honour, I derive no shame.

I had (and I hope I yet have) three brothers: the eldest is a shop-keeper, the second a farmer, and the youngest, if alive, is in the service of the Honourable East India company, a private soldier, perhaps, as I have been in the service of the king. I was born on the ninth of March 1766:[2] the exact age of my brothers I have forgotten, but I remember having heard my mother say, that there was but three years and three quarters difference between the age of the oldest and that of the youngest.

A father like ours, it will be readily supposed, did not suffer us to eat the bread of idleness. I do not remember the time when I did not earn my living. My first occupation was, driving the small birds from the turnip seed, and the rooks from the peas. When I first trudged a-field, with my wooden bottle and my satchel swung over my shoulders, I was hardly able to climb the gates and stiles, and, at the close of the day, to reach home was a task of infinite difficulty. My next employment was weeding wheat, and leading a single horse at harrowing barley. Hoeing peas followed, and hence I arrived at the honour of joining the reapers in harvest, driving the team and holding plough. We were all of us strong and laborious, and my father used to boast, that he had four boys, the eldest of whom was but fifteen years old, who did as much work as any three men in the parish of Farnham. Honest pride, and happy days!

I have some faint recollection of going to school to an old woman, who, I believe, did not succeed in learning me my letters. In the winter evenings my father learnt us all to read and write, and gave us a pretty tolerable knowledge of arithmetic. Grammar he did not perfectly understand himself, and therefore his endeavours to learn us that, necessarily failed; for, though he thought he understood it, and though he made us get the rules by heart, we learnt nothing at all of the principles.

Our religion was that of the Church of England, to which I have ever remained attached; the more so, perhaps, as it bears the name of my country. As my ancestors were never persecuted for their religious opinions, they never had an opportunity of giving such a singular proof of their faith as Doctor Franklin's grandfather did, when he kept his Bible under the lid of a close-stool. (What a book-case!) If I had been in the place of doctor Franklin, I never would have related this ridiculous circumstance, especially as it must be construed into a boast of his grandfather's having an extraordinary degree of veneration for a book, which, it is well known, he himself *durst* not believe in.

As to politics, we were like the rest of the country people in England; that is to say, we neither knew or thought any thing about the matter. The shouts of victory or the murmurs at a defeat, would now-and-then break in upon our tranquillity for a moment; but I do not remember ever having seen a news-paper in the house, and most certainly that privation did not render us less industrious, happy or free.

After, however, the American war had continued for some time, and the cause and nature of it began to be understood, or rather misunderstood, by the lower classes of the people in England, we became a little better acquainted with subjects of this kind. It is well known, that the people were, as to numbers, nearly equally divided in their opinions concerning that war, and their wishes respecting the result of it. My father was a partizan of the Americans: he used frequently to dispute on the subject with the gardener of a nobleman who lived near us. This was generally done with good humour, over a pot of our best ale; yet the disputants sometimes grew warm, and gave way to language that could not fail to attract attention. My father was worsted without doubt, as he had for [an] antagonist, a shrewd and sensible old Scotchman, far his superior in political knowledge; but he pleaded before a partial audience: we thought there was but one wise man in the world, and that that one was our father. He who pleaded the cause of the Americans had an advantage, too, with young minds: he had only to represent the king's troops as sent to cut the throats of a people, our friends and relations, merely because they would not submit to oppression, and his cause was gained. Speaking to the passions is ever sure to succeed on the uninformed.

Men of integrity are generally pretty obstinate in adhering to an opinion once adopted. Whether it was owing to this, or to the weakness of Mr. Martin's arguments, I will not pretend to say, but he never could make a convert of my father: he continued an American, and so staunch a one, that he would not have suffered his best friend to drink success to the king's arms at his table. I cannot give the reader a better idea of his obstinacy in this respect, and of the length to which this difference in sentiment was carried in England, than by relating the following instance.

My father used to take one of us with him every year to the great hop-fair at Wey-Hill. The fair was held at Old Michaelmas-tide, and the journey was, to us, a sort of reward for the labours of the summer. It happened to be my turn to go thither the very year that Long-Island was taken by the British. A great company of hop-merchants and farmers were just sitting down to supper as the post arrived, bringing in the extraordinary Gazette which announced the victory. A hop-factor from London took the paper, placed his chair upon the table, and began to read with an audible voice. He was opposed, a dispute ensued, and my father retired, taking me by the hand, to another apartment, where we supped with about a dozen others of the same sentiments. Here Washington's health, and success to the Americans, were repeatedly toasted, and this was the first time, as far as I can recollect, that I ever heard the General's name mentioned. Little did I then dream, that I should ever see the man, and still less that I should hear some of his own countrymen reviling him.

Let not the reader imagine, that I wish to assume any merit from this, perhaps mistaken, prejudice of an honoured and beloved parent. Whether he was right or wrong is not now worth talking about: that I had no opinion of my own is certain; for, had my father been on the other side, I should have been on the other side too, and should have looked upon the company I then made a part of as malcontents and rebels. I mention these circumstances merely to show that I was not "nursed in the lap of aristocracy," and that I did not imbibe my principles, or prejudices, from those who were the advocates of blind submission. If my father had any fault, it was not being submissive enough, and I am much afraid my acquaintance[s] have but too often discovered the same fault in his son.

It would be as useless as unentertaining to dwell on the occupations and sports of a country boy; to lead the reader to fairs, cricket-matches and hare-hunts. I shall therefore come at once to the epoch, when an accident happened that gave that turn to my future life, which at last brought me to the United States.

Towards the autumn of 1782 I went to visit a relation who lived in the neighbourhood of Portsmouth. From the top of Portsdown, I, for the first time, beheld the sea, and no sooner did I behold it than I wished to be a sailor. I could never account for this sudden impulse, nor can I now. Almost all English boys feel the same inclination: it would seem that, like young ducks, instinct leads them to rush on the bosom of water.

But it was not the sea alone that I saw: the grand fleet was riding at anchor at Spithead. I had heard of the wooden walls of Old England: I had formed my ideas of a ship and of a fleet; but, what I now beheld so far surpassed what I had ever been able to form a conception of, that I stood lost between astonishment and admiration. I had heard talk of the glorious deeds of our admirals and sailors, of the defeat of the Spanish Armada, and of all those memorable combats that good and true Englishmen never fail to relate to their children about a hundred times a year. The brave Rodney's victories over our natural enemies, the French and Spaniards, had long been the theme of our praise, and the burthen of our songs. The sight of the fleet brought all these into my mind; in confused order, it is true, but with irresistible force. My heart was inflated with national pride. The sailors were my countrymen, the fleet belonged to my country, and surely I had my part in it, and in all its honours: yet, these honours I had not earned; I took to myself a sort of reproach for possessing what I had no right to, and resolved to have a just claim by sharing in the hardships and the dangers.

I arrived at my uncle's late in the evening, with my mind full of my sea-faring project. Though I had walked thirty miles during the day, and consequently was well wearied, I slept not a moment. It was no sooner day-light than I arose and walked down towards the old castle on the beach of Spithead. For a sixpence given to an invalid I got permission to go up on the battlements: here I had a closer view of the fleet, and at every look my impatience to be on board increased. In short, I went from the castle to Portsmouth, got into a boat, and was in a few minutes on board the Pegasus man of war, commanded by the Right honourable George Berkley, brother to the Earl of Berkley.

The Captain had more compassion than is generally met with in men of his profession: he represented to me the toils I must undergo, and the punishment that the least disobedience or neglect would subject me to. He persuaded me to return home, and I remember he concluded his advice with telling me, that it was better to be led to church in a halter, to be tied to a girl that I did not like, than to be tied to the gang-way, or, as the sailors call it, married to *miss roper*. From the conclusion of this wholesome council, I perceived that the captain thought I had eloped on account of a bastard. I blushed, and that confirmed him in his opinion; but I declare to the reader, that I was no more guilty of such an offence than Mr. Swanwick, or any other gentleman who is constitutionally virtuous.[3] No; thank heaven, I have none of the Franklintonian crimes to accuse myself of; my children do not hang their hats up in other men's houses; I am neither patriot nor philosopher.

I in vain attempted to convince Captain Berkley, that choice alone had led me to the sea; he sent me on shore, and I at last quitted Portsmouth; but not before I had applied to the Port-Admiral, Evans, to get my name enrolled among those who were destined for the service. I was, in some sort, obliged to acquaint the Admiral with what had passed on board the Pegasus, in consequence of which my request was refused, and I happily escaped, sorely against my will, from the most toilsome and perilous profession in the world.

I returned once more to the plough, but I was spoiled for a farmer. I had, before my Portsmouth adventure, never known any other ambition than that of surpassing my brothers in the different labours of the field; but it was quite otherwise now; I sighed for a sight of the world; the little island of Britain seemed too small a compass for me. The things in which I had taken the most delight were neglected; the singing of the birds grew insipid; and even the heart-cheering cry of the hounds, after which I formerly used to fly from my work, bound o'er the fields, and dash through the brakes and coppices, was heard with the most torpid indifference. Still, however, I remained at home till the following spring, when I quitted it, perhaps, for ever.

It was on the sixth of May 1783, that I, like Don Quixotte, sallied forth to seek adventures. I was dressed in my holiday clothes, in order to accompany two or three lasses to Guildford fair. They were to assemble at a house about three miles from my home, where I was to attend them; but, unfortunately for me, I had to cross the London turnpike road. The stage-coach had just turned towards me at a merry rate. The notion of going to London never entered my mind till this very moment, yet the step was completely determined on, before the coach came to the spot where I stood. Up I got, and was in London about nine o'clock in the evening.

It was by mere accident that I had money enough to defray the expenses of this day. Being rigged out for the fair, I had three or four crown and half-crown pieces (which most certainly I did not intend to spend) besides a few shillings and half-pence. This my little all, which I had been years in amassing, melted away, like snow before the sun, when touched by the fingers of the inn-keepers and their waiters. In short, when I arrived at Ludgate-Hill, and had paid my fare, I had but about half a crown in my pocket.

By a commencement of that good luck, which has hitherto attended me through all the situations in which fortune has placed me, I was preserved from ruin. A gentleman, who was one of the passengers in the stage, fell into conversation with me at dinner, and he soon learnt that I was going I knew not whither nor for what. This gentleman was a hop-merchant in the borough of Southwark, and, upon closer inquiry, it appeared that he had often dealt with my father at Wey-Hill. He knew the danger I was in; he was himself a father, and he felt for my parents. His house became my home, he wrote to my father, and endeavoured to prevail on me to obey his orders, which were to return immediately home. I am ashamed to say that I was disobedient. It was the first time I had ever been so, and I have repented of it from that moment to this. Willingly would I have returned, but pride would not suffer me to do it. I feared the scoffs of my acquaintances more than the real evils that threatened me.

My generous preserver, finding my obstinacy not to be overcome, began to look out for an employment for me. He was preparing an advertisement for the news-paper, when an acquaintance of his, an attorney, called in to see him. He related my adventure to this gentleman, whose name was Holland, and who, happening to want an understrapping quilldriver, did me the honour to take me into his service, and the next day saw me perched upon a great high stool, in an obscure chamber in Gray's Inn, endeavouring to decypher the crabbed draughts of my employer.

I could write a good plain hand, but I could not read the pot-hooks and hangers of Mr. Holland. He was a month in learning me to copy without almost continual assistance, and even then I was of but little use to him; for, besides that I wrote a snail's pace, my want of knowledge in orthography gave him infinite trouble: so that, for the first two months I was a dead weight upon his hands. Time, however, rendered me useful, and Mr. Holland was pleased to tell me that he was very well satisfied with me, just at the very moment when I began to grow extremely dissatisfied with him.

No part of my life has been totally unattended with pleasure, except the eight or nine months I passed in Gray's Inn. The office (for so the dungeon where I wrote was called) was so dark, that, on cloudy days, we were obliged to burn candle. I worked like a galley-slave from five in the morning till eight or nine at night, and sometimes all night long. How many quarrels have I assisted to foment and perpetuate between those poor innocent fellows, John Doe and Richard Roe! How many times (God forgive me!) have I set them to assault each other with guns, swords, staves and pitch-forks, and then brought them to answer for their misdeeds before Our Sovereign Lord the King seated in His Court of Westminster! When I think of the *saids* and *soforths* and the counts of tautology that I scribbled over; when I think of those sheets of seventy-two words, and those lines two inches a part, my brain turns. Gracious heaven! if I am doomed to be wretched, bury me beneath Iceland snows, and let me feed on blubber; stretch me under the burning line and deny me thy propitious dews; nay, if it be thy will, suffocate me with the infected and pestilential air of a democratic club room; but save me from the desk of an attorney!

Mr. Holland was but little in the chambers himself. He always went out to dinner, while I was left to be provided for by the *Laundress*, as he called her. Those gentlemen of the law, who have resided in the Inns of court in London, know very well what a *Laundress* means. Ours was, I believe, the oldest and ugliest of the officious sisterhood. She had age and experience enough to be Lady Abbess of all the nuns in all the convents of Irish-Town. It would be wronging the witch of Endor to compare her to this hag, who was the only creature that deigned to enter into conversation with me. All except the name, I was in prison, and this Weird Sister was my keeper. Our chambers were, to me, what the subterraneous cavern was to Gil Blas: his description of the Dame Leonarda exactly suited my Laundress; nor were the professions, or rather the practice, of our master altogether dissimilar.

I never quitted this gloomy recess except on Sundays, when I usually took a walk to St. James Park, to feast my eyes with the sight of the trees, the grass, and the water. In one of these walks I happened to cast my eye on an advertisement, inviting all loyal young men, who had a mind to gain riches and glory, to repair to a certain rendezvous, where they might enter into His Majesty's marine service, and have the peculiar happiness and honour of being enrolled in the Chatham Division. I was not ignorant enough to be the dupe of this morsel of military bombast; but a change was what I wanted: besides, I knew that marines went to sea, and my desire to be on that element had rather increased than diminished by my being penned up in London. In short, I resolved to join this glorious corps; and, to avoid all possibility of being discovered by my friends, I went down to Chatham and enlisted, into the marines as I thought, but the next morning I found myself before a Captain of a marching regiment. There was no retreating: I had taken a shilling to drink his Majesty's health, and his further bounty was ready for my reception.

When I told the Captain (who was an Irishman, and who has since been an excellent friend to me), that I thought myself engaged in the marines: "By Jases, my lad," said he, "and you have had a narrow escape." He told me, that the regiment into which I had been so happy to enlist was one of the oldest and boldest in the whole army, and that it was at that moment serving in that fine, flourishing and plentiful country, Nova Scotia. He dwelt long on the beauties and riches of this terrestrial Paradise, and dismissed me, perfectly enchanted with the prospect of a voyage thither.

I enlisted early in 1784, and, as peace had then taken place, no great haste was made to send recruits off to their regiments. I remained upwards of a year at Chatham, during which time I was employed in learning my exercise, and taking my tour in the duty of the garrison. My leisure time, which was a very considerable portion of the twenty-four hours, was spent, not in the dissipations common to such a way of life, but in reading and study. In the course of this year I learnt more than I had ever done before. I subscribed to a circulating library at Brompton, the greatest part of the books in which I read more than once over. The library was not very considerable, it is true, nor in my reading was I directed by any degree of taste or choice. Novels, plays, history, poetry, all were read, and nearly with equal avidity.

Such a course of reading could be attended with but little profit: it was skimming over the surface of every thing. One branch of learning, however, I went to the bottom with, and that the most essential branch too, the grammar of my mother tongue. I had experienced the want of a knowledge of grammar during my stay with Mr. Holland; but it is very probable that I never should have thought of encountering the study of it, had not accident placed me under a man whose friendship extended beyond his interest. Writing a fair hand procured me the honour of being copyist to Colonel Debieg, the commandant of the garrison. I transcribed the famous correspondence between him and the Duke of Richmond, which ended in the good and gallant old Colonel being stripped of the reward, bestowed on him for his long and meritorious servitude.[4]

Being totally ignorant of the rules of grammar, I necessarily made many mistakes in copying, because no one can copy letter by letter, nor even word by word. The Colonel saw my deficiency, and strongly recommended study. He enforced his advice with a sort of injunction, and with a promise of reward in case of success.

I procured me a Lowth's grammar,[5] and applied myself to the study of it with unceasing assiduity, and not without some profit; for, though it was a considerable time before I fully comprehended all that I read, still I read and studied with such unremitted attention, that, at last, I could write without falling into any very gross errors. The pains I took cannot be described: I wrote the whole grammar out two or three times; I got it by heart; I repeated it every morning and every evening, and, when on guard, I imposed on myself the task of saying it all over once every time I was posted sentinel. To this exercise of my memory I ascribe the retentiveness of which I have since found it capable, and to the success with which it was attended, I ascribe the perseverance that has led to the acquirement of the little learning of which I am master.

This study was, too, attended with another advantage: it kept me out of mischief. I was always sober, and regular in my attendance; and, not being a clumsy fellow, I met with none of those reproofs, which disgust so many young men with the service.

There is no situation where merit is so sure to meet with reward as in a well disciplined army. Those who command are obliged to reward it for their own ease and credit. I was soon raised to the rank of Corporal, a rank, which, however contemptible it may appear in some people's eyes, brought me in a clear two-pence *per diem*, and put a very clever worsted knot upon my shoulder too. Don't you laugh now, Mr.

Swanwick; a worsted knot is a much more honourable mark of distinction than a *Custom-House badge*; though, I confess, the king must have such people as Tide-waiters as well as Corporals.

As promotion began to dawn, I grew impatient to get my regiment, where I expected soon to bask under the rays of Royal favour. The happy day of departure at last came: we set sail from Gravesend, and, after a short and pleasant passage, arrived at Hallifax [sic] in Nova Scotia. When I first beheld the barren, not to say hideous, rocks at the entrance of the harbour, I began to fear that the master of the vessel had mistaken his way; for I could perceive nothing of that fertility that my good recruiting Captain had dwelt on with so much delight.

Nova Scotia had no other charm for me than that of novelty. Every thing I saw was new: bogs, rocks and stumps, musquitoes and bullfrogs. Thousands of Captains and Colonels without soldiers, and of 'Squires without stockings or shoes. In England, I had never thought of approaching a 'Squire without a most respectful bow; but, in this new world, though I was but a Corporal, I often ordered a 'Squire to bring me a glass of grog, and even to take care of my knapsack.

We staid but a few weeks in Nova Scotia, being ordered to St. John's [sic], in the Province of New Brunswick. Here, and at other places in the same Province, we remained till the month of September, 1791, when the regiment was relieved, and sent home.

We landed at Portsmouth on the 3d of November, and on the 19th of the next month I obtained my discharge, after having served not quite eight years, and after having, in that short space, passed through every rank, from that of a private sentinel to that of Sergeant Major, without ever being once disgraced, confined, or even reprimanded.—But, let my superiors speak for me, they will tell my friends and all my readers what I was during my servitude.

By the Right Honourable Major Lord Edward Fitzgerald, commanding His Majesty's 54th Regiment of Foot, whereof Lieutenant General Frederick is Colonel.
These are to certify, that the Bearer hereof, WILLIAM COBBETT, Sergeant Major in the aforesaid regiment, has served honestly and faithfully for the space of eight years, nearly seven of which he has been a non-commissioned officer, and of that time he has been five years Sergeant Major to the regiment; but having very earnestly applied for his discharge, he, in consideration of his good behaviour

The Life and Adventures of Peter Porcupine [169]

and the services he has rendered the regiment, is hereby discharged. Given under my hand and the seal
of the regiment, at Portsmouth, this
19th day of December, 1791.

EDWARD FITZGERALD.

I shall here add the orders, issued in the garrison of Portsmouth on the day of my discharge.

Portsmouth, 19th Dec. 1791.
Sergeant Major Cobbett having most pressingly applied for his discharge, at Major Lord Edward Fitzgerald's request, General Frederick has granted it. General Frederick has ordered Major Lord Edward Fitzgerald to return the Sergeant Major thanks for his behaviour and conduct during the time of his being in the regiment, and Major Lord Edward adds his most hearty thanks to those of the General.

After having laid these pieces before my reader, I beg him to recollect what the *Argus* of New York and the *Aurora* of Philadelphia have asserted concerning Peter Porcupine's being flogged in his regiment for thieving, and afterwards deserting. The monstrous, disorganizing, democratic gang were not aware that I was in possession of such uncontrovertible proofs as these.

I hope, I may presume that my character will be looked upon as good, down to the date of my discharge; and, if so, it only remains for me to give an account of myself from that time to this.

The democrats have asserted . . . that I got my living in London by "garret-scribbling," and that I was obliged to "take a *French Leave* for France, for some *night work*."—Now, the fact is, I went to France in March, 1792, and I landed at New York in the month of October following; so that, I had but three months to follow "garret-scribbling" in London. How these three months were employed it is not necessary to say here,[6] but that I had not much leisure for "garret-scribbling" the ladies will be well convinced, when I tell them that I got a wife in the time. As to the charge concerning "night work," I am afraid I must plead guilty, but not with my "fingers," as these malicious fellows would insinuate. No, no, I am no relation to Citizen *Plato*: the French ladies do not call me, the *Garçon Fendu*.[7]

Before I go any further, it seems necessary to say a word or two about "French Leave." Did this expression escape the democrats in an unwary moment? Why "French Leave?" Do they wish to insinuate, that nobody but *Frenchmen* are obliged to fly from the hands of thief-catchers? The Germans, and after them the English, have applied this degrading expression to the French nation; but, is it not inconsistent, and even ungrateful, for those who are in the interest, and perhaps, in the pay, of that magnanimous republic, to talk about "French Leave?" It is something curious that this expression should find a place in a paragraph wherein I am accused of abusing the French. The fact is, the friendship professed by these people, towards the French nation, is all grimace, all hypocrisy: the moment they are off their guard, they let us see that it is the abominable system of French tyranny that they are attached to, and not to the people of that country.—"French Leave!" The leave of a *run-away*, a thief, a *Tom Paine*! What could the most prejudiced, the bitterest Englishman have said more galling and severe against the whole French nation? They cry out against me for "*abusing*" the cut-throats of Nantz and other places, and for accusing the demagogue-tyrants of robbery; while they themselves treat the whole nation as thieves. This is the democratic way of washing out stains; just as the sweet and cleanly Sheelah washes her gentle Dermot's face with a dishclout.

Leaving the ingenious citizens to extricate themselves from this hobble, or fall under the displeasure of their masters, I shall return to my adventures.—I arrived in France in March, 1792, and continued there till the beginning of September following, the six happiest months of my life. I should be the most ungrateful monster that ever existed, were I to speak ill of the French people in general. I went to that country full of all those prejudices, that Englishmen suck in with their mother's milk, against the French and against their religion: a few weeks convinced me that I had been deceived with respect to both. I met every where with civility, and even hospitality, in a degree that I never had been accustomed to. I found the people, among whom I lived, excepting those who were already blasted with the principles of the accursed revolution, honest, pious, and kind to excess.

People may say what they please about the misery of the French peasantry, under the old government; I have conversed with thousands of them, not ten among whom did not regret the change. I have not room here to go into an inquiry into the causes that have led these people to become the passive instruments, the slaves, of a set of tyrants such as the world never saw before, but I venture to predict, that, sooner or later, they will return to that form of government under which they were happy, and under which alone they can ever be so again.

My determination to settle in the United States was formed before I went to France, and even before I quitted the army. A desire of seeing a country, so long the theatre of a war of which I had heard and read so much; the flattering picture given of it by Raynal;[8] and, above all, an inclination for seeing the world, led me to this determination. It would look a little like coaxing for me to say, that I had imbibed principles of republicanism, and that I was ambitious to become a citizen of a free state, but this was really the case. I thought that men enjoyed here a greater degree of liberty than in England; and this, if not the principal reason, was at least one, for my coming to this country.

I did intend to stay in France till the spring of 1793, as well to perfect myself in the language, as to pass the winter at Paris; but I perceived the storm gathering; I saw that a war with England was inevitable, and it was not difficult to foresee what would be the fate of Englishmen, in that country, where the rulers had laid aside even the appearance of justice and mercy. I wished, however, to see Paris, and had actually hired a coach to go thither. I was even on the way, when I heard, at Abbeville, that the king was dethroned and his guards murdered. This intelligence made me turn off towards Havre de Grace, whence I embarked for America.

I beg leave here to remind the reader, that one of the lying paragraphs, lately published in the lying *Aurora*, states, that I was whipped at Paris, and that hence I bear a grudge against the French Republic. Now, I never was at Paris, as I can prove by the receipts for my board and lodging, from the day I entered France to that of my leaving it; and, as to the Republic, as it is called, I could have no grudge against it; for the tyrants had not given it that name, when I was so happy as to bid it an eternal adieu. Had I remained a few months longer, I make no doubt that I should have had reason to execrate it as every other man, woman, and child has, who has had the misfortune to groan under its iron anarchy.

Some little time after my arrival in this country, I sent Mr. Jefferson, then Secretary of State, a letter of recommendation, which I had brought from the American Ambassador at the Hague.[9] The following is a copy of the letter Mr. Jefferson wrote me on that occasion.

Philadelphia, Nov. 5th, 1792.

Sir,

In acknowledging the receipt of your favour of the 2d instant, I wish it were in my power to announce to you any way in which I could be useful to you. Mr. Short's assurances of your merit would be a sufficient inducement to me. Public Offices in our government are so few, and of so little value, as to offer no resource to talents. When you shall have been here some small time, you will be able to judge in what way you can set out with the best prospect of success, and if I can serve you in it, I shall be very ready to do it.

I am,
Sir,
Your very humble servant,
TH. JEFFERSON."

I will just observe on this letter, that it was thankfully received, and that, had I stood in need of Mr. Jefferson's services, I should have applied to him; but as that did not appear likely to be the case, I wrote him a letter some few months afterwards, requesting him to assist a poor man, the bearer of it, and telling him that I should look upon the assistance as given to myself. I dare say he complied with my request, for the person recommended was in deep distress, and a *Frenchman*.

With respect to the authenticity of this letter there can be no doubt. I have shown the original, as well as those of the other documents here transcribed, to more than fifty gentlemen of the city of Philadelphia, and they may, at any time, be seen by any person of credit, who wishes a sight of them. Nor have I confined the perusal of them to those who have the misfortune to be deemed aristocrats. Among persons of distant places, I have shown them to Mr. *Ketlatas* [sic] of New York, who, I must do him the justice to say, had the candour to express a becoming detestation of the base cut-throat author of the threatening letter sent to Mr. Oldden.[10]

I have now brought myself to the United States, and have enabled the reader to judge of me so far. It remains for me to negative two assertions which apply to my authoring transactions: the one is, that

The Life and Adventures of Peter Porcupine

"Mr. Bradford *put a coat upon my back*;" and the other, that I am, or have been, "in the pay of a British Agent."[11]

In the month of July, 1794, the famous Unitarian Doctor, fellow of the *Royal* Society, London, *citizen* of France, and delegate to the *Grande Convention Nationale* of notorious memory, landed at New-York. His landing was nothing to me, nor to any body else; but the fulsome and consequential addresses, sent him by the pretended patriots, and his canting replies, at once calculated to flatter the people here, and to degrade his country and mine, was something to me. It was my business, and the business of every man who thinks that truth ought to be opposed to malice and hypocrisy.

When the *Observations* on the Emigration of this "martyr to the cause of liberty" were ready for the press, I did not, at first, offer them to Mr. Bradford. I know him to retain a rooted hatred against Great Britain, and concluded, that his principles would prevent him from being instrumental in the publication of any thing that tended to unveil one of its most bitter enemies. I therefore addressed myself to Mr. Carey.[12] This was, to make use of a culinary figure, jumping out of the frying-pan into the fire. Mr. Carey received me as booksellers generally receive authors (I mean authors whom they hope to get but little by): he looked at the title from top to bottom, and then at me from head to foot.—"No, *my lad*," says he, "I don't think it will suit"—*My lad!*—God in heaven forgive me! I believe that, at that moment, I wished for another yellow fever to strike the city; not to destroy the inhabitants, but to furnish me too with *the subject of a pamphlet*, that might make me rich.—Mr. Carey has sold hundreds of the *Observations* since that time, and therefore, I dare say he highly approved of them, when he came to a perusal. At any rate, I must not forget to say, that he behaved honourably in the business; for, he promised not to make known the author, and he certainly kept his word, or the discovery would not have been reserved for the month of June, 1796. This circumstance, considering Mr. Carey's politics, is greatly to his honour, and has almost wiped from my memory that contumelious "*my lad*."

From Mr. Carey I went to Mr. Bradford, and left the pamphlet for his perusal. The next day I went to him to know his determination. He hesitated, wanted to know if I could not make it a little *more popular*, adding that, unless I could, he feared that the publishing of it would endanger *his windows*. *More popular* I could not make it. I never was of an accommodating disposition in my life. The only alteration I would consent to was in the title. I had given the pamphlet the double title of, "*The Tartuffe Detected*; or, *Observations, &c.*" The former was suppressed, though, had I not been pretty certain that every press in the city was as little free as that to which I was sending it, the *Tartuffe Detected* should have remained; for, the person on whom it was bestowed merited it much better than the character so named by Moliére [sic].

These difficulties, and these fears of the bookseller, at once opened my eyes with respect to the boasted liberty of the press. Because the laws of this country proclaim to the world, that every man may write and publish freely, and because I saw the news-papers filled with vaunts on the subject, I was fool enough to imagine that the press was really free for every one. I had not the least idea, that a man's windows were in danger of being broken, if he published any thing that was *not popular*. I did, indeed, see the words *liberty* and *equality*, the *rights of man*, the *crimes of kings*, and such like, in most of the bookseller's windows; but I did not know that they were put there to save the glass, as a free republican Frenchman puts a cockade tricolor in his hat to save his head. I was ignorant of all these *arcana* of the liberty of the press.

If it had so happened that one of the Whiskey-Boys had went over to England, and had received addresses from any part of the people there, congratulating him on his escape from a nation of ruffians, and beseeching the Lord that those ruffians might "tread back the paths of *infamy* and *ruin*;" and if this emigrating "*Martyr*" in the cause of whiskey had echoed back the hypocritical cant, and if he and all his palavering addressers had been detected and exposed by some good American, in London, would not such an American have received the applause of all men of virtue and sense? And what would, or rather what would not, have been said here against the prostituted press of Great Britain, had an English bookseller testified his fears to publish the truth, lest his windows should be dashed in?

The work that it was feared would draw down punishment on the publisher, did not contain one untruth, one anarchical, indecent, immoral, or irreligious expression; and yet the bookseller feared for his windows! For what? Because it was not *popular enough*. A bookseller in a *despotic* state fears to publish a work that is *too popular* and one in a *free* state fears to publish a work that is not *popular enough*. I leave it to the learned philosophers of the "Age of Reason" to determine in which of these states there is the most liberty of the press; for, I must acknowledge, the point is too nice for me: fear is fear, whether inspired by a Sovereign Lord the King, or by a Sovereign People.

I shall be told, that Mr. Bradford's fears were groundless. It may be so; but he ought to be a competent judge of the matter; he must know the extent of the liberty of the press better than I could. He might be mistaken, but that he was sincere appeared clearly from his not putting his name at the bottom of the title page. Even the *Bone to Gnaw for the Democrats*, which did not appear till about six months afterwards, was "Published for the Purchasers." It was not till long after the public had fixed the seal of approbation on these pamphlets, that they were honoured with the bookseller's name. It was something curious that the second and third and fourth editions should be entitled to a mark of respect that the first was not worthy of. Poor little innocents! They were thrown on the parish like foundlings; no soul would own them, till it was found that they possessed the gift of bringing in the pence. Another singularity, is, they got into better paper as they advanced. So the prudent matron changes the little dirty ragged wench into a fine mademoiselle, as soon as she perceives that the beaux begin to cast their eyes on her.

But, it is time to return, and give the reader an account of my gains. The pecuniary concerns of an author are always the most interesting.

The terms on which Mr. Bradford took the *Observations*, were what booksellers call *publishing it together*. I beg the reader, if he foresees the possibility of his becoming author, to recollect this phrase well. *Publishing it together* is thus managed: the bookseller takes the work, prints it, and defrays all expenses of paper, binding, &c. and the profits, if any, are divided between him and the author.——Long after the Observations were sold off, Mr. Bradford rendered me an account (undoubtedly a very just one) of the sales. According to this account, my share of the profits (my share only) amounted to the sum of *one shilling and seven-pence half-penny*, currency of the State of Pennsylvania (or, about eleven-pence three farthings sterling), quite entirely clear of all deductions whatsoever!

Now, bulky as this sum appears in words at length, I presume, that when 1s./$7\frac{1}{2}$d. is reduced to figures, no one will suppose it sufficient to put a coat upon my back. If my poor back were not too broad to be clothed with such a sum as this, God knows how I should bear all that has been, and is, and is to be, laid on it by the unmerciful democrats. Why! 1s./7½d. would not cover the back of a Lilliputian; no, not even in rags, as they fell here.

Besides, this clothing story will at once fall to the ground, when I assure the reader (and Mr. Carey will bear witness to the truth of what I say), that, when I offered this work for publication, I had as good a coat upon my back, as ever Mr. Bradford or any of his brother booksellers put on in their lives; and, what is more, this coat was my own. No taylor nor shoemaker ever had my name in his books. . . .

Indeed these booksellers, in general, are a cruel race. They imagine that the soul and body of every author that falls into their hands, is their exclusive property. They have adopted the birdcatcher's maxim: "a bird that can sing, and wont [sic] sing, ought to be made to sing." Whenever their devils are out of employment, the drudging goblin of an author must sharpen up his pen, and never think of repose till he is relieved by the arrival of a more profitable job. Then the wretch may remain as undisturbed as a sleep-mouse in winter, while the stupid dolt whom he has clad and fattened, receives the applause.

I now come to the assertion, that I am, or have been, in the pay of the British government.

In the first place the democrats swear that I have been "frequently visited by a certain Agent," meaning I suppose Mr. Bond:[13] to this I answer, that it is an abominable lie. I never saw Mr. Bond but three times in my life, and then I had business with him as the interpreter of Frenchmen, who wanted certificates from him, in order to secure their property in the conquered colonies. I never in my life spoke to, corresponded with, or even saw, to my knowledge, either of the British Ministers, or any one of their retinue. Mr. Bradford once told me, that Mr. Allen, the father-in-law of Mr. Hammond,[14] said he was acquainted with me. If this gentleman did really say so, he joked, or he told a lie; for he never saw me in his life, that I know of. . . .

It is hard to prove a negative; it is what no man is expected to do; yet, I think I can prove, that the accusation of my being in British pay is not supported by one single fact, or the least shadow of probability.

When a foreign government hires a writer, it takes care that his labours shall be distributed, whether the readers are willing to pay for them or not. This we daily see verified in the distribution of certain blasphemous gazettes, which, though kicked from the door with disdain, flies [sic] in at the window. Now, has this ever been the case with the works of Peter Porcupine? Were they ever thrust upon people in spite of their remonstrances? Can Mr. Bradford say that thousands of these pamphlets have ever been paid for by any agent of Great Britain? Can he say that I have ever distributed any of them? No; he can say no such thing. They had, at first, to encounter every difficulty, and they have made their way supported by public approbation, and by that alone. Mr. Bradford, if he is candid enough to repeat what he told me, will say, that the British Consul, when he purchased half a dozen of them, insisted upon having them *at the wholesale price*! Did this look like a desire to encourage them? Besides, those who know any thing of Mr. Bradford, will never believe, that he would have lent his aid to a British Agent's publications; for, of all the Americans I have yet conversed with, he seems to entertain the greatest degree of rancour against that nation.

I have every reason to believe, that the British Consul was far from approving of some, at least, of my publications. I happened to be in a bookseller's shop, unseen by him, when he had the goodness to say, that I was a "*wild fellow*." On which I shall only observe, that when the King bestows on me about five hundred pounds sterling a year, perhaps, I may become a *tame fellow*, and hear my master, my countrymen, my friends and my parents, belied and execrated, without saying one single word in their defence.

Had the Minister of Great Britain employed me to write, can it be supposed that he would not furnish me with the means of living well, without becoming the retailer of my own works? Can it be supposed that he would have suffered me ever to appear on the scene? It must be a very poor king that he serves, if he could not afford me more than I can get by keeping a book-shop. An Ambassador from a king of the Gypsies could not have acted a meaner part. What! where was all the "gold of Pitt?" That gold which tempted, according to the democrats, an American Envoy to sell his country, and two-thirds of the Senate to ratify the bargain:[15] that gold which, according to the Convention of France, has made one half of that nation cut the throats of the other half; that potent gold could not keep Peter Porcupine from standing behind a counter to sell a pen-knife, or a quire of paper!

Must it not be evident, too, that the keeping of a shop would take up a greater part of my time? Time that was hardly worth paying for at all, if it was not of higher value than the profits on a few pamphlets. Every one knows that the Censor has been delayed on account of my entering on business; would the Minister of Great Britain have suffered this, had I not been in his pay?[16] No; I repeat, that it is downright stupidity to suppose, that he would ever have suffered me to appear at all, had he even felt in the least interested in the fate of my works, or the effect they might produce. He must be sensible, that, seeing the unconquerable prejudices existing in this country, my being known to be an Englishman would operate weightily against whatever I might advance. I saw this very plainly myself; but, as I had a living to get, and as I had determined on this line of business, such a consideration was not to awe me into idleness, or make me forego any other advantages that I had reason to hope I should enjoy.

The notion of my being in British pay arose from my having now-and-then taken upon me to attempt a defence of the character of that nation, and of the intentions of its government towards the United States. But, have I ever teazed my readers with this, except when the subject necessarily demanded it? And if I have given way to my indignation when a hypocritical political divine attempted to degrade my country, or when its vile calumniators called it "an insular Bastile," what have I done more than every good man in my place would have done? What have I done more than my duty; than obeyed the feelings of my heart? When a man hears his country reviled, does it require that he should be paid for speaking in its defence?

Besides, had my works been intended to introduce British influence, they would have assumed a more conciliating tone. The author would have flattered the people of this country, even in their excesses; he would have endeavoured to gain over the enemies of Britain by smooth and soothing language; he would have "stooped to conquer;" he would not, as I have done, rendered them hatred for hatred, and scorn for scorn.

My writings, the first pamphlet excepted, have had no other object than that of keeping alive an attachment to the Constitution of the United States and the inestimable man who is at the head of the government, and to paint in their true colours those who are the enemies of both; to warn the people, of all ranks and descriptions, of the danger of admitting among them, the anarchical and blasphemous principles of the French revolutionists, principles as opposite to those of liberty as hell is to heaven. If, therefore, I have written at the instance of a British agent, that agent must most certainly deserve the thanks of all the real friends of America. But, say some of the half democrats, what right have you to meddle with the defence of our government at all?—The same right that you have to exact my obedience to it, and my contribution towards its support. Several Englishmen, not so long in the country as I had been, served in the militia against the western rebels, and, had I been called on, I must have served too. Surely a man has a right to defend with his pen, that which he may be compelled to defend with a musquet.

As to the real, bloody, cut-throats, they carry their notion of excluding me from the use of the press still further. "While" (says one of them)

> While I am a friend to the *unlimited* freedom of the press, when exercised by *an American,* I am an implacable foe to its prostitution to a *foreigner,* and would at any time assist in hunting out of society, any meddling foreigner who should dare to interfere in our politics. I hope the apathy of our *brethren* of Philadelphia will no longer be indulged, and that an exemplary *vengeance* will soon burst upon the head of such a presumptuous fellow.—*Justice, honour,* national *gratitude,* all call for it.—May it no longer be delayed.
>
> *An American.*

Are not you, Mr. Swanwick, the President of the Emigration Society? Well, then, Sir, as your institution is said to be for the information of persons emigrating from foreign countries, be so good as to insert the little extract, above quoted, in your next dispatches for a cargo of emigrants. Above all, Sir, be sure to tell those who are disposed to emigrate from England, those martyrs in the cause of liberty; be sure to tell them that this is the land of *equal* liberty; that here, and here alone, they will find the true unlimited freedom of the press, but that, if they dare to make use of it, "*justice, honour,* national *gratitude,* will call for exemplary *vengeance* on their heads."

I should not have noticed this distinction between *foreigners* and *Americans,* had I not perceived, that several persons, who are, generally speaking, friends to their country, seem to think that it was impertinent in me to meddle with the politics here, because I was an Englishman. I would have these good people to recollect, that the laws of this country hold out, to foreigners, an offer of all that liberty of the press which Americans enjoy, and that, if this liberty be abridged, by whatever means it may be done, the laws and the constitution and all together is a mere cheat; a snare to catch the credulous and enthusiastic of every other nation; a downright imposition on the world. If people who emigrate hither have not a right to make use of the liberty of the press, while the natives have, it is very ill done to call this a country of *equal* liberty. *Equal*, above all epithets, is the most improper that can be applied to it; for, if none but Americans have access to the press, they are the masters and foreigners are their subjects, nay their slaves. An honourable and comfortable situation upon my word! The emigrants from some countries may be content with it, perhaps: I would not say, that the "Martyrs in the cause of liberty" from England, would not quietly bend beneath the yoke, as, indeed, they are in duty bound to do; but, for my part, who have not the ambition to aspire to the crown of martyrdom, I must and I will be excused. Either the laws shall be altered, or I will continue to avail myself of the liberty that they held out to me, and that partly tempted me to the country. When an act is passed for excluding Englishmen from exercising their talents, and from promulgating what they write, then will I desist; but, I hope, when that time arrives, no act will be passed to prevent people from emigrating back again.

Before I conclude, it seems necessary to say a word or two about the miserable shift, which the democrats have recourse to, respecting the infamous letter of *Citizen Hint*.[17] They now pretend, that I fabricated it myself, though I have publicly declared, that it was delivered into my hands by a gentleman of reputation, whose name I have mentioned. Can any one be stupid enough to imagine, that I would, particularly at this time, have run the risk of being detected in such a shameful business? And, how could it have been undertaken without running that risk? Had I written it myself, there would have been my hand-writing against me, and had I employed another, that other might have betrayed me; he might have ruined me in the opinion of all those, whom it is my interest as well as my pride to be esteemed by; or, at best, I should have been at his mercy for ever afterwards.

Besides the great risk of detection, let any one point out, if he can, what end I could propose to myself by such a device. As to making my shop and myself known, I presume I did not stand in need of a scare-crow, to effect that, when the kind democrats themselves had published to the whole Union, that I had taken the house in which I live, for the purpose of retailing my "poison," as they called it, and had even the candour to tell the world, that I had paid my rent in advance.[1] They affect to believe, sometimes, that the letter was a mere

---

[1] It was to Mr. Franklin Bache's creditable and incorruptible Gazette, that I was indebted for this volunteer advertisement. This was generous in a declared foe; but those will not be astonished at the editor's candour and *tolerating principles*, who are acquainted with the following anecdote.

trick to bring in the pence, and, in one of their latest paragraphs, they call me a "catch-penny author." But, let them recollect, that I am now a bookseller, whose trade it is to get money; and if I am driven to such shifts as the Scare-Crow, to get a living, let them reconcile this circumstance with their assertions concerning my being liberally paid by Great Britain. A man in British pay, rolling in "the Gold of Pitt," could certainly never be so reduced as to venture every thing for the sake of collecting a few eleven-penny bits. It is the misfortune of the democrats ever to furnish arguments against themselves.

Those who reason upon the improbability of the democrat's sending the threatening letter, do not recollect the extract I have above quoted from the *Aurora*, in which the people of Philadelphia are called upon to murder me, and are told, that "*justice, honour*, and national *gratitude* demand it." Is it very improbable that men, capable of writing paragraphs like this, should, upon finding the people deaf to their *honourable* insinuations, attempt to intimidate my landlord by a cut-throat letter?

Their great object is to silence me, to this all their endeavours point: lies, threats, spies and informers, every engine of Jacobinical invention is played off. I am sorry to tell them, that it is all in vain, for I am one of those whose obstinacy increases with opposition.

I have now to apologize to my indulgent reader, for having taken up so much of his time with subjects relating chiefly to myself. The task, has, to me, been a very disagreeable one; but it was become necessary, as well for the vindication of my own character as for the satisfaction of my friends; yes, in spite of envy, malice and falsehood, I say, my numerous and respectable friends, who, I trust, will be well pleased to find, that there is nothing in the history of Peter Porcupine to raise a blush for the commendations they have bestowed on his works, or to render them unworthy of their future support.

From the European Magazine, for Sept. 1795, page 156.

"When Voltaire arrived at Paris, an interview took place between him and Franklin. After the first compliments, which by the way were more adulative than comported with the character of an American, and above all of a stern Republican, the Doctor presented his grandson to Voltaire, in soliciting for him his *blessing*. The philosopher of impiety relished the pleasantry; and to render the farce complete, he rose from his chair, and with a patriarchal air, laid his hands on the head of *the child*, and solemnly pronounced, in a loud voice, these three words: *God, Liberty*, and *Toleration*. All the pious were shocked at the American, who, they said, burlesqued Religion in asking the *blessing* of Voltaire."

[6]

History of the American Jacobins

IN 1795, THE ENGLISH LOYALIST WILLIAM PLAYFAIR WROTE HIS *History of Jacobinism, Its Crimes, Cruelties, and Perfidies*, one of the most influential counterrevolutionary works of the decade. Cobbett printed an American edition, which he sold from his Philadelphia bookstore; his own *History of the American Jacobins* initially appeared as the Appendix to Playfair's book, and was subsequently issued as a separate pamphlet.

Cobbett began by caricaturing the "American Jacobins, commonly denominated democrats," as anti-federalists whose opposition to the Constitution of 1787 had been symptomatic of their hatred of government in general. The French, he argued, were trying to use these disaffected people to overthrow Washington's administration and push the United States into war with Britain. Genet's mission, the Democratic Societies, and the Whiskey Rebellion were all seen as manifestations of an international Jacobin conspiracy, centered in Paris. Fortunately for the stability and prosperity of America, Cobbett continued, the firmness of the government saved the day. But the disease of democracy lurked just beneath the surface, ready to break out again if the conditions proved favorable; it was imperative that "the friends of the General Government, of order, of peace and of general happiness and prosperity" remain vigilant and be ready to act against the first signs of a Jacobin revival.

In the course of his polemic, Cobbett provided colorful descriptions of Genet's reception in Philadelphia, the "civic *fête*" in 1794 celebrating the second anniversary of the overthrow of monarchy in France, and the spread of Jacobin fashions in the United States. He ridiculed the American adoption of French styles of address, in which democrats went around greeting each other as "Citizen" and "Citess." He wrote of the destruction of "aristocratic" statues, the renaming of streets (in New York, for example, King Street became Liberty Street), the guillotining in effigy of Louis XVI, the insidious influence of English democrats in America, and the new breed of Jacobin women who "began to talk about liberty and equality in a good masculine style." And he related examples of the influence of Jacobinism in the church and in the University of Philadelphia, where one professor even attempted to cut out the monarchical references in Shakespeare and replace them with pro-French democratic sentiments.

HISTORY OF THE AMERICAN JACOBINS, COMMONLY DENOMINATED DEMOCRATS.

BY PETER PORCUPINE.

"History, who keeps a durable record of all our acts, and exercises her awful censure over *all sorts of sovereigns*, will not forget these events."
Burke.

Dedication. To Mr. William Playfair,
Author of the History of Jacobinism.

Dear Sir,

I have seldom known a greater pleasure than I now feel, in rendering you my thanks, in this public manner, for your spirited efforts in the cause of order and *true* liberty. Your work, Sir, has met with the approbation of all who have read it on this side the Atlantic, the enemies of mankind excepted; and, as to myself, I presume I could not give a more unequivocal proof of my high opinion of it, than by submitting it to the perusal of the people of the United States of America.

The History of the American Jacobins, commonly denominated Democrats, which I have attempted in the following pages, seemed necessary to supply a deficiency, which, undoubtedly, is to be attributed to your want of authenticated materials. I am well aware, that the reader will, at every step, regret that this part of the task also did not fall to your lot; but, the experience I have had of the indulgence

of the public, emboldens me to trust to it once more, though under the enormous disadvantage of following such a writer as Mr. Playfair.
    I am,
        Sir,
        Your most obliged humble servant,
                PETER PORCUPINE.
Philadelphia,
10th Nov. 1796

History of the American Jacobins, &c.

When the Jacobins of Paris sent forth their missionaries of insurrection and anarchy, their professed object was to enlighten the ignorant and unchain the enslaved. There was something preposterous in the idea of Frenchmen giving liberty to the world; but, had it been possible for men in their senses to believe, that a club of distracted Monsieurs, who knew not the meaning of the word liberty, were calculated for this arduous task and were serious in their professions, such credulous persons must have been at once undeceived, when they observed, that the newly-enlightened missionaries were dispatched to those countries alone where the greatest degree of civil liberty was already to be found. Had the Propagande at Paris been sincere in their professions, why were not their envoys directed towards Russia and Turkey, instead of England, America, and other free states? The fact is, Brissot and his philanthropic colleagues wanted to draw as many foreign nations as possible within the vortex of their own savage system, and they well knew, that where the voice of the people has the most weight in public affairs, there it is most easy to introduce novel and subversive doctrines.[1]

In such states too, there generally, not to say always, exists a party, who, from the long habit of hating those who administer the government, become the enemies of the government itself, and are ready to sell their treacherous services to the first bidder. To this description of men the sect of the Jacobins have attached themselves, in every country they have been suffered to enter. They are a sort of flesh flies, that naturally settle on the excremental and corrupted parts of the body politic. It is well known what aid they have received from the disaffected of several European nations; but, neither the Malcontents in Geneva, the Patriots in Holland, nor the Reformers in Great Britain

A Peep into the Antifederal Club. A somewhat unflattering depiction of the Democratic Society of Pennsylvania, which was founded in 1793; Cobbett's "History of the American Jacobins" was a verbal equivalent of the caricature. (Courtesy of the Library Company of Philadelphia.)

and Ireland, were half so well adapted to the reception of Jacobinical doctrines and Louis d'ors as the *Anti-federalists* in America.[2] This faction was co-existent with the General Government of the Union. Notwithstanding the necessity of establishing this government, and its mild and equitable principles, it did not fail to meet with a formidable opposition. The persons who composed this opposition, and who thence took the name *Anti-federalists*, were not equal to the Federalists, either in point of riches or respectability. They were, in general, men of bad moral characters, embarrassed in their private affairs, or the tools of such as were. Men of this cast naturally feared the operation of a government endued with sufficient strength to make itself respected, and with sufficient wisdom to exclude the ignorant and wicked from a share in its administration.

However, the *Anti-federalists* attracted notice, and acquired consequence. A hypocritical anxiety for the preservation of the liberties of the people made up for a want of every real virtue. Some of the states refused, for a long time, to accede to the new Confederation, and many individuals, in those states which did accede to it, remained obstinately opposed to its principles.

Thus did the Federal Government receive, at its birth, the seeds of a disease, which, unless its friends discover more zeal than they have hitherto done, will one day accomplish its destruction. It began its career in defiance of a party, organized and marshalled, and ready to seize the favourable moment for attacking it with open force. We shall soon see that this moment was at no great distance.

The happy effects of the new system, which were almost instantaneously felt, operated so forcibly on the minds of the people at large, that the Anti-federalists began to feel themselves abashed. Seeing their numbers daily diminish, they found it prudent to hide their discontent; nor would their clamors have since been revived, had they not been encouraged and backed by the usurpers in France. The successful example, the promises, and, above all, the gold of these latter, have emboldened them again to shew their heads; as the rays of the sun draw the adder from the loathsome retreat, where he has lain engendering and bloating over his poison.

The French usurpers, from the moment they had got a firm grasp of the reins of power, lost no time in engaging this desperate faction in their views, which were, to acquire a perfect command of the American government, and force it into the war of Liberty and Equality. Monsieur Ternant, the then ambassador here, was, besides his being sent by a king, very justly looked upon as unfit for managing the intrigues of Brissot and his brother regicides. He had ever been accustomed to live on terms of friendship with the officers of government, and to treat their communications with becoming respect. Citizen Genet was therefore dispatched to supply his place: a man every way qualified for the mission he had to execute.[3] Educated in the subaltern walks of the most intriguing court in Europe, he was versed in all the menial offices of corruption; and unencumbered with the family pride of the French Chevaliers, he could visit a democratic club, and give the fraternal buss to its shirtless members, with that kind of cordiality, which gives a zest to flattery, and seldom fails to gain the affections of the grovelling heart. If the Citizen has hitherto failed of ultimate success, we must attribute his failure to the deep penetration and inflexible integrity he had to encounter, rather than to any want of cunning, industry or *liberality* on his part.

The attachment of the Federal Government to a pacific system was well known in France. Genet was therefore instructed, in case he should not be able to shake this attachment either by promises or threats, to apply himself to the sovereign people themselves, whose partiality, it had been represented, and with but too much truth, had received a strong bias in favour of the usurpers. In order to pave the way for acting in the last resort, he disembarked at a point the most distant from the seat of government, that he might have it in his power to act on some part of the people at least, before the sentiments of their government respecting him and his mission were known. He accordingly landed at Charleston, South Carolina, where he remained caballing for some time, and then proceeded to Philadelphia.

The inhabitants of Charleston, and, indeed, of most parts of South Carolina, were admirably disposed for a warm reception of Genet. Not long before his landing, a proposition had been published for a solemn abolition of the use "of all aristocratical terms of *distinction* and *respect*." The levellers had even proposed having an engagement to this effect, printed and stuck up in the market-places, court-houses, &c. for the signature of the citizens. In a state where sans-culottism had already made such a progress, the animating presence of the Parisian Missionary was all that could be wanted to complete the farce. The Carolinians had cut the strings of their culottes, and the Citizen pulled them down about their heels.

The frigate, L'Ambuscade, that brought Genet to America, brought also the news of war being declared by France against England. The inhabitants of Southern climes have never been famous for their wisdom; accordingly, the people of Charleston looked down upon a prize, which the Ambuscade brought in with her, as an earnest of success, and an indubitable indication of French naval superiority.

No sooner was Genet on shore, than he began to exercise his powers, as sovereign of the country. He commissioned land and sea officers, to make war upon the Spanish and English; he fitted out privateers, and opened rendezvouses for the enrolling of both soldiers and sailors. The French flag was seen waving from the windows in this sans-culotte city, just as if it had been a sea-port of France. Genet was sent expressly to engage the country to take part in the war, and such was his contempt for the government, that he did not look upon its consent as a thing worth asking for, or thinking about.[4]

The Citizen found more volunteers than he knew what to do with, particularly of the higher ranks: Captains and Commodores, Majors and Colonels, flocked to his standard in such crowds, that had he a hundred reams of paper in blank commissions, he might have filled them all up in the State of Carolina. Whether these men of high rank and empty purses were encouraged by the confidence they had in the power of the French, or by their own instinctive bravery, I know not; but as to the end they had in view, there can be little doubt. For one of them, who was actuated by a love of liberty, there were five hundred who were actuated by a love of plunder. Some of them longed for a dive into the Spanish mines, and, in idea, already heard the chinking of the doubloons; while others were eyeing the British merchant-men with that kind of savage desire, with which the wolf surveys a herd of fat oxen.

After having remained at Charleston from the 9th to the 19th of April 1793, the *Sans-culotte corps Diplomatique*, marched off for Philadelphia, where it arrived on the 9th of May.

I avoid mentioning the processions, banquets, &c. that attended the Citizen during his journey; nor should I think it worth while to give an account of his reception at the capital, were I not assured that the civilians of the Rights of Man will hereafter quote it as a precedent in the laws of their ceremonial.

The city had been duly prepared for this famous public entry by paragraphs in the papers, announcing the Citizen's arrival at the different stages on the road. Expectation was kept on tip-toe for several days. The best penmen among the patriots were at work composing congratulatory addresses, and their choicest orators were gargling their throats to pronounce them. At last, on the happy 16th of May, a *salve* from the cannons of a frigate lying in the port, gave notice that the Citizen would soon be arrived [in] a place called Gray's Ferry, about three miles distant from the city. Thither all the patrioticly disposed went, to meet him, and escort him to his dwelling. In the evening of the same day there was, what was called, a meeting of the citizens of Philadelphia, when it was agreed to appoint a committee to draft an address to him. An address was accordingly prepared, submitted to the sovereign citizens, at a second meeting, highly approved of, and another committee, consisting of about half a hundred persons, appointed to carry it up. But I must now avail myself of their own account of the business, feeling a total want of capacity to do it justice.

The citizens assembled expressing a desire to accompany their committee in presenting the address to the Citizen minister; two gentlemen were dispatched to know what time it would be convenient for him to receive it, and they returned in a few minutes with the following report: "That Mr. Genet had expressed a high sense of the compliment intended to be paid him by the citizens of Philadelphia; that he was solicitous to avoid giving them the trouble of another meeting, and that if they would accept the spontaneous effusions of his heart, which, however deficient in point of form, would not be deficient in sincerity, as an answer to the address, he would be happy to receive it immediately, leaving to the ensuing day the ceremony of a written reply."—The citizens testified their approbation of the minister's proposition by *reiterated shouts of applause.*

The committee, headed by their chairman, and followed by an immense body of citizens, walking three abreast, having arrived at the City-tavern, were introduced into the presence, and after the *acclamations, as well in the house as in the streets,* had ceased, the address was delivered, at the close of which *the house and streets again resounded with congratulations and applause.*

Citizen Genet, evidently *affected with the warmth of the public attachment,* thus conveyed, delivered, an extemporaneous reply, in terms which *touched the feelings* of every auditor, &c.—It is impossible to describe, with adequate *energy,* the scene that succeeded. *Shouts* and *salutations* were not unattended with *other evidences* of the effect, which this interesting interview had *upon the passions* of the parties who were engaged in it.—From the citizens in the room the minister turned his attention to the citizens in the street, and addressed them in a few short but emphatic sentences, from one of the windows.

In this instance we see the sovereign people taking the liberty to act for themselves, while their servants, the officers of government, stand looking on. What right, I would be glad to know, had the people of Philadelphia, even supposing them all assembled together, to acknowledge any man as a public minister, before he had been acknowledged and received as such by the General Government? No wonder that this insolent missionary should conceive, that the government was a mere cypher; and many of those who afterwards complained of his appeal to the people, should have recollected, that they had encouraged him so to do.

For some time after the Citizen's arrival, there was nothing but addressing and feasting him. It may not be amiss to give an account of one of these treats; the memory of such scenes should be preserved, and often brought into view.

> On Saturday last a *republican dinner* was given at Oellers's hotel, to *Citizen Genet*, by a respectable number of French and American citizens. After dinner a number of patriotic toasts were drunk, of which the following is a translation:
> 1. Liberty and Equality.
> 2. The French Republic.
> 3. The United States, &c. &c.
> After the third toast, an *elegant ode*, suited to the occasion, composed by a young Frenchman, was read by Citizen *Duponceau*, and universally applauded. The society, *on motion* {to be sure, *on motion*} ordered that *Citizen Freneau* should be requested to translate it into English verse, and that the original and translation should be published.
> After a short interval, the *Marseillois's Hymn* was, upon the request of the citizens, sung by Citizen *Bournonville*, with great taste and spirit, the *whole company joining in the chorus.*

——I leave the reader to guess at the harmony of this chorus, bellowed forth from the drunken lungs of about a hundred fellows, of a dozen different nations. Who would have thought five and thirty years ago, when the inhabitants of Pennsylvania were petitioning King George for protection against the French and their allies, the scalping Indians, that in the year 1793, the people of Philadelphia would carry their complaisance to a French minister so far, as to ape his outlandish howling in the chorus of a murderer's song! But, let us proceed with the feast.——

> Two additional stanzas to the *Marseillois's Hymn*, composed by *Citizen Genet*, and suited to the *navy* of France, were then called for, sung, and encored.

Before the singing of the Hymn, it should be mentioned, that a *deputation from the sailors* of the frigate, L'Ambuscade, made their appearance, *embraced*, and took their seats.

The table was decorated with the tree and cap of liberty, and with the French and American Flags. The last toast being drunk, the cap of liberty was placed on the head of *Citizen Genet*, and then it *travelled from head to head*, round the table {just as the guillotine has since travelled round France} each wearer enlivening the scene with a patriotic sentiment.

These tokens of liberty, and of American and French fraternity, were delivered to the officers and mariners of the frigate, L'Ambuscade, who promised to defend them till death.

Thus rolled Genet's time away, in a variety of such nonsensical, stupid, unmeaning, childish entertainments, as never were heard or thought of, till Frenchmen took it into their heads to gabble about liberty.

On the very day that this liberty-cap feast took place, the citizen minister was formally received, and acknowledged in his diplomatic capacity, by the President of the United States. There, indeed, his reception was not quite so warm. He afterwards complained, that the first object that struck his eye in the chamber, was the bust of Louis XVI. I never heard whether he started back or not, at the sight; but it is certain he looked upon it as an ill omen. He saw that he had not to do with a man, whose friendship shifted with the changes of fortune. He saw that the President had not been deceived by the calumnies heaped on the unfortunate king; and that, though the welfare of his country induced him to receive an envoy from his murderers, he was far from approving of their deeds.

This silent reproof, which must, however, be attributed to mere accident, stung the insolent Genet to the soul. His resenting it is a striking instance of that overbearing spirit which the rulers of the deluded French have ever discovered. Because they had killed their king, hurled down the statues of his ancestors, and dug their rotten bones from the tomb, they had the presumption to think, that the governors of other nations ought to follow the savage example.

But, a cold reception was not the rub that Genet most complained of. The Federal Government, informed of his bold beginnings at Charleston, made no doubt that his instructions went to the engaging it in the war. Indeed these instructions were made known from the moment of his landing; and it cannot be doubted but this had an influence on the conduct of the government; for an article appeared in the Charleston papers, the day after, specifying that a report had gained ground, that the Federal Government *must* take part in the war; and this article made its appearance at Philadelphia, on the very day that the President's proclamation, declaring it the resolution of the United States to remain neuter, was first promulgated.

This wise and determined step Genet's masters had not foreseen; or, if they did foresee it, they were not aware that it would be taken, before their missionary could find time to make his warlike proposals. This was a most cruel disappointment to the Citizen, and completely baffled all his projects. In vain did he endeavour to draw the old General from his ground, neither promises nor threats had any effect on him, and Genet soon found, that he had no hope but in rousing the people to oppose their government.

A man of more penetration than Genet might have conceived such a project feasible, from the violent partiality that every where appeared towards the French, from the little respect testified for the opinion of the government, and particularly from the freedom, not to say audacity, with which its conduct, in issuing the proclamation of neutrality, was arraigned. Besides, the Anti-federal faction began to appear with more boldness than ever. Genet was continually surrounded with them; and, as they sighed for nothing so much as for war, they strengthened him in the opinion, that the people would ultimately decide in his favour.

But, there wanted something like a regular plan to unite their forces, and bring them to act in concert. A dinner here and a supper there, were nothing at all. The drunkards went home, snorted themselves sober, and returned to their employments. It was not as in France, where a single tap upon a drum head, would assemble *canaille* enough to overturn forty Federal Governments in the space of half a night. In America there existed all the materials for a revolution, but they were scattered here and there; affiliated clubs were wanting to render them compact, and manageable, as occasion might demand.

Genet did not judge it prudent to give to the American Jacobins the same name, that had been assumed by those in France: that would have been too glaring an imitation. *Democratic* was thought less offensive, at the same time that it was well adapted to a society of men, who were about to set themselves up for the watch-dogs of a government, which they pretended was already become *too aristocratic*, and was daily growing more so; but that a Democrat was but another name for a Jacobin no one had the folly to deny, when, afterwards, some of these very clubs were known to send petitions for having their names entered on the registers of the Jacobin club at Paris.[5]

The Mother Club, in America, met at Philadelphia on the 3d of July, 1793, about six or seven weeks after Genet's arrival in the city, during which space, it is well ascertained, more than *twenty thousand Louis d'ors* had been distributed.

As it is here, properly speaking, that the History of the American Jacobins, or Democrats, begins, it seems necessary to give some account of their *constitution*, as they termed it. This anarchical act sets out with a preamble containing the principles under which the members had united, and it then proceeds to the rules and regulations for transacting the business of the institution.

Art. I.

The Society shall be co-extensive with the State; but, for the conveniency of the members, there shall be a separate meeting in the city of Philadelphia, and one in each county, which shall choose to adopt this Constitution. A member admitted in the city, or in any county, shall of course be a member of the Society at large; and may attend any of the meetings, wherever held.

Art. II.

A meeting of the Society shall be held in the city of Philadelphia, on the first Thursday in every month, and in the respective counties as often, and at such times as they shall by their own rules determine. But the President of each respective meeting may *convene the members on any special occasion.*

Art. III.

The election of new members, and of the officers of the society, shall be by ballot, and by a majority of the votes of the members present. The names of the members proposing any candidate for admission shall be entered in a book kept for that purpose. Every member on his admission shall subscribe this Constitution, and pay the sum of half a dollar to the treasurer for the use of the Society.

Art. IV.

The officers of the meeting in the city of Philadelphia shall consist of a *President*, two *vice Presidents*, two *Secretaries*, one *Treasurer*, and one *corresponding committee* of five members; and the meetings of the respective counties shall choose a *President* and such other officers as they think proper.

Art. V.

It shall be the duty of the corresponding committee, to correspond with the various meetings of the Society, *and with all other societies, that may be established on similar principles, in any other of the United States.*

Art. VI.

It shall be the duty of the Secretaries to keep minutes of the proceedings of the several meetings; and of the treasurer to receive and account for all monies to them respectively paid.

Now, what was the object of all this balloting and corresponding and meeting? This we are to look for, they tell us, in their first circular letter: here it is then.

> Fellow Citizen,
> We have the pleasure to communicate to you a copy of the constitution of the *Democratic Society*, in hopes that after a candid consideration of its principles, and objects, you may be induced to promote its adoption, in the county of which you are an inhabitant.
>
> Every mind, capable of reflection, must perceive, that the present crisis in the politics of nations is peculiarly interesting to America. The European Confederacy, transcendent in power, and unparalleled in iniquity, menaces the very existence of freedom. Already its baneful operation may be traced in the tyrannical destruction of the Constitution of Poland: and should the glorious efforts of France be eventually defeated, we have reason to presume, that, for the consummation of monarchical ambition, and the security of its establishments, this country, the only remaining depository of liberty, will not long be permitted to enjoy in peace, the honours of an independent, and the happiness of a republican government.
>
> Nor are the dangers arising from a foreign source, the only causes, at this time, of apprehension and solicitude. The *seeds of luxury* appear to have taken root in our domestic soil: and the *jealous eye of patriotism* already regards the *spirit of freedom and equality*, as eclipsed by the *pride of wealth* and the *arrogance of power*.
>
> This general view of our situation has led to the institution of the *Democratic Society*. A constant circulation of useful information, and a

liberal communication of republican sentiments, were thought to be the best antidotes to any political poison, with which the vital principles of civil liberty might be attacked: for by such means, a fraternal confidence will be established among the citizens; every symptom of innovation will be studiously marked; and a standard will be erected, to which, in danger and distress, the friends of liberty may successfully resort.

To obtain these objects, then, and to cultivate on all occasions, the love of peace, order, and harmony; an attachment to the constitution, and a respect to the laws of our country, will be the aim of the *Democratic Society*, &c.

Never did a piece of political hypocrisy come forth to public view under such a flimsy disguise as this circular letter. People stared to see that there were men amongst them possessed of impudence enough, thus to invite them to revolt against the constitution, under the pretext of preserving it in its purity. The Americans can swallow a pretty comfortable dose of any thing that is strongly seasoned with *liberty and equality*, but there were few, above the vulgar, whose stomachs did not turn at this.

How *democratic societies* were to protect the country against the monarchs of Europe seemed a mystery. What standard were they to raise for the people to find shelter under, in the hour of danger and distress? Nothing is clearer, than that the combination was intended to operate against the General Government, and against that alone. They set out with talking about the dangers to be apprehended from foreign powers, but they soon came to the point; the spirit of *freedom and equality*, they say, is eclipsed by the *pride of wealth* and *arrogance of power*. It is to combat these, that they invoke the aid of their fellow citizens.

Indeed a political club, if it is not intended to strengthen the government, must be intended to act against it. The very foundations of such a club must imply a systematic opposition to the lawful rules of the land; it is an act of rebellion, unpunishable by law 'tis true, but which will ever be punished by the abhorrence of all peaceable and honest men.

No one can read the concluding paragraph of this letter, without calling to mind the professions of the French and English Jacobins: the former united themselves under the name of, "*Les Amis de la Constitution*" (the friends of the Constitution), and the latter, under that of, "*The Constitutional Society.*" What sort of *friends* to the Constitution (of 1791) the Jacobins were, their subsequent conduct, and the fate of that Constitution, have fully proved; and it would be sinning against conviction to suppose, that those of England and America exceeded them in sincerity. The patriots, or *reformers* (call them which you please) who emigrate from England, throw off the disguise as soon as their feet touch the shore. They tell you, that their intention was to destroy "the old rotten constitution of Britain," from which they took their name; and there is not the least doubt, but the Democrats would be as candid with respect to the American constitution, were they landed in France.

As to those who placed themselves at the head of the Democrats, speaking of them generally, they were very little esteemed, either as private or public characters. Few of them were men of property, and such as were, owed their possessions to some casual circumstance, rather than to family, industry, or talents. The bulk of political reformers is always composed of needy, discontented men, too indolent or impatient to advance themselves by fair and honest means, and too ambitious to remain quiet in obscurity. Such, with very few exceptions, are those who have appeared among the leaders of the American Jacobins.[1]

The effects of the institution soon became apparent from one end of the United States to the other. The blaze did not, indeed, communicate itself with such rapidity as it had done in France, nor did it rage with so much fury when it had caught; but this must be ascribed to the nature of the materials, and not to any want of art or malice on the part of the incendiaries. The Americans are phlegmatic, slow to act; extremely cautious and difficult to be deceived. However, such was

---

[1] The *Officers,* as they were called, of the Mother Club, and who must ever be looked upon (under Genet) as the chief instruments in founding the sect, were:

DAVID RITTENHOUSE,	President.
WILLIAM COATS, CHARLES BIDDLE,	Vice-Presidents.
JAMES HUTCHINSON, ALEXANDER J. DALLAS, MICHAEL LEIB, JONATHAN SERGEANT, DAVID JACKSON,	Committee of Correspondence.
ISRAEL ISRAEL,	Treasurer.
J. PORTER, P. S. DUPONCEAU,	Secretaries.

These names should never be forgotten.

the indefatigableness of the Democratic Clubs, that I venture to say, without running the risk of contradiction, that more enmity to the General Government was excited in the space of six months, by the barefaced correspondencies and resolves of these clubs, than was excited against the colonial government at the time of the declaration of Independence.

The leading object was to stimulate the people to a close imitation of the French Revolutionists, who had just then begun the career of pure unadulterated sans-culottism. Every act or expression that bore the marks of politeness or gentility soon began to be looked upon, to use their own words, as a sort of *leze republicanism*. All the new fangled terms of the regenerated French were introduced and made use of. The word *citizen*, that stalking horse of modern liberty-men, became almost as common in America as in France. People, even people of sense, began to accustom themselves to be-citizen each other in as shameful a manner as the red-headed ruffians of the Fauxbourg St. Antoine.

The news-printers were in some sort the teachers of this new cant; and it was diverting enough sometimes to observe their embarrassment in rendering the French political jargon into English. One of them having a wedding to announce, found himself at a stand when he came to the word *citoyenne*. Our good ancestors had not foreseen these days of equality, and had therefore never thought of a termination to express the *feminine* of a *free-man*. To say that *citizen* A. was married to *citizen* B. would have had a brutal sound, even in the ears of a Jacobin, and therefore the ingenious news-man invented a termination, and his paragraph ran thus: "On———Citizen———was married to *Citess*———by *Citizen*———."[2]

The *citizens* of France had just given signal proof of their patriotic valour, in making war upon the old busts and statues of their kings and nobles, and those of America were determined not to be behind hand with them, as far as lay in their power. Lord Chatham's statue, erected by the people of Charleston, South Carolina, as a mark of their esteem for the part he took in pleading the cause of America, was drawn up into the air, by means of a jack and pullies, and absolutely hanged, not till it was dead, but till the head separated from the body. The statue of Lord Bettertout, a piece of exquisite workmanship, which stood in the town house of Williamsburgh in Virginia, was

---

[2] This article is to be found in the *Federal Gazette*, for the year 1793.

beheaded by the students of that place, and every mark of indignity, such as ignoble minds can show, was heaped on the resemblance of a man, to whom the fathers of these students had yielded all possible testimony of love and esteem.

The rage for *re-baptism*, as the French call it, also spread very far. An alley at Boston, called *Royal Exchange Alley*, and the stump of a tree, in the same town, which had borne the name of *Royal*, were rebaptized with a vast deal of formality; the former was called *Equality Lane*, and the latter *Liberty Stump*. At New York the names of several streets and places were changed; *Queen Street* became *Pearl Street*, and *King Street*, *Liberty Street*.

Those who were unacquainted with the influence of the Democratic Clubs, were astonished at these marks of political insanity. Indeed, the follies of the French seemed to be wafted over the instant they had birth, and the different districts seemed to vie with each other in adopting them. The delirium seized even the women and children; the former began to talk about liberty and equality in a good masculine style: I have heard more than one young woman, under the age of twenty, declare that they would willingly have dipped their hands in the blood of the Queen of France. A third part of the children, at least, were decorated, like their wise sires, in tricolored cockades. "*Dansons la Carmagnole*," pronounced in a broken accent, was echoed through every street and every alley of Philadelphia, by both boys and girls. Some ingenious democratic poet had composed the following lines:

> "Englishman no bon for me,
> Frenchman fight for liberty."

This distich, which at once shows the prevailing sentiments, and exhibits an instance of that kind of jargon which has become fashionable, was chanted about by young and old. Poor devils! thought I when I used to hear them, little do you know about liberty.

Nor were marks of ferocity wanting. At a dinner at Philadelphia (at which *a man high in office* was present) a *roasted pig* became the representative of Louis XVI and it being the anniversary of his murder, the pig's head was severed from his body, then carried round to each of the convives, who, after placing the liberty-cap upon his head, pronounced the word *tyrant*, and gave the poor little grunter's head a chop with his knife.

Never was the memory of any man so cruelly insulted as that of this mild and humane monarch. He was guillotined in effigy, in the capital of the union, twenty or thirty times every day, during one whole winter, and part of the summer. Men, women, and children, flocked to this tragic exhibition, and not a single paragraph appeared in the papers to shame them from it.—Much has been said about the *cruelty of English sports*, and the *humane* French have now-and-then stigmatized them as barbarians, for the delight they take in seeing a pair of courageous animals spur each other to death; nay, the charge has been often repeated by Americans, and I must confess, that nothing can be said in its defence; but I defy both French and Americans to bring me an instance of cruelty from the English sports, that will bear a comparison with the exhibition above mentioned.

One cannot think of this exhibition without reflecting on the honours that Louis formerly received on the same spot. On the triumphal arch that was erected at Philadelphia, in 1783, was a bust of Louis XVI with this motto:

MERENDO MEMORES FACIT.
His merit makes us remember him.

On another part of the arch were the *Three Lillies*, the arms of France, with this motto:

GLORIAM SUPERANT.
They exceed in Glory.

When a representation of this Triumphal Arch was sent to the King of France, what would he have done to one of his courtiers, who should have said to him: "Sire, be not too vain; depend not too much on the sincerity of the Americans; for, ten years from this day, they will shake hands with your murderers, and on the very spot where this arch was erected, they will murder you in effigy; and these Lillies, now surpassing in glory, will they trample under foot."

It is just, however, to observe, that a very great majority of the people of America, abhorred these demonstrations of a sanguinary spirit; nor would it be going too far to assert, that two-thirds of the Democrats were foreigners, landed in the United States since the war. The charge that attaches to the people in general, is, that these things were suffered to pass unreproved. The friends of order and of humanity were dilatory; like persons of the same description in France, they seemed to be waiting, till the sons of equality came to cut their throats; and if they have finally escaped, it is to be ascribed to mere chance, or to any thing, rather than to their own exertions.

While the Democratic Societies were thus poisoning the minds of the people, familiarizing them to insurrection and blood, Genet was not idle. He had surrounded himself with a troop of horse, enlisted and embodied in Philadelphia. These were, in general, Frenchmen, and no one can doubt but they were intended to act, either on the offensive or defensive, as occasion might require. This force rendered his adherents bold; they threw off all reserve, and issued their invitations to rebellion with an unsparing hand. The clubs at a distance followed the example, and, in some instances, improved upon it.

As the Democrats increased in strength and impudence, other men grew timid. No one ventured to whisper his disapprobation of the conduct of the French; every one, even of their most savage acts, was applauded: robbery and murder were called *national justice* in America as well as in France. The people, properly so called, were fairly cowed down, and things seemed as ripe for revolution here, as they were in France, in the month of July, 1790.[6]

The country was saved from this dreadful scourge by the hasty indiscretion of the Citizen Minister. The light-headed Frenchman was intoxicated with his success, and conceived that the moment was arrived for him to set the government at defiance, and call on the people for support. But no sooner had he expressed his intention of "appealing from the President to the sovereign people," than he found he had been too sanguine. He found that the *people of America* were yet more attached to General Washington than to the French Minister or the French nation. Their love and veneration for their old and tried friend seemed to be revived by this insult; and though the Democratic Clubs defended the conduct of their founder, they found themselves too weak to take any decided step in his favour.

When Genet discovered that he had been too rash, he strove to recover himself by denying that he had threatened the government with an appeal to the people, and his friend *Dallas*, who, as Secretary of the State of Pennsylvania, had been the bearer of the threat, was prevailed on to deny that it was made. *Dallas* published an explanation of his contradictory account of the matter, endeavouring to exculpate both the Frenchman and himself; but this explanation had no other effect than that which a lie added to an offence never fails to produce.

From this time forward the clubs were a little more cautious in their resolves. When they met it was by night, and *under lock and key*. Genet became timid, attempted to justify himself, and seemed to tremble for his fate. He saw that his resources decreased, and that the remainder would be wanted for other purposes than that of nourishing a nest of hungry Democrats. The vital principle being extinct, the body began to dwindle: the old leaders skulked off one by one, and at last none remained but the mere tools.

Among these were the Democrats from England, a set of mortals whose stupidity is equalled by their obstinacy, and by that alone. They, poor devils, who had never been suffered even to smell the loaves and fishes, persevered with as good heart as ever, after the feast was all over; and wondered why others abated in their zeal. Englishmen are said to be changeable and fickle minded; but when foreigners lay this to our charge, they should make an exception of one case, and that is, *when we are in the wrong*. No men on earth abandon their errors with so much reluctance as the inhabitants on the south of the Tweed.

One *Pearce*, who had had the honour to be a delegate to the *London Corresponding Society*, and who, on that account, was admitted a member of the Jacobin club of Philadelphia, proposed a *negro man* as worthy of a seat. Pearce was a philanthropist, a true equality man, a disciple of Winchester.[7] He was silly enough to suppose that the Democrats were really what they professed to be, and therefore he foresaw no kind of opposition to the introduction of his charcoal-faced friend, and having an extraordinary degree of zeal for the increase of the society, took the earliest opportunity to propose him. The club being met and the doors locked, he rose in all the pride of conscious sans-culottism, and proposed brother Pompey as a member; but he soon found that the American Democrats did not carry their ideas of equality quite so far as he did. "No, no, no," resounded from every quarter, and when the votes came to be taken, there appeared but two or three, out of about fifty, in favour of the admission; and thus Pompey, whom Pearce describes as a d——d honest fellow, escaped inevitable corruption and disgrace.

This refusal, however, lost them the Delegate: he told them, that he had joined the club in the persuasion that it was composed of pure Democrats, and that his conscience would not permit him to remain among them a moment, after what he had been a witness of that night.

The business of the clubs was reduced to trifling discussions of this sort, when the recall of Genet seemed to forebode their total extinction. Genet's insolence had produced a complaint on the part of the American Government, and this complaint had produced his recal [sic]. The corner stone of the Jacobin affiliation being removed, every one expected the superstructure to fall to the ground; how deceitful appearances were we shall see by-and-by, after having made a remark or two on this act of "friendly condescension," as it has been termed, of the French usurpers.

First, it must be remembered, that at the time the complaint was made, the faction, by whom Genet had been sent out, were hurled from their thrones, and another had got possession of them. Robespierre and Marat were glad of having an opportunity to accuse their rivals of having offended the American Government, and to take to themselves the credit of healing the wound. Displacing Genet instantly, upon application, was a step, too, which they knew would render them popular in America, and silence those who began to arraign the conduct of the Convention. Thus, by the means of this "condescension," they secured to themselves three advantages: it furnished them with one more crime to heap on the heads of their rival faction; they completely supplanted that faction in the partiality of the people of the United States; and, which was of still greater importance, they pursued the same treacherous manoeuvres, without being suspected. These were the motives of this act of "friendly condescension."

That they did not, in their hearts, disapprove of the proceedings of Genet, is clear from their suffering him to remain in the United States. When did they forgive those who offended them? Had they demanded him, the government must, and, they knew, would, have given him up; but no such demand was ever made, and this circumstance alone sufficiently proves, that, had he succeeded, a *civic crown* would have been the mede of his machinations.

Fauchet, the successor of Genet, trod exactly in his steps, but with a little more caution.[8] The Democratic Clubs made not the least hesitation in transferring their obedience from one minister to another. Indeed, all the disciples of the new-light philosophy are made of the same commodious kind of stuff. All that they do is, to ask who directs the storm of anarchy, and they instantly become his ardent admirers, if not his tools. In this respect no set of beings, I cannot call them men, ever approached so near to the herd of Paris, as did the Democrats of America. One day saw the faction of Brissot exalted to the skies, and the very next, saw the same compliments, the very same turgid effusions of patriotic admiration, heaped on their murderers. From the first assembling of the States General to this very hour, every leader, while he continued such, has been the god of those wretches who now-a-days style themselves patriots. I have now a bundle of gazettes before me, published all by the same man, wherein Mirabeau, Fayette, Brissot, Danton, and Robespierre, are all panegyrized and execrated in due succession; nor do I yet despair of living to see Talien and Louvet added to the list. The versatile mob of Paris, who first canonized Mirabeau and Voltaire, and afterwards scattered their remains to the winds; and who, after having given Marat's ugly carcass a place in their temple of fame, and his name to a city, dug him up, put his ashes into a chamber-pot, by way of urn, and then threw them into the common sewer; this versatile, stupid and venal mob, does not surpass in either quality, the Democratic news-printers in the United States of America; and sorry am I to say, that they are not few in number.[3]

[3] At the head of these we may venture to place *Benjamin Franklin Bache*, a grand-son (whether in a *straight or crooked line*, I know not) of Old Doctor Franklin. This is the man whom the doctor left his books and printing-office to, and good use has he made of them. The history of the types of this office would be an amusing performance: it would be curious to trace them from the opposition of the British Colonial government to as determined an opposition against the government raised on its ruins; from the old saws of hypocritical morality, contained in the pages of *Poor Richard's* Almanac, to the blasphemous nonsense of the French Republican Calendar. Those types were, indeed, a rich legacy. Their proprietor may, with a trifling change, join in chorus with the highwayman in the Beggar's Opera.

> See the types I hold!
> See the types I hold!
> Let the chemists toil like asses,
> My ink their fire surpasses,
> And *turns my lead to gold!*
> And *turns my lead to gold!*

It must be confessed, however, that, in one instance, he did, for a moment, discover more consistency than the rest of his fellow labourers. He did defend his friends *Barrere, Collot d'Herbois*, and *Billaud de Varennes*, even after he looked upon them as dead! Of "the three" says he, "*Barrere* is most to be regretted."—And why?—"Because *he presided in the convention when Louis was condemned*, and expressly declared, that *the Tree of Liberty must be watered with the blood of the Tyrant*."——These are the *humane* and *grateful* Citizen Bache's reasons for regretting the fall of *Barrere!* Would not one imagine that he must have been suckled with blood? His friends defend him (God defend me from the defence of such friends) by insisting that he is a fool, and the mere cat's-paw of the *supporters* of his paper. Of the two, I must confess, that a *hireling* is less detestable than a *savage*, and as I wish to excite as little detestation against Bache, as justice will admit of, I leave him to take his choice of the two characters.

A circumstance that strongly seconded the endeavours of *Fauchet* and the Clubs, was, the discontents that existed among the people of the Western Counties of Pennsylvania, on account of the excise on whisky. These discontents were, in some measure, done away, or at least, they produced no serious consequences, before the institution of the Democratic Societies: with this institution they revived, and assumed a more determined aspect; the malcontents had now a rallying point; by means of the affiliation they communicated their pretended grievances to every corner of the Union, from whence they instantly received assurances of aid and support of the clubs. Thus encouraged, they proceeded from one excess to another, till, at last, several counties were officially declared to be in a state of actual insurrection.

To give a detailed account of this insurrection, were it consistent with my circumscribed plan, would be of little use. That *fifteen thousand* men were obliged to quit their homes and business, to encounter a campaign of uncommon hardship and toil; that many of these peaceable, orderly citizens (citizens in the true sense of the word) lost their lives in consequence of the fatigues they underwent, leaving their ashes to be trod on by the vile insurgents; that the expenses of the armament to a million and a half of dollars, are to be deducted from the fruits of industry; these are well known, and will be long remembered facts, and therefore need no historian. It is to the influence that the Democratic Clubs had in producing the insurrection, and its consequent calamities, that I wish to direct the reader's attention.[9]

As soon as the Club at Philadelphia was formed, similar ones were formed in the Western Counties, composed entirely of men, who were not only opposed to the excise law, but to the government which had enacted it. Messengers and emissaries passed continually between the clubs in the East and those in the West. From this time the *resolves* of the malcontents assumed another tone. These refractory people had hitherto confined their demands to a repeal of the excise law; but they now talked of forcing the government to open the navigation of the Mississippi, and complained, in the style of Genet and the Clubs, against the Proclamation of Neutrality, and, in short, against the whole of the conduct of the Federal Government.

Let any one read their *toasts* and *resolves*, and observe their manner of proceeding, and compare these with those of the Democratic Societies; and then believe, if he can, that they were not both actuated with the same spirit, and had not the same objects in view; namely, a war with Britain, and the destruction of the General Government. During two years had the Western complaints existed: the complainants had often assembled, and had passed resolves without number about their detestable drink; but never till now did they join their cause to that of France: never till now did they wear national cockades, or rally under the *tree of liberty* mounted with a bloody Parisian cap. Will any man in his senses believe that these were mere whims, freaks of fancy, that came athwart their brains by chance, without the least advice or prior instruction from their friends in the East?

Let us hear our old friend *Citizen Fauchet's* opinion on this subject.[10] In giving his masters an account of the breaking out of the insurrection, he says: "In the mean time *popular societies are formed*; political ideas concentre themselves; the *patriotic party unite* and more closely connect themselves, &c."—Then, after giving them a description of the Western people and the nature of their drink, &c. he adds: "Now, as the common dispatches inform you, these complaints *were systematizing* by the *conversations of influential men, who retired into these wild countries*, and who, from *principle*, or by a series of *particular heart-burnings, animated discontents* already near effervescence. At last, the *local explosion is effected*. The Western people calculated on being supported by *some distinguished characters in the East*, and even imagined they had in the bosom of the government some abettors, who might share in their grievances or their principles."

I shall not attempt to point out these *distinguished characters in the East*; but let the reader recollect that *Mr. Dallas* was one in the leaders of the Mother,[11] and then let him read the following extract from another part of *Fauchet's Letter*.

"Of all the governors, whose duty it was to appear at the head of the requisitions, the *governor of Pennsylvania* alone enjoyed *the name of Republican*; his opinion of the Secretary of the Treasury and of his systems was known to be unfavourable. The *Secretary of this state possessed great influence in the Popular Society of Philadelphia*, which in its turn influenced those of other states; of course he merited attention. It appears therefore that these men, with others unknown to me, all having without doubt Randolph at their head, were balancing to decide on their party. Two or three days before the proclamation was published, and of course before the cabinet had resolved on its measures, Mr. Randolph came to see me with an air of great eagerness, and made to me the overtures, of which I have given you an account in my No. 6. Thus, with some thousands of dollars, the Republicans could have decided on civil war or on peace! Thus the consciences of the pretended patriots of America have already their prices! It is very true that the certainty of these conclusions, painful to be drawn, will for ever exist in our archives! What will be the old age of this government, if it is thus early decrepid!"[12]

From the conduct of the democrats prior to the breaking out of the insurrection, we naturally come to that which they observed subsequent to that event; and here we shall find nothing but what tends to strengthen the charge against them. Immediately upon the issuing of the President's proclamation, all the papers devoted to the French Minister and his clubs, and particularly *Bache's*, which might be looked upon as the mirror of their sentiments, attacked, with all their malice, both those who issued, and those who were ready to obey it. Every art was used to instil into the minds of the militia, that they were called on to cut the throats of their fellow citizens merely to support the rich creditors of the State; and, of course, that they ought not to obey the summons to attend. "As violent means," (says Bache's paper of the 20th of August) "As *violent means* appear the desire of high-toned government men, it is to be hoped that those who derive the most benefit from our revenue laws, will be the foremost to march against the Western Insurgents. Let stock-holders, bank directors, speculators, and revenue officers arrange themselves immediately *under the banners of the treasury*, and try their prowess in arms, as they have done in calculation. The prompt recourse to hostilities will no doubt operate upon the *knights* of our country to appear in military array, and then the *poor but industrious citizen* will not be *obliged to spill the blood of his fellow citizen to gratify certain resentments*, and expose himself to the loss of life and of limb to *support a funding order*." In the same paper of the 26th of August: "The discontents which have taken place in the Western Counties, and which have appeared in the form of open hostility to law, and indeed the dissatisfactions that are to be found in every part of the continent, may be readily accounted for, by a reference to the proceedings of our government *from its birth*. The bantling fancied itself *something royal*, before it was able to stand alone, and since it has been progressing towards manhood, the State dignity, superciliousness and manners of a monarch have characterized its actions. To support itself in royal pomp, arose the funding and banking systems, *excises*, &c. Nothing but coronets and stars are wanting, to the stockholders. Is this a land of liberty? Is this a land where citizens are *equal? It would be no wonder* if every citizen, who is not immediately interested in the funding system, *should rise up*, and with one word *exclaim against its iniquity*," or, in other words, *join the insurgents*.

Such was the language of the democrats, at the very moment that the insurrection wore the most threatening aspect, and such was the effect it had on some descriptions of the people, that it was with the utmost difficulty a sufficient number of men were collected to make up the quota of the State of Pennsylvania.

Mr. Findley, the ingenious historian of the Western Insurrection, and a principal actor in it, insists, with a *modesty* becoming his country, that the insurrection ought to be attributed entirely to the irritable *heat of the weather*, during the dog-days of 1794; and, of course he wishes us to believe, that it was quelled by the returning coolness of October and November.[13] It must be confessed that the insurgents were afflicted with a sort of canine malady, for they snapped at the hand that yielded them protection; but, I believe, few people, after what has been said above, will not remain well convinced, that the insurrection was fomented by democratic fuel, paid for with French Gold; and that it was cooled again by the approach of General Washington, at the head of fifteen thousand men.

For the sake of preserving connection, some striking traits of sans-culottism, which took place prior to the epoch at which we are now arrived, have been omitted; but they are too characteristic of the sect whose history I am writing, to pass altogether unnoticed.

As I have more than once observed, that the Democrats aped the regenerated French in all their follies, and in all their crimes as far as they were able, it will be understood, that they made a boast of being atheists or deists as the Convention changed its creed. When the faction of Danton seemed to preponderate, and members exclaimed against the "aristocracy of heaven;" when the infamous *Dupont* exclaimed: "Oh! shame, Legislators of the Universe! You have hurled down the thrones of kings, and you yet suffer the altars of God to remain!"[14] Then the Democrats made an open profession of Atheism. But when *Robespierre* obtained the ascendency, and ordered the Convention *to decree*, that there was a *Supreme Being* (Etre Supreme): then did our good sans-culottes burn incense on the altars of deism, with as much devotion as the ragged groups of *St. Marceau* and the whores and bullies of the *Palais de L'Egalite*.

It has been often observed, that, however widely atheism and deism may differ in theory, in practice, that is in their effects, they were nearly the same. So it happens now; for, whether they professed the opinions of Danton or those of his bloody successor, they still testified the same hatred of the Christian Religion, and persecuted, with every insult they durst offer, all those who had courage enough to stand forward in its defence.

The first assault of this kind was on the Reverend Mr. Abercrombie of the Episcopal Church, Philadelphia. This gentleman had preached a sermon, warning his congregation against the contagion of French atheism and deism. For this instance of becoming zeal in the discharge of the most imperious of all duties, he was attacked in the public papers; accused of *bigotry*, of being *an enemy to the cause of liberty*, and of the *French people*. There was not a worthy man in the city, who did not feel an indignation against the authors of this unprovoked calumny, and who did not regret, that the injured clergyman should see the necessity of answering it. Dreadful times indeed are those, when the servants of the Lord are brought to the bar of the public, for daring to obey the commands of their master! For daring to defend him against those, who brand him with the name of cheat and imposter![4]

This pulpit evesdropping having, in some measure succeeded, they cast their scrutinizing scowling eyes over the out-side of the church. Here they found a small wooden bust of George II. This bust, like the *Old Stump* at Boston, had remained very quiet during the American revolution; but could not endure the fiery ordeal of the French revolution. Trifling circumstances like these show the difference in the influence which these revolutions have had on men's minds, in a stronger light than the most important events can do, and prove what I have always asserted; namely, that the moderation which marked the American character in the last revolution, must not be counted upon, should another take place.

The discovery of the bust was no sooner made, than the Democrats formed the resolution of destroying it; or, in the language of *Gregoire*,

---

[4] About the same time that this insult was offered to Mr. Abercrombie, a paragraph appeared in the Philadelphia Gazette, published by one Brown, containing a list of eminent men, who had arisen on "the democratic floor," and concluding with, *Marat, St. Paul,* and *Jesus Christ.*

I have mentioned this scandalous paragraph in so many places, that I should not have done it here, had not its existence been denied in a pamphlet lately published by a Scotch run-away, whose name is *Calender,* and who was, it seems, the editor of the gazette at the time. The paragraph appeared in the paper above-mentioned, on the 20th of June, in the memorable 1794.

of committing an act of *vandalism*. They accordingly published the following card, as they called it, in their printer Bache's gazette of the 21st July, 1794.

> *To the Clergy and Vestry of Christ Church.*
> GENTLEMEN,
> It is the wish of many respectable *citizens*, that you would cause the image and crown of GEORGE II to be removed as readily as possible. It has nothing to do with the worship of the most high God, nor the government under which we exist: it has a tendency to cause that church to be disliked, while *bearing the mark of infamy*; it has a tendency, to the knowledge of many, to keep *young* and *virtuous men* from attending public worship; it is therefore a public nuisance.
> M.

One is at a loss which to admire most, the logic, the impudence, or the hypocrisy of this intimation. How exactly, too, does it imitate the style of the Convention; "*young* and *virtuous men!*" Canting rascals! How willingly would you have led those *young* and *virtuous men* to cut the throats of their fathers and mothers, and of the ministers to whom they were attached!

In consequence of the democratic *card*, which was rightly looked upon as a threat, a vestry was called, and it was thought more adviseable to abandon the bust to the fury of the *vandals*, than to expose the church itself to danger. Accordingly, the *barbarians* assembled with ladders, mallets and chissels. The crown and the projecting part of the bust were chipped off; but the profile, with G on one side of it and II. on the other, are still as conspicuous as ever. All that the Democrats effected, was, a change in the ideas awakened by the sight of the bust. From a monument of well-placed esteem and gratitude, it is become a monument of democratic folly and baseness and rancour and undistinguishing revenge.

It was easy to perceive, that they did not mean to stop here, and therefore few people were surprised at their next pointing out the propriety of taking the *mitre* from the steeple.[5] This demand was not made in such direct and positive terms, and therefore it was not complied with; but there is little doubt but both mitre and church would have had a tumble long ago, had not the Western Insurrection

---

[5] See Bache's gazette of the 21st August, 1794.

excited a general hatred against the clubs, and thus rendered them less daring and insolent.

At the same time that we are recording the violences of the clubs against Christian institutions, truth requires that we should confess, that but too many of the clergy appeared either contaminated with French principles, or cowardly enough not to attempt an opposition to their progress. All that can be said in the defence of such men, is, that they feared to offend their congregations, on whom they were totally dependent for support. This is surely a very weak defence; but, I am afraid, it is one that must often be made, where the pastor is removable at the pleasure of his flock.

But, there were others who were not merely passive; who were not ashamed to mingle in the bacchanalian orgies of the civic festivals, held to celebrate the successes of atheists over the religion of which they professed to be believers, and of which they were teachers. Among these the *Reverend Citizen Prentiss*, of Reading, Massachusetts, and the *Reverend Citizen Doctor McKnight*, of New York, claim the scandalous pre-eminence.

Nor were the places dedicated to the instruction of youth securely guarded against the approaches of sans-culottism. Of this the conduct of Doctor Rogers, a teacher in the University at Philadelphia, exhibits a striking proof. He gave the boys of his class a speech out of Shakespeare's Harry V. to get by heart. It was the king's animating address to his army before Harfleur: "Once more to the breach, dear friends," &c. which, in Shakespeare ends thus:

> "Follow your spirit, and, upon this charge,
> Cry—God for Harry! England! and St. George!"

—This conclusion the Doctor parodied:

> "Cry—God for *Freedom! France!* and *Robespierre!*"

All the class repeated it with the democratic emendation, except a little English boy about ten or eleven years of age, who boldly said:

> "Cry—God for *Harry! England!* and *St. George!*"

Nor could he be prevailed upon to alter the text. This brave little fellow's name is Whitlock, who, though a child, certainly possessed more taste, more sense, more patriotism and more piety than his Reverend teacher.

When the sweet Warwickshire bard put this noble speech into the mouth of his favourite hero, he was not blessed with the hope, that, hundreds of years afterwards, and thousands of miles distant, it would call forth such a noble spirit in a child ten years of age.

Before I return to take my leave of the Democratic Societies, I trust the reader will not be displeased with an account of the civic *fete* of the 23d *Thermidor* (10th of August, "style of the slaves"), which was celebrated at Philadelphia in 1794.

To ward off every charge of misrepresentation, I shall confine myself to a literal translation of the *Proces Verbal* (Minutes of the proceedings), sent to the Convention, and which may be seen in the French Philadelphia gazette of the 25th *Thermidor*, 12th of August, "style of the slaves," as the *humane* French Governor of Gaudaloupe calls it.

> At sun-rise the *fete* was announced by a *salve* of 22 guns, in allusion to the 22d of Sept.—At eight o'clock another *salve* of 10 guns, at once announced the *fete* of the 10th of August, and the hour of assembling.[15]
>
> The French and *American* citizens now repaired to the centre square, where the order of march was to be settled on: the greatest part of the citizens wore oak-boughs, and little bunches of ears of wheat, ornamented with *tricolored* ribbons.
>
> In the middle of the square there was an obelisk {*made of pasteboard*}, decorated with attributes of liberty. On the four sides of the obelisk were *engraven* {engraven on paste-board mind} the following inscriptions:
>
>> To Immortality.
>> The French Republic one and indivisible.
>> Liberty, Equality, Fraternity.
>> Tremble Tyrants, your reign is over.
>
> A deputation of French citizens then went to the French Minister's where the *chiefs civil and military of the state of Pennsylvania* were assembled. A deputy announced to the minister that the good people were waiting for their *representatives*. They immediately came to the square preceded by the flags of the two nations, marching to the noise of drums and cannons, and amidst the cries, a hundred times repeated,

of *Vive la Republique Françoise*! {I will not disgrace our language by translating the vile acclamation}; and war-like music played, by intervals, airs analogous to the transports which burst forth from every quarter.

When everything was ready, ten guns were fired as a signal for the march. Two pieces of cannon, followed by French and American cannoneers, took the lead. The hatred that we were going to swear against tyrants, was written on every countenance. The anniversary of the destruction of despotism painted on every face patriotism, liberty, and equality.

The *obelisk was carried by four citizens*, two French and two American, in red liberty caps: these were followed by a French grenadier, bearing a *pike* surmounted with a liberty cap.

Now comes the prettiest part of the procession.

Twelve young *citoyennes* {or she citizens}, dressed in pure white, adorned with civic crowns and cestuses tricolor, each bearing a little basket of flowers, surrounded the obelisk.

What a contrast there was between these little innocent lambs, with their flower-baskets, and the swarthy grenadier with his bloody pike and cap!

The French Minister, the Consuls, the *chiefs civil and military of Pennsylvania*, marched in the centre of the procession.

Indeed it was diverting enough to see these great personages, the good sober-looking, pot-bellied chiefs of Pennsylvania, come squeezing, and shouldering, and zigzaging along, like so many raw recruits at drill. They were formed into what military men call a platoon, and never did my eyes behold so awkward a squad.

There is a small omission in this part of the *Proces Verbal*, which I shall supply.—Before the procession left the centre square, the *English flag*, which had been brought thither *reversed*, under the flags of France and America, was *burnt* before the obelisk, amidst the triumphant hootings of the brave sons of liberty and equality.—This was by way of retaliation for Lord Howe's victory over the sans-culotte fleet, the news of which had arrived the day before.

The procession advanced to the garden of the Minister François, where there was an altar erected to the country, on which stood the goddess of liberty. The flags of the two nations were planted on each side of her, while the little she citizens were ranged round the altar.

Patriotic hymns were now sung, accompanied with music; and while the most tender and melting invocations were put up, the citizens made to the goddess a sweet smelling offering of the flowers they had brought, with which they covered her altar, with an innocent zeal peculiar to their age.

The patriotic hymns being ended, an oration was made by a Citizen François[6] and then the Minister François made another, and then the whole swore to be faithful to the Republic. The best of this was, three-fourths of the audience did not understand a word of what they heard, of what they swore to, or even of the oath they took.

The Minister had hardly time to conclude, when the cries {or howlings} of *Vive la Republique François une et indivisible*! burst forth from every throat.

A discharge of cannon, a war-like march, and a roll of the drums, expressed the joy of the people, and signified that every heart was glad.—Instantly the ranks broke off, and dances were formed round the altar of liberty, and over all the enclosure.

These dances were the finest fun I ever enjoyed. The patriotic hymns were well enough; four hundred fellows howling out French bombast, without understanding a word of it, was not a bad specimen of fraternal dissonance; but to behold fifty or sixty groupes, promiscously [sic] formed, whistling, singing and capering about they knew not why nor wherefore; and to see the "*chiefs civil and military of Pennsylvania*," heaving up their legs, and endeavouring to ape the light-heeled mounseers, was a spectacle which, I trust, has been seldom equalled.— In one part of the garden you heard the chorus of the bloody

---

[6] It is well worthy of remark, that this oration, which was sent to the convention, contained a high strained compliment to *Robespierre*, just at the very time that the convention and their mob were hacking and shooting and guillotining him.—Had the *virtuous civic feters* known this, they would have cursed him most heartily; as, indeed, they did two months afterwards.—What a pity it is, that there is no means by which our sans-culottes can come at the exact state of things in France at the moment they are framing their toasts and resolves!

> Ah! ça ira, ça ira, ça ira,
> Les Aristocrats a la Lanterne.

In another:

> Dansons la carmagnole,
> Vive le son, vive le son
> Du canon.

While in another,

> Alons enfans de la patrie

seemed to issue from the lungs of twenty infernals. But what was still most ludicrous, was, to hear all this uttered, by the greatest part of the chanters, in an accent barbarous beyond description. But, to proceed with my translation:

"During the rest of the day, public joy was manifested all over the city."—That's a lie. One half of the people of the city cared nothing at all about the *fete*, and were astonished and ashamed that the cannons of the state should be employed on such an occasion; and I venture to affirm, that not one-twentieth part of those who assisted at it, would have assisted, had they known they were celebrating the anniversary of the fall of Louis XVI and the horrid and cowardly murder of the Swiss guards. This remark justice demanded in defence of those who attended through ignorance. With regard to the "*chiefs, civil and military of Pennsylvania,*" as I have too much respect for them to accuse them of ignorance, I leave them to themselves.

We must now return to the Democratic Clubs. In what remains to be said of them I shall be very concise.

Though they were instituted for the express purpose of clogging the wheels of government, weakening its power, and exciting a spirit of discontent among the people, that might acquire strength enough to force it into a war on the side of France, or totally annihilate it; yet there were three measures in this continued opposition, against which the Democrats made a bolder stand than usual, and called forth more than ordinary exertions; namely, the *Proclamation* of *Neutrality*, the enforcing obedience to the *Excise-Law*, and the sanctioning of the *British Treaty*. They had entered their solemn protest against the two former, and had used every means in their power to effect a forcible, and even an armed opposition to them; and their conduct with respect to the latter was exactly of the same description. But, of every part of this conduct, their resolves against the appointment of the man best calculated to bring about an accommodation; their publishing the treaty in a mutilated form with their own invidious misrepresentations; their dispatching runners to all the principal towns, to exasperate the discontented, and deceive the weak; their dishonourable means of obtaining petitions to Congress against it; the intrigues of Randolph and Fauchet, and the embarrassment and alarm their machinations spread through the country; all these are so fresh in every one's memory, that it is useless to dwell on them here. Certain it is that they ought not to be forgotten, nor will they be, while *Peter Porcupine's* writings are remembered; and though these latter are assuredly not destined to long life, I hope they will outlive the infernal sect of the Jacobins, and if this hope be to be [sic] realized, I sincerely wish they may sink into oblivion to-morrow.

The Western Insurrection and its effects had already rendered the Democrats extremely odious; here their mischievous efforts touched the pockets and the lives of the people; and their failure in the last attempt to trouble the peace of the Union, obliged them to hide their heads. The dark caballing clubs do, indeed, still exist; but they either never meet, or they dare not publish their resolves. However, let not the friends of the General Government, of order, of peace and of general happiness and prosperity, imagine that the sect is annihilated. They only wait for a more favourable moment, and should the indiscretion or supineness of the sound part of the community suffer that moment to arrive, they will obtain an ascendency that will enable them to inflict signal vengeance for their past disappointments. From their reign God defend me and mine! . . .

[7]

Pen Portraits

"I NEVER COULD SEE," WROTE COBBETT IN 1799, "HOW ABUSES WERE to be corrected, without attacking those to whom they were to be attributed. If swindling and debauchery prevails, how are you to check it without exposing the *swindler* and the *debauchee*? And how are you to expose them without attacking their private characters?" Throughout his career, Cobbett hectored and harassed his political enemies, on the grounds that flawed principles flowed from flawed personalities. He justified his initial attack on Joseph Priestley by arguing that once a person became involved in political debate, "his opinions, his principles, his motives, every action of his life, public or private, become the fair subject of public discussion." And he attacked "all the reforming philosophers of the present enlightened day" for possessing a speculative kind of humanity which "never breaks out into action." "Hear these people," he wrote, "and you would think them overflowing with the milk of human kindness. They stretch their benevolence to the extremities of the globe: it embraces every living creature—except those who have the misfortune to come into contact with them. They are all citizens of the world: country and friends and relations are unworthy the attention of men who are occupied in rendering all mankind happy and free."

These extracts are taken from the vast number of ad hominem attacks and asides in Cobbett's writings between 1796 and 1800. The targets range from Thomas Paine ("the old broken exciseman"), through the leading British and Irish radicals, or "trans-Atlantic traitors," in the United States, to prominent American figures such as Noah Webster (the "spiteful viper"), Benjamin Rush ("Doctor Sangrado") and Thomas McKean ("Mrs. McKean's husband"). This chapter also includes Cobbett's mock "Will and Testament" of March 1797, in which he ridicules leading members of the American political and literary intelligentsia; it is Cobbett at his satirical sharpest.

[Cobbett on Thomas Paine]

[THE *AGE OF REASON*][1] CANNOT BE BETTER DESCRIBED THAN BY SAYING that it is as stupid and despicable as its author. The wretch has all his life been employed in leading fools astray from their duty, and, as nothing is more easy, he has often succeeded. His religion is exactly of a piece with his politics; one inculcates the right of revolting against government, and the other that of revolting against God. Having succeeded against the Lord's anointed (I mean his and our *ci-devant*[2] friend the most Christian king) he turned his impious arms against the Lord himself. This process is perfectly natural, as has been exemplified in the conduct of others as well as that of Paine.

How Tom came to think of exercising his clumsy battered pen upon the Christian Religion is what has excited a good deal of curiosity, without ever being well accounted for in this country; notwithstanding, the circumstances under which a man writes ought to be attended to in forming a judgement of his opinions, particularly if those opinions are new and extraordinary. For this reason, I shall endeavour to trace this raggamuffin deist from America to his Paris dungeon, and to account for his having laid down the dagger of insurrection in order to take up the chalice of irreligion.

Thomas, after having retailed out a good deal of very *Common Sense*, commonly called *Nonsense*, found himself rather richer than when he began.[1] This gave him a smack for revolutions; but finding himself sinking fast into his native mud, and pretty universally despised and neglected by the people of this country: finding, in short, that the Americans were returning to order, and feeling that his element was confusion, he crossed the Atlantic to bask in the rays of the French revolution.

---

[1] In his second Part of the Rights of Man, he says he has a *place* in the State of Delaware. Whether this be a lye or not I cannot tell; but, if it be true, it was certainly the product of the revolution; for every one knows he had nothing before. This was encouragement for him to try his talent in other countries. A confiscated castle in France, or some Abbey where he might join sacrilege to robbery, was a sufficient temptation to lead him across the ocean.

The *Propagande* at Paris, that is, the society instituted for the propagation of the vile and detestable principles of the *Rights of Man*, as laid down in the famous French Constitution, fixed their Jacobinical eyes on Tom, as an excellent missionary for great Britain and Ireland. Off goes Tom with his Rights of Man, which he had the abominable impudence to dedicate to *General Washington*.[2] The English Jacobins stared at him at first: he went a step further than they had ever dreamed of: his doctrines, however, grew familiar to their ears: they took him under their wing, and he made sure of another revolution. This security was his misfortune, and had nearly cost him a voyage to the South Sea.

From the thief-catchers in England Tom fled, and took his seat among the thieves of Paris. After having distinguished himself in execrating the Constitution he had written in defence of, he, and two or three others, set to work and made a new one; quite brand new, without a single ounce of old stuff.[3] This covered Tom with glory soon after, when it was unanimously accepted by the rich, free, generous and *humane* French nation.

This may be looked upon as the happiest part of Tom's life. He had enjoyed partial revolts before, had seen doors and windows broken in, and had probably partaken of the pillage of some aristocratic stores and dwelling houses; but, to live in a continual state of insurrection, "sacred, holy, organized insurrection;"[4] to sit seven days in the week issuing decrees for plunder, proscription and massacre, was a luxurious life indeed! It was, however, a short life and a merry one: it lasted but five months. The tender-hearted philanthropic murderer, Brissot, and his faction, fell from the pinnacle of their glory: poor Tom's wares got out of vogue and his carcass got into a dungeon.

This was a dreadful reverse for old Common Sense. To be hurled, all in a moment, from tip top of the *Mountain* of the *Grande Convention Nationale* down to the very bottom of a stinking dungeon, was enough to give a shock to his poor unsteady brain. But this was not all; he well knew that the national razor was at work, and had every reason to suppose that his days were numbered. He laid extended on the dirt like a sheep or a calf in a slaughter-house, expecting every moment that the Butcher would come for him.

How Thomas came to escape is something that will probably remain

---

[2] The *Second Part* was dedicated to *Lafayette*, to which nobody had any kind of objection.

a mistery. It was said, that *Danton* (the new chief tyrant) spared his life at the request of certain Americans; but this is improbable, not that some Americans might be found silly enough to petition for it, but because, when his enlargement was afterwards demanded upon the score of his being an American, the ruling tyrants answered, that he was a *sacré Anglois*, a d——nd Englishman. The fact is, I believe, Danton and his party despised Tom too much to run any risk of disobliging their friends in great Britain and America by taking away his worthless life. Be the motive what it might, he was kept in his cage, and there he wrote the first part of his *Age of Reason*.[5]

Now to the motive that led him to the composition of this blasphemous work; which was no other than that of saving his ugly uncombed head from the guillotine.

The reader will recollect, that it was under the reign of *Danton* that the Christian Religion was abolished by decree. A few days before Tom's imprisonment the famous festival of Reason was held. A common strumpet was dressed up as the *Goddess Reason*,[3] seated on a throne of turf, and, while incense was burnt before her altar at some little distance, the idolatrous populace, with the Convention at their head, prostrated themselves before her. Not many days before this, the *constitutional* Bishop of Paris[4] with his vicars and three rectors, came to the Convention and abdicated their religion, declaring themselves to have been cheats, and that in future they would profess no other worship than that of *Reason*. In short, *Danton*, and *Robespierre* (then second in command) were incessantly occupied in extirpating the small remains of Christianity from the minds of the poor brutified and enslaved French. It was a necessary preparation to the bloody work they intended they should execute.

Citizen Common Sense knew this, and therefore it was not wonderful that he should attempt to soften his lot, by something from his pen, calculated at once to flatter their vanity and further their execrable views. Thomas had long railed against the baseness of courtiers, but when the moment of trial came, he was found as base as the basest. The high-minded republican Paine, who had set Lords and Kings at defiance, was glad to bend the knee before a vile, low-bred, French pettifogger. He descended to make use of the very phrases that the new tyrants had introduced. The Goddess was called *Reason*,

---

[3] She was guillotined soon after.
[4] The *constitutional* clergy means the *new clergy*, the *clergy of the revolution, the apostates.*

the church which was profaned by her worship was called the *Temple of Reason*, and the inscription on the banners carried at the festival was "*The Age of Reason*" (Le Siècle de la Raison), the very title of Tom's book. Base adulation! adulation not to be excused even by the situation in which he was. The old French clergy, with the daggers at their breast, scorned to purchase life at such a price.

I would by no means be understood as believing that Paine's book was a desertion of his principles; for, as before observed, he had been corrupted years before. It is the disgraceful motive for publishing his creed that I am exposing. That it was done to make his court to the tyrants of the day, cannot be doubted; for in all his former works, if he has occasion to speak of the Christian religion, he does it in decent, if not respectful language. In his Rights of Man, for instance, he extols toleration, and observes, that *all religions are good*; but as soon as he had got into his new-fashioned study, a dungeon, he discovered that *they were all bad*, or at least the Christian religion, and it was of the divers denominations of that religion that he before *pretended* to speak.[6] When he said that all religions were good, he was an abominable hypocrite, or he is one now, when he tells us that the Christian religion is a very bad one. Either he disguised his sentiments to deceive the English, or he has since done so to deceive *Danton* and *Robespierre*. Tom knows the value of a character for consistency too well to run the risk of losing it unless upon a pressing emergency: but, the guillotine was yet red with the blood of his comrades, and he well knew that there was but this one way of keeping his own corrupted streams within his veins.

It will be said, by Tom's deistical Friends, that the *Second Part* of the Age of Reason was written after his releasement, and at a time when he was in no danger. Very true; but the die was cast; the *First Part* was out, and there was no recalling it. He had openly attacked both heaven and earth; he could do no more. One essay at blasphemy was as good as a thousand for establishing his new pretensions to infamy; but Thomas had now something else to attend to besides his reputation; I mean his belly. The usual means of subsistence had failed: he was no longer *a great* Representative of a *great* and *free* people. The handful of assignats he received daily were gone to some more staunch patriot, and the old Rights of Man was left to dine where he could. As to political drugs[,] Thomas's were grown out of vogue in France as much as they now are in this country: his constitution was declared to be the most stupid performance that ever issued from a sick brain, and its author fell into discredit as rapidly as he had risen to fame.⁵ Among thousands of others, he experienced the sudden change in the opinions of the volatile Parisians: from being a sort of demi-god he was become the most degraded thing in nature, a poor, half-starved despised pretender to renown. Besides, the constitution that was now coming into play, with a council of youngers and a council of elders and five kings, elected by *people of some property*, or at least, some *qualification*, was what Tom never could defend with his right of universal suffrage and continual insurrection, and, for once, he had the prudence to hold his tongue.[7]

Tom's fate in France was nearly what it had been in America; when it was no longer necessary to employ him he sunk into neglect. Happy if he could have ceased eating when his insurrection talents became useless; but as he could not, he must continue to write, and as he was in a country where he was permitted to revile none but the Almighty, the Almighty he reviled. The present of poison he has sent to his "fellow citizens" of America, is not therefore, so much the work of choice as of necessity. The Second Part of the Age of Reason he wrote for a living and the First part he wrote for his life.

Those who prefer a few years of life to every thing else, may find an excuse for this degraded man: it is impossible for any of us to say how we should act at the foot of the guillotine. But, what shall be said to those, who, pressed by neither danger nor want, make uncommon exertions to spread his infamous performance among the ignorant part of their countrymen, and thereby sow in their minds the seeds of vice[,] inquietude, and despair? Again; deists may find some apology for doing this; but who will dare to become the apologist of those book-sellers, who, professors of the Christian faith, throw out this bait of blasphemy to catch unwary comers, and, smiling at their simplicity, pocket the dirty pence. Such men (and they are but too numerous) are like the Hollander on the coast of Japan, who, to outstrip others in trade with the natives, tramples on the cross of his Saviour.⁶

---

⁵ *Insurrection, revolution, constitution,* a knowledge in all these seems to be a necessary qualification in a professor of the *Rights of Man.* Tom Paine understood the first perfectly well, he had a smattering of the second, but as to the third he was, and, if alive is, totally ignorant.

⁶ I know a printer and book-seller who has taken, for his sign, the picture of the blasphemer Paine. This undoubtedly is to inform the *amateurs* of insurrection and infidelity that they may be supplied within. It is no more than fair to impute this intention to him who hangs out such a sign. When *Caterfelto* placed the picture of the Devil over his door, it was to inform people that hell was to be seen in the house.

[Cobbett on Transatlantic Radicals]

Emigrated Patriots.[8]—It has been, I believe, about ten thousand times averred, that the *emigrated patriots*, particularly those who come from any part of the British dominions, are the cause of a very great portion of the happiness and honour of America. Among thousands of instances, the following may be mentioned.

HANCOCK was a republican Briton; he fled from England hither for *liberty*, and he *counterfeited Bank notes.*

HARPER was a burning patriot of the same stamp. When war was expected between this country and his, he invented a machine for destroying his countrymen; it was not wanted—and he *counterfeited the current coin.*

CALLENDER fled from Scotland for libelling the Government, the King and his family. He says Mr. *Jefferson* encouraged him to republish his libels here—and *he has called the Congress thieves.*

DOCTOR REYNOLDS was a United Irishman. He fled hither *for repose.* He assisted at the hanging of King George in effigy, on board the ship in which he came passenger—*and he had assisted in a most base attempt to vilify the character of the American Secretary of State.*

MATTHEW LYON came from Ireland. He not long ago drank "Success to the *United Irishmen,*" then in open rebellion against their King—*and he spit in the face of an American Member of Congress.*

If the public papers and the arts of land-jobbers have invited traitors to the country, the people have, on their arrival, uniformly treated them with every mark of abhorrence; and it is a well-known truth, that, of the vast horde who have fled hither since the beginning of the French revolution, not one has met with confidence or encouragement.

Reynolds, the seditious United Irishman, who was obliged to fly from Ireland to save his neck, now stands prosecuted for a libel on the American Secretary of State. Go where he will, still he must be a malecontent. He is, however, now reduced so low, that no one will associate with him, except he be of the very dregs of the mob. He called himself Doctor for some time; but the title has been laid aside, as of no use. This wretch, in his passage to America, guillotined the king in effigy.

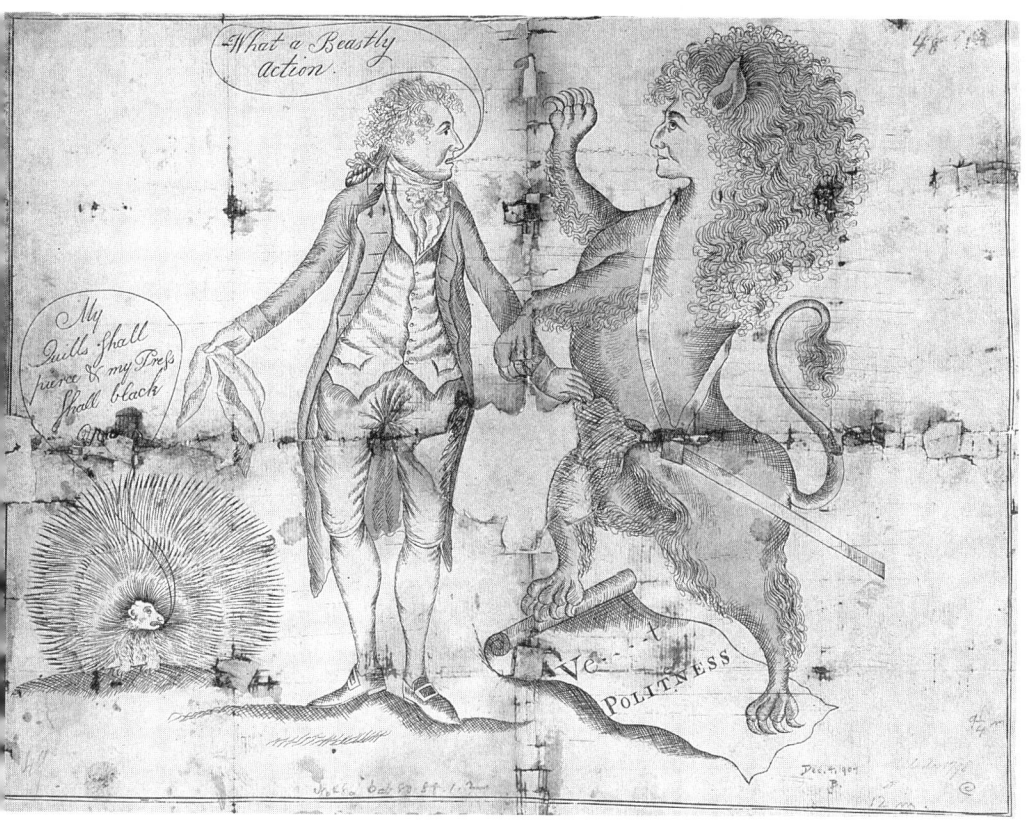

What a Beastly Action. In February 1798, Matthew Lyon, the Irish-American Republican Congressman from Vermont, responded to an insult from Federalist Roger Griswold by spitting in Griswold's face; a few days later, they came to blows in the House of Representatives. In this cartoon, Griswold confronts the "Spitting Lyon," while Peter Porcupine prepares his quills before going to press. Cobbett repeatedly reminded his readers that Lyon had brought Congress into disrepute, and he used the incident to attack Irish-American radicalism in particular and republican manners in general. (Courtesy of the Boston Public Library, Print Department.)

Archibald Hamilton Rowan[9] makes spruce beer, and drives it about for sale in a wheelbarrow. He lives in the borough of Wilmington.

Daniel Isaac Eaton, of hog's-wash memory, was quite bold on his first arrival.[10] He advertised pamphlets for sale by "Daniel Isaac Eaton, *six times tried for sedition*;" but the *Alien law* soon made him withdraw both his advertisement and himself from the notice of the public. He some time ago lived in a log-hut over the Schuylkill, where he cohabited with an Indian squaw. The proprietor of the hut, finding what gentry he had got for tenants, turned them out bag and baggage. I happened to be going out on a shooting party, when the miscreant and his yellow hided frow were coming into Camp-town, trapsing through the dirt. "And is that," I thought, "the PRINTER TO HIS MAJESTY, THE PEOPLE!"—He has brought his *hogs* to a fine market!

Citizen Lee first attempted a magazine, then a book, and then he tried what could be got by travelling; and he is, at last, comfortably lodged in *New-York jail*.[11]

[Cobbett on Thomas Muir]

"*Muir* has lately written a letter to the French Directory from Cadiz, where he is still detained by the wounds he received in the engagement that took place between the Spanish frigate, on board of which he was, and an English ship. He *has lost an eye*, and one side of his face *is totally disfigured*. In other respects he is out of danger, and will soon set out for Paris."[12]

Soon set out for Paris! Yes, that is the traitor's rendezvous; the assassin's general home. If I remember well, this miscreant Muir, on his trial, pretended that he disapproved of the French principles, and that he was even persecuted at Paris. How comes the villain now to write to the Directory? Would he write to persons by whom he was disliked, and amongst whom he met with persecution, to inform them that he was about to take refuge under their wings?

The rascal has lost one eye. So far so good; but he should have lost two. However, to be continually tormented with the sight of his "*totally disfigured*" visage may, for aught I know, be a greater punishment than blindness itself; and if so, I am glad he has got one eye left.

He was a fine rosy-gilled fellow, when he stood, like an impudent villain as he was, and dared the Court of Session in Scotland. He has now got the marks of liberty and equality: an empty purse, lank sides, and a mutilated face. A thousand blessings on the ball that caused his wounds! May such never be wanting while there is a Jacobin traitor on earth!

[Cobbett on Noah Webster]

The power of a rooted prejudice is incredibly great. This Webster is, in the common concerns of life, a man of a good sound understanding; on certain subjects he has shown that he possesses considerable talents; but the moment the name of Great Britain is mentioned, he seems to lose his reason; this hated name is to him what water is to one bitten by a mad dog. The wretch was a Whig of the revolution; he flattered himself with the hope of seeing Britain ruined for ever, and America reign in her stead. He finds himself grossly deceived, and his disappointment and mortification has increased his hatred against Great Britain.[13]

The more I see of NOAH's conduct at this critical juncture, the more I am convinced that he is a tool in the service of sans-culottism. He cries aloud sometimes against the French; but, he takes good care to endeavour to *damp the spirit of the country*, to espouse every measure of *delay*, to sow the seeds of discord, by reviving that old term of reproach *Tory*, and to produce a breach, if possible, with Great Britain, by abusing her government, reviling her maritime commanders, and calling her king *"little better than an idiot."*—What can France desire more, in the most zealous and costly of her partizans? An *undisguised* tool cannot serve her half so effectually. Few persons, except those who are totally devoted to France, will listen to BACHE or GREENLEAF;[14] whereas NOAH may, and does, obtain a hearing, and makes many *converts* to the cause. In the manufactory of Sans Culottes, NOAH is the first artizan; he takes them in the rough material and shapens them to the hand of BACHE, GREENLEAF, &c. who finish them off, and send them into the world fit for service.

This poor creature ["that *pestilential* writer, Noah Webster, jun. '*Esq.*'"], who had he been content to move in that sphere for which alone Nature intended him, would, by this time, have been a very tolerable teacher, and would have gained an honest and reputable livelihood, has, by his vanity and presumption, rendered himself, successively, an object of indignation and contempt, ridicule and pity. From the collision of two such bodies as [Benjamin] Rush and Webster, one might naturally expect something strongly expressive of emptiness; and accordingly a farcical anecdote of their first meeting in Philadelphia, where Webster had just been appointed a teacher in the Episcopal Academy, is worth relating.

SCENE THE STREET
Enter Rush and Webster

Rush.—How do you do, my dear friend? I congratulate you on your arrival in Philadelphia.

Webster.—You may, if you please, Sir, congratulate Philadelphia on the occasion!!!——(*They embrace.*)

[Cobbett on Benjamin Rush]

The loathsome subject now before me, is not taken up from choice, but from a sense of duty.[15] I am actuated by neither malice nor revenge; but, in holding up, in their true light, the *Rushes*, the *Hopkinsons*, the *Meases*,[16] and the rest of the tribe, I look upon myself as acting in the capacity of a public executioner, who, while he performs the dreadful behests of justice, secretly bewails the ignominious fate of the sufferer. . . .

Had Rush's pleaders . . . not, in numerous instances, gone out of their way to extol the *family* and *character* of their client, and to traduce and vilify mine; had they not held him up as an "*Hippocrates*" and a "*saving angel*," while they represented me as a "*wretch cast up from the very dregs and slime of the community, that ought to have rotted in obscurity*;" had they not thus insolently (and I may add foolishly) provoked an inquiry, the family and character of Rush would have remained, with me, objects of as perfect insignificance as the poverty-bred plant, the name of which he bears, and the worthlessness of which is proverbial.

No herald, reader, proclaimed the birth of the Pennsylvanian "*Hippocrates.*" The "*saving angel*" was born (and, I believe, in the usual way) in the city of Philadelphia. His father, honest John, was, I am sorry to say it, of English extraction, and was, by calling, a Blacksmith. . . .

Rush is remarkable for insinuating manners, and for that smoothness and softness of tongue, which the mock quality call *politeness*, but which the profane vulgar call *blarny*. To see and hear him, you would think he was all friendship and humanity. He shakes hands with all he meets; every one is his *dear friend*, all the people his *dear fellow-citizens*, and all the creation his *dear fellow-creatures*. The lamp of his philanthropy is constantly burning, and it burns with equal brightness, whether whites, yellows, or blacks are the objects of his affection. . . .

Some persons, however, notwithstanding this pleasing talent in the Doctor, have ventured to call his *sincerity* in question. . . . As to the Doctor's *mildness* and *candour*, so boldly insisted on by his pleaders[,] . . . a few facts, fresh in the memory of every Philadelphian, will afford a most satisfactory illustration.

Rush called *Doctor Wistar* an *assassin*, because Wistar denied the virtue of his grand specific, the *mercurial purges*. I have this fact from *Doctor Glentworth*, who, though a native Philadelphian, and a staunch republican, is a very candid, honest, and brave man. Doctor Glentworth also told me (and he will tell the same to any one), that Rush attended him in the yellow fever of 1793; that he bled him till he was extremely weak, and ordered *several other bleedings*, which Glentworth's knowledge made him omit, without, however, telling Rush of the omission; that he came one day, and finding his patient sitting up in the bed, ran to him, squeezed his hand, called him his "*dear* Glentworth," and congratulated him on the salutary effects of his bleeding system; "But," said he, "my *dear* friend, you must lose a little MORE BLOOD."—"Lose *more blood!*" replied Glentworth, "when I am so faint I can hardly support myself."—Upon this, Rush started from the bed-side, caught up his hat, called his "*dear* friend" an *assassin*, told him he was leagued with Wistar to ruin his reputation, and ran down stairs bawling out, "You're a dead man! you're a dead man! you'll be buried before to-morrow night."

There was an instance of *mildness, candour* and *humanity!* Doctor Glentworth did, however, disappoint him. He recovered his health, without losing more blood, and lived to laugh very heartily at the charitable predictions of the *Pennsylvanian* "Hippocrates."

Rush, in his Account of the Yellow Fever of 1793, accuses *Doctors Kuhn, Stevens*, and others, of having "*slain more than the sword*," merely because they rejected his practice. Nor does he, when speaking of his opponents, confine his charges to their *practice*; but, in the excess of his *mildness* and *candour*, attacks their *motives*. He says, that "it requires an uncommon portion of charity, to ascribe their conduct to *humane and benevolent motives;*" which is, to say the least of it, a very broad insinuation, that they were actuated by motives both *selfish* and *cruel*. . . .

So intolerant was he, and yet is, towards those who would not, or will not, acknowledge the infallibility of his system of bleeding and mercurial purges, that he has, since 1793, refused to consult with any physician who has not been weak enough to adopt his practice. . . . Rush, in his Account of the Yellow Fever of 1793 attempts to justify his conduct in refusing to consult with any physician, except those of his own school, on the ground of the *disagreement in opinion*; but, what a senseless excuse! If the opinions of all physicians were settled, there would be no use in calling a consultation. In fact, this was no more than a miserable apology for the most insolent pretension to superiority ever set up by mortal man. . . .

A Bitter Pill for the Rushites

In the last Number of Porcupine's Gazette, I observed that it was somewhat singular (and it really was so) that, on the 14th of December [1799], on the same day, and in the very *same hour*, that a ruinous fine was imposed on me for endeavouring to put a stop to the practice of Rush, General Washington was expiring under the operation of *that very practice*. . . . I doubt not, that, in order to keep themselves in countenance, they [the Philadelphians] will deny that any other treatment would have saved the General. I dare say they will deny that he was not treated according to the practice of their "Hippocrates." But, whatever the silly Philadelphians may believe, or pretend to believe, on this subject, I beg that other people will observe, and remember it well, that General Washington was not only treated precisely according to the famous *System of Depletion*, but that *Doctor Dick*, one of the physicians, was *a pupil of Rush*.

[Cobbett on Thomas McKean]

His grandfather was an Irishman, who *emigrated* by the consent of his Majesty and *twelve good and true men*. He himself was born in this State, in Chester county, and was for some years an *hostler*. He was successively a Constable, a Sheriff, a Justice of the Peace, and a Pettyfogger: in which last capacity the revolutionists found him a man fit for their purposes. After having seen MARAT a Legislator, and DANTON a Minister of Justice in France, no one will be surprised that M'KEAN should have become a Congress-man, and Chief Justice of Pennsylvania, during the American revolution.[17] Of the character he exhibited in those times the reader may judge by the following extracts from "SMYTH'S TOUR in the United States."[18] SMYTH was an old English officer settled in Virginia, very much attached to the royal cause. He was driven from his home, taken prisoner, and confined *as a spy*, merely because the Congress feared the effect of his zeal and his talents. The cruelties he endured at Philadelphia are almost beyond imagination; and this brings us to his character of M'KEAN. In a letter, dated Dec. 17th, 1778, addressed to the Congress, after having described the savage treatment he and his fellow-prisoners had received, and the horrid situation in which they were when their dungeon was inspected by a Committee of Congress, he says, "At the same time I must do three of your members the justice to say, that they behaved with politeness, and appeared much shocked at our treatment: but the injurious, cruel measures of the persecuting, violent incendiary M'Kean, overpowered moderation and humanity." Thus has he ever been. It was he who was guilty of the legal murder committed on two Quakers, ROBERTS and CARLISLE: he has been a persecutor of this inoffensive sect from that day to this: he was the principal promoter of all the cruel laws and confiscations in Pennsylvania, and he *now lives in a confiscated house*. He was, in a word, the FOUQUIER TINVILLE of America.[19] His private character is infamous. He beats his wife, and she beats him. He ordered a wig to be imported for him by Mr. KID, refused to pay for it, was sued before the Mayor's Court; the dispute was referred to the Court of *Nisi Prius*; where (merely for want of the *original invoice*, which KID had lost) the Judge came off victorious! He is a notorious drunkard. The whole bar, one lawyer excepted, signed a memorial, stating, that so great a drunkard was he, that, *after dinner, person and property were not safe in Pennsylvania*. He has been horsewhipped in the City Tavern, and kicked in the street for his insolence to particular persons; and yet this degraded wretch is *Chief Justice of the State!*

Reader, comparisons are odious you know, and therefore don't you go to ask me what the people at Westminster would have thought, if they had seen Lord Mansfield[20] boozing and bawling in a public house along with thirty or forty of the rabble, headed by a foreign agent, at open enmity with the government. What suits very well in one country, does not suit at all in another; and therefore I beg you will not ask me any such sneering questions as this.

However, every one may speak for himself, and I will say, that if ever I should become a judge (of which I see no reason to despair), and should so far forget the dignity of my station as to become the companion of a herd of sottish malcontents, may all the world that moment forget what is due to me. May my family disown my sway; may my own rib rise up against my lawful authority; may she be the cursedest shrew that ever wielded a broomstick; may she belabour me *with the tongs*, cut me *over the eye*, rib-roast me, till I am obliged *to call in the neighbours* to shelter me from the effects of her wrath.

I *know* M'Kean, and I know that it is my duty, my bounded duty, to my subscribers in this State, to use all my feeble efforts to preserve them from the power of such a man. From private considerations, there is no man, who need care less about the issue of the election [for Governor of Pennsylvania, in 1799] than myself. It is out of M'Kean's power to hurt me. *I will never live six months under his sovereign sway.* As soon as he is safe in his saddle, I shall begin to look out for a horse. Nor will a migration of this sort give me a moment's uneasiness. It would be a durable source of satisfaction to me, that I had scorned to live amongst a set of beings, who could voluntarily and deliberately choose such a man to reign over them.

Will and Testament

Since I took up the calling that I now follow, I have received about forty threatening letters; some talk of fisticuffs, others of kicks, but far the greater part menace me with outright murder. Several friends (whom, by the by, I sincerely thank) have called to caution me against the lurking cut-throats; and it seems to be the persuasion of every one, that my brains are to be knocked out the first time I venture from home in the dark.

Under these terrific circumstances, it is impossible that death should not stare me in the face: I have therefore got myself into as good a state of preparation as my sinful profession will, I am afraid, admit of; and as to my worldly affairs, I have settled them in the following *Will*, which I publish, in order that my dear friends, the legatees, may, if they think themselves injured or neglected, have an opportunity of complaining before it is too late.

IN the name of Fun, Amen. I PETER PORCUPINE, pamphleteer and newsmonger, being (as yet) sound both in body and in mind, do, this fifteenth day of April, in the year of our Lord one thousand seven hundred and ninety-seven, make, declare, and publish this my LAST WILL AND TESTAMENT, in manner, form, and substance following, to wit;

IN PRIMIS, I leave my body to Doctor Michael Leib,[21] a member of the Legislature of Pennsylvania, to be by him dissected (if he knows how to do it) in presence of the Rump of the Democratic Society. In it they will find a heart that held them in abhorrence, that never palpitated at their threats, and that, to its last beat, bade them defiance. But my chief motive for making this bequest is, that my spirit may look down with contempt on their cannibal-like triumph over a breathless corpse.

Item, As I make no doubt that the abovesaid Dr. Leib (and some other Doctors that I could mention) would like very well to skin me, I request that they, or one of them, may do it, and that the said Leib's father may tan my skin; after which I desire my executors to have eight copies of my works complete, bound in it, one copy to be presented to the five Sultans of France; one to each of their Divans; one to the Governor of Pennsylvania; to Citizens Maddison, Giles, and Gallatin, one each; and the remaining one to the Democratic Society of Philadelphia, to be carefully preserved among their archives.[22]

Item, To the Mayor, Aldermen, and Councils of the city of Philadelphia, I bequeath all the sturdy young hucksters, who infest the market, and who, to maintain their bastards, tax the honest inhabitants many thousand pounds annually. I request them to take them into their worshipful keeping—to chasten their bodies for the good of their souls; and, moreover, to keep a sharp lookout after their gallants; and remind the latter of the old proverb, *Touch pot, touch penny*.

Item, To Thomas Jefferson, philosopher, I leave a curious Norway spider, with a hundred legs and nine pairs of eyes; likewise the first black cut-throat general he can catch hold of, to be flayed alive, in order to determine with more certainty the real cause of the dark colour of his skin: and should the said Thomas Jefferson survive Banneker the almanack-maker,[23] I request he will get the brains of said Philomath carefully dissected, to satisfy the world in what respect they differ from those of a white man.

Item, To the Philosophical Society of Philadelphia, I will and bequeath a correct copy of Thornton's Plan for abolishing the Use of the English Language, and for introducing in its stead a republican one, the representative characters of which bear a strong resemblance to pot-hooks and hangers; and for the discovery of which Plan, the said Society did, in the year 1793, grant to the said language-maker 500 dollars premium.—It is my earnest desire, that the copy of this valuable performance, which I hereby present, may be shown to all the travelling literati, as a proof of the ingenuity of the author, and of the wisdom of the Society.[24]

Item, To Dr. Benjamin Rush, I will and bequeath a copy of the Censor for January, 1797; but upon the express condition, that he does not in any wise or guise, either at the time of my death, or six months after, pretend to speak, write, or publish an eulogium on me, my calling or character, either literary, military, civil, or political.[25]

Item, To my dear fellow-labourer, Noah Webster, "gentleman-citizen," Esq. and newsman, I will and bequeath a prognosticating barometer of curious construction and great utility, by which, at a single glance, the said Noah will be able to discern the exact state that the public mind will be in the ensuing year, and will thereby be able to trim by degrees, and not expose himself to detection, as he now does by his sudden lee-shore tacks. I likewise bequeath to the said "gentleman-citizen," six Spanish milled dollars, to be expended on a new plate of his portrait at the head of his spelling-book, that which graces it at present being so ugly that it scares the children from their lessons; but this legacy is to be paid him only upon condition that he leave out the title of Squire, at the bottom of said picture, which is extremely odious in an American school-book, and must inevitably tend to corrupt the political principles of the republican babies that behold it. And I do most earnestly desire, exhort, and conjure the said Squire newsman to change the title of his paper, *The Minerva*, for that of *The Political Centaur*.

Item, To F. A. Muhlenburgh, Esq. Speaker of a late House of Representatives of the United States, I leave a most superbly finished statue of Janus.[26]

Item, To Tom the Tinker,[27] I leave a liberty-cap, a tri-coloured cockade, a wheelbarrow full of oysters, and a hogshead of grog: I also leave him three blank checks on the Bank of Pennsylvania, leaving to him the task of filling them up; requesting him, however, to be rather more merciful than he has shown himself heretofore.

Item, To the Governor of Pennsylvania, and to the late President and Cashier of the Bank of the said State,[28] as to joint legatees, I will and bequeath that good old proverb: *Honesty is the best policy*. And this legacy I have chosen for these worthy gentlemen, as the only thing about which I am sure they will never disagree.

Item, To Tench Coxe, of Philadelphia, citizen,[29] I will and bequeath a crown of hemlock, as a recompense for his attempt to throw an odium on the administration of General Washington; and I most positively enjoin on my executors, to see that the said crown be shaped exactly like that which this spindle-shanked legatee wore before General Howe, when he made his triumphal entry into Philadelphia.

Item, To Thomas Lord Bradford (otherwise called Goofy Tom), bookseller, printer, newsman, and member of the Philosophical Society of Philadelphia,[30] I will and bequeath a copy of the Peerage of Great Britain, in order that the said Lord Thomas may the more exactly ascertain what probability there is of his succeeding to the seat which his noble relation now fills in the House of Lords.

Item, To all and singular the authors in the United States, whether they write prose or verse, I will and bequeath a copy of my Life and Adventures; and I advise the said authors to study with particular care the fortieth and forty-first pages thereof; more especially, and above all things, I exhort and conjure them never *"to publish it together,"* though the bookseller should be a saint.[31]

Item, To Edmund Randolph, Esq. late Secretary of State, to Mr. J. A. [sic] Dallas, Secretary of the State of Pennsylvania, and to his Excellency Thomas Mifflin, Governor of the said unfortunate State, I will and bequeath, to each of them, a copy of the sixteenth paragraph of Fauchet's intercepted letter.[32]

Item, To Citizen J. Swanwick, Member of Congress, by the will and consent of the sovereign people, I leave bills of exchange on London to an enormous amount; they are all protested, indeed, but, if properly managed, may be turned to good account. I likewise bequeath to the said John, a small treatise by an Italian author, wherein the secret of pleasing the ladies is developed, and reduced to a mere mechanical operation, without the least dependence on the precarious aid of the passions: hoping that these instances of my liberality will produce, in the mind of the little legislator, effects quite different from those produced therein by the King of Great Britain's pension to his parents.[33]

Item, To the editors of the Boston Chronicle, the New-York Argus, and the Philadelphia Merchants' Advertiser, I will and bequeath one ounce of modesty and love of truth, to be equally divided between them. I should have been more liberal in this bequest, were I not well assured, that one ounce is more than they will ever make use of.

Item, To Franklin Bache, editor of the Aurora of Philadelphia, I will and bequeath a small bundle of French assignats, which I brought with me from the country of equality. If these should be too light in value for his pressing exigencies, I desire my executors, or any one of them, to bestow on him a second part to what he has lately received in Southwark; and as a further proof of my good will and affection, I request him to accept of a gag, and brand new pair of fetters, which if he should refuse, I will and bequeath him in lieu thereof—my malediction.[34]

Item, To my beloved countrymen, the people of Old England, I will and bequeath a copy of Dr. Priestley's Charity Sermon for the benefit of poor Emigrants; and to the said preaching philosopher himself, I bequeath a heart full of disappointment, grief, and despair.

Item, To the good people in France, who remain attached to their sovereign, particularly to those among whom I was hospitably received, I bequeath each a good strong dagger; hoping, most sincerely, that they may yet find courage enough to carry them to the hearts of their abominable tyrants.

Item, To Citizen Munro,[35] I will and bequeath my chamber looking-glass. It is a plain but exceeding true mirror: in it he will see the exact likeness of a traitor, who has bartered the honour and interest of his country to a perfidious and savage enemy.

Item, To the republican Britons, who have fled from the hands of justice in their own country, and who are a scandal, a nuisance, and a disgrace to this, I bequeath hunger and nakedness, scorn and reproach; and I do hereby positively enjoin on my executors to contribute five hundred dollars toward the erection of gallowses and gibbets, for the accommodation of the said imported patriots,

A Political Sinner.

A Political Sinner. As a leading Republican politician, Albert Gallatin was one of Cobbett's most familiar and frequent targets, and thus earned a place among Cobbett's "beneficiaries" in the "Will and Testament." This cartoon first appeared in Cobbett's *Political Censor*, April 1796; the guillotine in the background may be a visual pun on Gallatin. The nickname "A Political Sinner" came from Gallatin's support for the radical Pittsburgh Resolutions against the whiskey exercise in 1791; three years later, Gallatin wrote that his action in Pittsburgh was his "only political sin." Cobbett put the words "stop de wheels of government" into Gallatin's mouth in a report on Gallatin's opposition to Jay's Treaty in 1796. See *Porcupine's Works*, vol. 3, pp. 253–56. (Courtesy of the Rare Books and Manuscripts Division, the New York Public Library, Astor, Lenox, and Tilden Foundations.)

when the legislators of this unhappy State shall have the wisdom to countenance such useful establishments.

Item, My friend, J. T. Callender, the runaway from Scotland, is, of course, a partaker in the last-mentioned legacy; but, as a particular mark of my attention, I will and bequeath him twenty feet of pine-plank, which I request shall be made into a pillory, to be kept for his particular use, till a gibbet can be prepared.

Item, To Tom Paine, the author of Common Sense, Rights of Man, Age of Reason, and a Letter to General Washington, I bequeath a strong hempen collar, as the only legacy I can think of that is worthy of him, as well as best adapted to render his death in some measure as infamous as his life: and I do hereby direct and order my executors to send it to him by the first safe conveyance, with my compliments, and request that he would make use of it without delay, that the national razor may not be disgraced by the head of such a monster.

Item, To the gaunt outlandish orator, vulgarly called the Political Sinner,[36] who, in the just order of things, follows next after the last-mentioned legatee, I bequeath the honour of partaking in his catastrophe; that, in their deaths, as well as in their lives, all the world may exclaim, "*See how rogues hang together!*"

Item, To all and singular the good people of these States, I leave peace, union, abundance, happiness, untarnished honour, and an unconquerable everlasting hatred to the French revolutionists and their destructive abominable principles.

Item, To each of my subscribers I leave a quill, hoping that in their hands it may become a sword against every thing that is hostile to the government and independence of their country.

Lastly, To my three brothers, Paul, Simon, and Dick, I leave my whole estate, as well real as personal (first paying the foregoing legacies), to be equally divided between them, share and share alike. And I do hereby make and constitute my three brothers the executors of this my Last Will; to see the same performed, according to its true intent and meaning, as far as in their power lies.   P. PORCUPINE.

Witnesses present,
Philo Fun.
Jack Jocus

[8]

Detection of a Conspiracy

THIS PAMPHLET WAS PUBLISHED IN MAY 1798, AGAINST THE background of the Quasi-War with France and the debates in Congress over the Alien and Sedition Bills. In this atmosphere, conspiracy theories ran wild. People like Jedidiah Morse and Dr. Robison argued that the French Revolution and the slave rising in San Domingo had been brought about by the Society of the Illuminati, a supposedly worldwide secret organization dedicated to the destruction of all religious establishments and existing governments. And Cobbett himself had long believed that a kind of Jacobin International was attempting to subvert the United States from within and deliver the country to France. Central to this conspiracy, he believed, were the "restless rebellious tribe" of United Irishmen; "Detection of a Conspiracy" was designed to expose their activities and eradicate their influence.

After reading the constitution of the American Society of United Irishmen, Cobbett believed that he had found proof of an Irish-inspired plot to bring down the American government. He attempted to decode the document to bring out its hidden meaning. First, he noted that the society was open to all democrats, whether Irish or not, and was dedicated to promoting the principles of liberty and equality in all countries, including the United States itself. Under the guise of seeking "liberty" for Ireland, Cobbett contended, the society sought to impose its ideology on America. Second, this interpretation appeared to be strengthened by the society's emphasis on secrecy—a sure sign, in Cobbett's view, that its members were working in devious ways to realize dangerous intentions. Third, the nature of these intentions was given away, according to Cobbett, by the document's discussion of the need to facilitate communication among members during "cases of urgency." Such cases, he argued, could have nothing to do with getting the British government out of Ireland. In the American context, he concluded, "cases of urgency" could only mean one thing—a French invasion, which would be the signal for an internal insurrection against the government of the United States.

From a modern perspective, Cobbett's arguments appear forced and strained, with a strong streak of paranoia. But in the circumstances of 1798, with the threat of war, the fear of a French invasion, and the existence of a pro-French faction in the United States, his conspiracy theory could appear alarmingly accurate. And there is little doubt that in the summer of that year, as the war fever intensified, Cobbett caught the mood of much of the country.

DETECTION OF A CONSPIRACY, FORMED BY THE UNITED IRISHMEN, WITH THE EVIDENT INTENTION

Of Aiding the Tyrants of France

IN SUBVERTING THE GOVERNMENT OF THE UNITED STATES OF AMERICA.

BY PETER PORCUPINE.

PHILADELPHIA:

PUBLISHED BY WILLIAM COBBETT.

May 6, 1798.

I HAVE LONG THOUGHT, THAT THE FRENCH HAVE FORMED A REGULAR plan for organizing an active and effective force within these States; and I am persuaded, that after what I am now going to lay before the public shall have been read with attention, few people will be so blind as not to perceive, that my opinion was well founded. The Parisian Propagande have, in every country that they wished to ruin, found villains in abundance ready to engage in their service. The ambitious they have allured by the prospect of power, and the needy by that of pillage. In America there is less ambition and less poverty than in most other countries, and therefore, though some traitors have been found amongst them, the *natives* were not much to be relied on, in the prosecution of any design, evidently hostile to the interests and honour of their country. They might be deceived, they might be duped to lend their aid indirectly to some such design; but no man, who is led on in the dark, can be safely confided in; because, at the first dawn of light, it is a thousand to one but he makes his retreat.

The French seem to have been fully aware of this. Indeed, they have learnt this truth from the mortifying defection of the AMERICAN DEMOCRATIC SOCIETIES. There were many well-meaning men, who became members of these seditious meetings from ignorance, and who discovered no inconsiderable zeal in propagating their principles; but, the bandage was torn from their eyes and no sooner did they perceive the real views of DALLAS[1] and the other leaders, than they turned their backs on them with detestation.

This lesson induced the French to exert their *"diplomatic skill"* in choosing instruments more fit for their purpose. Ignorance when allied with honesty was no tool for them to work with. Real, sincere, villainy, then without property, without principles, without country and without character; dark and desperate, unnatural and bloodythirsty ruffians; these were what they wanted; and where could they have sought them with such certainty of success, as amongst that restless rebellious tribe, the emigrated UNITED IRISHMEN? The wretches known by this name, had escaped from their country to avoid punishment justly due to their multitude of crimes. *Here* they expected to find an organized system of perpetual anarchy: the needy anticipated a life of laziness and plunder, the ambitious thought to grasp on power already moulded to their hands; they all counted upon a state of things, congenial to their own wicked dispositions.

Happily for us, they were deceived. They found a government, which, if too weak (like their own) to punish conspirators according to their deserts, was yet too sturdy to fall prostrate at their feet. They found a government protected from their fraternizing clutches; they saw their hopes of political consequence vanish like a dream; and, instead of caresses, condolence and applause, from the people, they meet with the same virtuous abhorrence that had followed them from the shores of their native land.

Thus disappointed, thus mortified, thus humbled and disgraced, it was not to be wondered at, that they conceived a hatred against America equal to that which they entertained against their own country, and it is still less to be wondered at, that they enrolled themselves in the treacherous service of France.

The first I heard of the existence of a Society of United Irishmen *here*, was by a printed paper (a copy of which the reader will see by-and-bye dated the 18th December last, and signed Js. REYNOLDS.[2] It was envelloped in a piece of paper addressed to me, and was left by an unknown hand, at the house of a person in Market-street. It was on the 16th of January that I received this paper, and in about three weeks afterwards, the *plan* of the conspiracy was conveyed to me through the same channel.

This *plan*, which is called a *constitution*, is printed in a small octavo pamphlet, bearing date the 8th of August last. The imprint imports, that it was printed at Philadelphia, for the society; but the *printer's name* is very cautiously omitted. The person who enclosed me the pamphlet, has, indeed, written in the margin the name of a printer, who, from the villainous publications which have come from his press, I make no doubt was really the man; but this evidence is too weak for me to proceed upon in publishing his name to the world, as guilty of an offence, which amount to treason against the United States.— Here follows the *plum* of the *conspiracy*.

DECLARATION and CONSTITUTION *of the* AMERICAN SOCIETY *of* UNITED IRISHMEN.—Philadelphia; printed for the Society, August 8, 1797.

Declaration.

Six hundred years have past, since division and fraud reduced Ireland to colonial subserviency; the division of her people have ever since subjected them to the lash and to the goad of a foreign tyranny; a tyranny more odious than Asiatic despotism.

In our day and generation we have seen and we have felt; it is not necessary, there is not now time cooly to count over the long black catalogue of her baleful wrongs; there is not now time to argue and complain. THIS IS THE TIME TO ACT; *to act with energy we must act with unison: Irishmen are united at home, we will not be disunited abroad.*

Our love for freedom has not been lessened by what we have experienced of its effects, or for Ireland by our distance. Under the sacred influence of devotion to the Union, EQUALITY AND LIBERTY *of* ALL *men, we gladly embrace the solemn ties by which we wish to be bound to one another, and hereby form ourselves into an association,*

UNDER THE NAME OF
THE AMERICAN SOCIETY
OF
UNITED IRISHMEN,
ADOPTING THE FOLLOWING
CONSTITUTION.

The declared intention of procuring *"equality and liberty to* ALL *men,"* is a clear proof Ireland alone was not in their view. But, as we go on, we shall perceive that neither that country nor its concerns are at all included in the objects of these people. The words *Ireland, Irishmen,* &c. are mere substitutes for other words, like the cant of the pickpockets, according to which a *hog* means a *shilling*, a *pig* means a *sixpence*, and so on. This will clearly appear from the articles and TEST of the precious constitution.

Section I. That ALL SUCH PERSONS and such only, shall be eligible to this Society of United Irishmen, as shall have suffered in the cause of freedom, or who, by their zeal for THE RIGHTS OF MANKIND, shall have rendered themselves distinguished and worthy of attachment and trust.

Thus, you see, it is not IRISHMEN alone, who are eligible to this Society; but ALL SUCH PERSONS as shall, according to their cant, have *suffered in the cause of freedom,* or have shown their zeal for *the rights of mankind!!* In other words, every scoundrel of whatever nation, is eligible, provided he has been manacled or transported, or has rendered himself worthy of the gibbet, for some attempt at rebellion or some act of treason, no matter under what government or on what occasion; or, provided his seditious principles are so well known and established as to leave no room to doubt of his attachment to the cause. *Americans,* then, and *Britons,* and *Frenchmen,* and men of every country being eligible to the Society, can any one be silly enough to suppose, that the conspiracy had *Ireland* in view? What had any of these people to do with *Ireland?* But, on the absurdity of this we shall have time to remark by-and-by. Indeed, the TEST itself gives the lie to this cant about Ireland. All that is necessary to remark on this section, is, *that it provides for the admission of every discontented, factious man in the United States*; and that the latter part of it is no more than a copy of the qualification clause of the Jacobin Club at Paris, except that the latter required positive proof from every new member of his having *actually committed some crime deserving the halter*, while our liberal conspirators, thinking it unjust to exclude a villain merely because he has failed of success, are willing, in some cases, to admit the *intention* as equal in merit to the deed.

Section 2. That no person shall be proposed for admittance but by a member in his place.

Section 3. That no proposition for the admittance of a member shall be received, unless it be seconded by another member present, and that it shall likewise be necessary for the proposer and seconder, to vouch for the moral character and CIVISM of the person proposed; in defect of which, no election shall take place.

Section 4. Members shall have the privilege of proposing, or seconding the proposal of candidates, in any Section, as well as that to which they belong.

Section 5. A candidate proposed agreeable to the 2d, 3d, and 4th elections, shall not be ballotted for, until the next meeting after that in which he has been proposed, unless known to two-thirds of the members present, (two black beans to reject without a reason, and one with reasons), but, upon his election, he shall be immediately admitted, under the following forms:—

Section 6. Before a person elected shall be considered a member, the President shall put to him the following questions; an affirmative to the 1st, 5th and 6th, and a negative answer to the 2d, 3d, and 4th, shall be indispensable to admission as such:

Section 7. I. Do you believe a free form of government, and uncontrouled opinion on all subjects, to be the common rights of all the human species?

II. Do you think the people of Ireland are in possession of these rights?

III. Do you think the government of Great Britain ever was, or is now disposed, to acknowledge, or assent, to the freedom of Ireland?

IV. Do you think Great Britain ought, of right, to govern Ireland?

V. Are you willing to do all that in you lies to promote the emancipation of Ireland, and the establishment of a republican form of government there?[3]

VI. Are you willing to bind yourself, by a solemn *obligation*, to the principles you have acknowledged?

Section 8. That upon the candidate answering these questions, as required by the sixth section, the following shall be admitted as a test, all present standing:

TEST.

I. A. B. *in the presence of the* SUPREME BEING *do most solemnly swear, that I will, to the utmost of my power, promote the emancipation of Ireland from the tyranny of the British Government:—That I will use the like endeavours for increasing, and perpetuating, the warmest affection among all religious denominations of men, and for the attainment of* LIBERTY, *and* EQUALITY TO MANKIND, IN WHATEVER NATION I MAY RESIDE. *Moreover, I do swear, that I will, as far as in me lies, promote the interest of this, and every other Society of United Irishmen, and of each of its members—and that I will never, from fear of punishment, or hope or reward, divulge any of its* SECRETS *given to me as such.*

Section 9. That the TEST of this Society, the INTENTION of this INSTITUTION, (in all other respects than as a *social body*, attached to freedom,) be considered as SECRET AND INVIOLABLE in all cases, but between members, and in the body of the Society.

Section 10. That nevertheless, a member of the Society shall not be considered as divulging its secrets, who shall propound to persons disposed to become members, the sense of the six propositions which *precede the test.*

Here we see that Ireland is almost dropped out of sight. It is just mentioned in order to introduce the British government; but the initiated is to swear, that he will do the utmost of his power for the attainment of LIBERTY and EQUALITY, to MANKIND; and, these efforts does he swear to make, IN WHATEVER NATION HE MAY RESIDE! Ireland, therefore, if not totally dismissed by the TEST, is no more contemplated by it than America is, taking the words in their literal sense: and we shall see in the sequel, that this blessed liberty and equality is intended for America alone.

The criminality of the purpose and end of the combination is most amply proved by the section that immediately follows the TEST.— "The TEST of this society and the INTENTION of the institution shall be kept SECRET AND INVIOLABLE."—The members may tell the world that it is a "*social body*, attached to freedom;" that is, they may give out that its principles are friendly to general liberty; they may represent it as one of those collections of individuals that men of sense usually laugh at, but they must not say a word about the INTENTION of the institution, nor must they discover the nature of the OATH.

Now, if nothing more were meant than an association against *the government of Great Britain*, which they must well know would excite contempt and ridicule, why all this *secrecy?* Why conceal the nature of the oath? and, particularly, why conceal the *intention* of the institution?

By the 9th Section we see, that the discoveries, made even to those who offer themselves as members, are to extend no further than "the sense of the six propositions *preceding* the TEST." The Test itself they are to know nothing of, 'till they have gone too far to retreat, and then they are bound not to divulge what they have learnt. First the initiated member swears, that he "will never, from *fear of punishment*, or *hope of reward*, divulge any of the *secrets*, given to him as such?" and then the INTENTION of the institution is immediately given to him as one of those *inviolable secrets!* If there were nothing wicked, nothing highly criminal, nothing dark and traiterous in this INTENTION, why is the discovery of it thus guarded against? Men never *"fear punishment"* for concealing what is not criminal. Indeed, this TEST stamps the character of the combination: a Test of secrecy, as to the *motives* of the members, is essential to a conspiracy; and it is that which distinguishes this society from "*a social body*," which is the character they wish to appear under in the eyes of the world.

Here again we perceive the plan to be little more than a copy of that of the Jacobin club in France. The *Christian Religion* is discarded, and the initiated wretch swears by the "SUPREME BEING." Next *Liberty and Equality to mankind* is the object, *in whatever country they may reside;* the world are to be told, that the society is merely a *social body;* but its real INTENTION is to be kept a secret under the most solemn injunctions. Thus proceeded the Jacobins at Paris, that *social body* who overturned the government of France. PLAYFAIR[4] says, they had *two creeds*, one to *amuse the public*, and another that, for [a] long time, never was known but to the members.

The oath of secrecy necessarily forbids a communication of one of the pamphlets containing the TEST, &c. [T]he person who made this communication to me must, therefore, have broken his oath, or must have purloined the pamphlet. I rather think the former; because had he not thus committed himself; were it not that he was ashamed to own himself one of the conspirators, and at the same time, incurred the odium of having betrayed his companions, it is pretty clear that possessing an inclination to make the discovery he would long ago have come forward as the instrument of an effectual prosecution. He tells me in a note which covered one of the papers, that he has *found a clue* to all their secrets, and, as I before observed, he writes down the name of the printer in the margin. This latter circumstance was enough; for, if the printing could be proved, or if it can be proved now, the printer at least, can be punished as a conspirator, and this may lead to a discovery of his employers.

Having thus remarked on the design of the conspirators, I should now come to the means provided for *insuring its success*, by which the reader will at least see the extent of the plan, and will be fully convinced that its real object is the destruction of the American Government. . . .

Now, leaving the mere formalities and other trifling things aside, let us take th[eir] plan and look at it in its substance. . . .

"*The General* EXECUTIVE *Committee*" (which, I have not the least doubt, is now sitting in Philadelphia) keeps up a constant communication with the State-Committees, and from it, the whole Society, or rather *army*, receives "directions" when and how to act. It has returns made to it of the numbers enrolled in each State, of the names, residence, and occupation, of the persons enrolled; by this mean it is at all times informed of its strength, and of where that strength lies.

When it is necessary TO ACT, the General *Executive* Committee are to dispatch their orders to the State Committees; these to their sections, and these again (by their committee of *secrecy*) to their *sub-sections*. Here the orders reach the *active troops*, and that there may be no confusion in their movements, these *sub-sections* consist of only *eight* men each, all *living near one another*, and one of these eight is a sort of non-commission officer, who (to use the very words of the conspirators) is to "have the *charge* of the other seven, and is to WARN them IN CASES OF URGENCY"!!!

Now, I appeal to any man of common sense, whether this infernal combination can possibly have any other object in view than an insurrection against the government of America. What "*cases of urgency*" can arise *in this country*, what opportunity can offer itself *here*, for *overturning the British Government in Ireland?* Were the villains, indeed furnished with *wings*; could they like other birds of passage, assemble in a flock and take their flight to Ireland; then the ostensible motive of the association would have something like plausibility about it; but, as they are, this ostensible motive is a palpable absurdity, a mere trick which has been invented in order to inveigh ignorant persons to take the TEST, and, in case of detection, to avoid the punishment which the law awards to *traitors* and *spies*; or at least, to leave room for doubt and contention in the courts of justice; a bad chance being better than none, and ten years imprisonment better than death.

That this conspiracy is intended *to aid the cause of France*, it is hardly necessary to insist on; every one must perceive it at the first glance.— What can these ragged ruffians expect to do *alone*? How can they alone support their current expences, exclusive of "*cases of urgency*," of arms, ammunitions, &c. &c. By an attention to the financial part of their plan, you will perceive, that the money they collect from the members is barely sufficient to defray the charges which must necessarily be incurred for rooms to meet in. Who is to pay for printing their CONSTITUTIONS, their CERTIFICATES (which I hear is from an engraved copper plate); who is to pay for the time and travelling expences of all their Delegates from the Sections to the State Committee at Philadelphia; who is to pay a sum amounting to not less than *forty thousand dollars* annually? Who but those who boast of their "*Diplomatic Skill*," and of their "*powerful faction in this country*;" those who have long had in pay the leading *patriots* in Ireland, and who have constantly supported a hireling press in each of the principal Cities of America?

Next, observe that the closest intimacy exists between the sansculotte French, who are here, the most distinguished of the emigrated United Irishmen, and a base American printer, notoriously in the service of France.[5] Observe too, that NAPPER TANDY went from New York to France, and that the conspiracy, as appears by its date, was not formed, 'till *after we heard of his arrival at Paris*.[6]

The leaders in this conspiracy are the very same persons, who conducted that in Ireland. When a section of their deluded partizans, in that country, were taken unawares by the King's troops, no money but *French* was found upon them, and this in a retired part of the kingdom, where it was impossible these infatuated wretches could have come at it through any other channel than that of the despots of Paris and their wicked agents. And, if a conspiracy could be so effectually paid there, in a country at open war with France, with an *alien law*, vigorously enforced, how easy must it be for them to maintain a hired and regularly paid conspiracy here, when there is no check whatsoever to their machinations!

This diabolical plan was formed on the 8th of August last, immediately before the YELLOW FEVER commenced its ravages in this city; with this in his recollection the reader will form his opinion respecting the following, which is a copy of the *printed paper*, before mentioned.

American Society,
OF
UNITED IRISHMEN.

WHEN the Society of United Irishmen was formed here, men were found emulous of crouding to the Irish Standard, for the aspect of Ireland then, afforded hope that her wrongs would soon be redressed.—That view so consoling to humanity, has for a moment been obscured; but it is not honourable to desert a deserving friend in distress, it is not honourable to abandon a meritorious cause, which when prosperous we have sworn to support.

The society is happy to find, that there is still reason to think, the fire and the scourge, will not long be exercised over our brethren with impunity, that the tyrannical imprisonments, the rapes, the arsons, the tortures, and the military murders are about to be avenged, and, that a manly people, whom six hundred years slavery could not debase, are about to be restored to their rights.

We have cause to deplore the loss we have sustained by the disease which lately suspended our meetings; and, we are unwilling to ascribe the present neglect of attendance of some members, to unworthy motives—but, it is deemed a duty, to notify you, that those who in future absent themselves, cannot conformably to the 18th Article of the Constitution, be regarded as belonging to the association.

The next meeting will be held at 7 o'clock on the evening of the 21st instant, in the African School-room, Willing's-alley, which lies between Third, Fourth, Walnut, and Spruce-streets.

Signed by Order of the committee,
Js. REYNOLDS.

Philadelphia, December 18th, 1797.

This is the man, who began his canting letter, respecting his attack on Mr. Pickering, with declaring that he was come *here* in search of "REPOSE"!![7]—I will just remark further on this notice, that I would lay my life it was translated from the French.—"That view so consoling to humanity."—This is French in English words.—"a manly people whom six hundred years slavery could not debase, are about to be restored to their right."—A very awkward translation of French cant.

This notice, I would have the reader believe, I have not published without good proof of its being signed by REYNOLDS, the seeker of "REPOSE." His name is *written*, and the hand writing has not only been carefully compared with the signature to a letter of his, now in my possession; but has also been compared and verified before one of the judges in this city. All that is now wanted is, good proof of the person who *printed*, or who *authorized printing*, the plan of the conspiracy, which is called the CONSTITUTION, and if any American, *native or adopted*, is in possession of the means of producing such proof, and neglects to produce it, he is to all intents and purposes a TRAITOR.

I shall, now, briefly state, what I have lately gathered respecting the members of which the conspiracy now consists, and respecting the manner in which they are to ACT, and on what occasions. In the mean time, I would have THOSE, in whose power alone it is to counteract the baleful effects of this hellish combination, to recollect, that any ALIEN LAW, which extends only to ALIENS of a *nation committing hostilities on the United States*, will not reach the members of this affiliation.[8]

I am informed, by one of the persons who manage the affairs of the AFRICAN SCHOOL, that the United Irishmen have not assembled there, for some time past, and that the reason of this was, their number was become *too great* for so small a room. I am also well informed, that two *Englishmen* have been admitted into the Society (I dare say there are two hundred), and that they earnestly solicited *another Englishman* to join it. Their strength, at this time, in this city and twenty miles around, consists of above *fifteen hundred*; no contemptible number, if we consider how short the space is, since they began to enlist. A *section* has been formed at New-York, another at Baltimore, and another is either formed, or about to be formed, at Chambersburgh, in this state. Indeed, there is very little doubt, but we shall very soon receive satisfactory information of their being organized in every state, and in every principal city and town in the Union.

With respect to their calling their troops into *actual service*, it is clear that they would proceed in the same manner as the Jacobins in every other country have done. Conspirators are always cowards: besides this, they know too well their weakness to attempt an attack on the Government, unaided by any other party, and unprotected by a foreign power. Their whole business therefore, at present, is, to organize themselves; to enlist and number their troops, and to lie in wait for what they very properly call, "*cases of* URGENCY."

If the "*diplomatic skill*" of France had been exercised with such complete success as the tyrants of that wretched country supposed it was; if it had been found, upon trial, that she possessed a very numerous and formidable faction here entirely devoted to her orders, these "*cases of* URGENCY" might have arisen from internal commotions. This source now seems to be dried up. The dispatches from France[9] have robbed the "Sister Republic" of all her adherents, except the most abandoned and infamous miscreants amongst the Americans, her own sans-culottes, and the half-gibbeted democrats from Great Britain and Ireland. Nothing then, can give rise to one of those "*cases of* URGENCY" short of an invasion by France either from the Spanish territory, or from the sea; and, for an event of this kind the conspirators are looking for with hopes much more sanguine than [the] wandering seed of Abraham ever looked for the coming of the Messiah.

An invasion on the coast is a thing naturally to be expected, unless an alliance is formed with Great Britain: from Louisiana or the Floridas [it] is to be expected, whether such an alliance takes place or no. This, then, would be the "*case of* URGENCY," and thus the conspirators would act. Before the panic would be over, (for there are your panic people in all countries) the whole affiliation would be in movement. They would thwart, threaten, or collect mobs; openly oppose, or secretly betray, just as it suited their several situations. They are not visible now, but then they would be seen and felt too. I make no doubt but they have members, in some capacity or other, in every public department. I should not wonder if they had at this time fifty in the different branches of the Post-office. Thus has it proved in every country, which the infamous sans-culottes have invaded with success. In Holland, for instance, few people feared their invaders. The barriers were well fortified, well garrisoned, well supplied with ammunition and provisions, and the people appeared *unanimous* in their hatred of the enemy. But the fortresses fell, nobody could tell how; the French arrived as if it were *by appointment*, and many of those who had been the loudest in their expressions against them, were the first that they took by the hand. These villains had held a correspondence with them, and afterwards made a boast of their treason; the jacobin affiliation ran through all the United Provinces; its members had crept into every department, civil and military; the mine was completed, and, at the approach of the enemy it was sprung. Just so was it in Italy, in Geneva, in Venice; so was it in Switzerland; so will it be in Spain, and would it have been in Britain long ago, had it not been for her insular situation and the watchfulness and vigour of her government.

To the danger of such a conspiracy America is peculiarly exposed. Her *distance from France* is often, and, I must add, very stupidly held out as a guarantee for her safety. I might insist that there is no barrier between her and the Spanish territory, which nobody would deny; but, waving that, what, without the interference of Great Britain, is there to prevent twenty thousand sans-culottes from landing in this country? And, if they should do this, how many circumstances has America against her which no state in Europe knew any thing of!

From various causes these United States have become the resting place of ninety nine hundredths of the factious villains, which Great Britain and Ireland have vomitted from their shores. They are all schooled in sedition, are adepts at their trade, and they must certainly bear as cordial a hatred to this government as they did to their own. The French sans-culottes now here, capable of bearing arms, amount to at least thirty thousand, all furious ruffians, puffed up with vanity, starving with hunger, and fighting for conquest and pillage.

Great numbers of these wretches, of all countries, are what are called CITIZENS; so that no *alien laws* will touch them. Several hundreds of French have very lately been admitted to this destructive privilege and it is well known, that REYNOLDS is not only a citizen, but the *political father* of other citizens; for he has been suffered to vouch for their "good moral character and *their attachment to [the]* "*Constitution,*" a necessary prelude to their admission. The penal code has been softened down, till it has no terrors, except for the honest man, who stands in need of *protection*. There are sixteen governments, all in some measure independent of the general government, to whom the safety of the nation is committed, and these sixteen are very far from being all in the hands of such men as would lend their cordial support to that general government. The villain, who would get his neck stretched in the Federal courts, would very probably escape through other hands. In such a state of things the civil magistrate must hold a blunted, if not a broken, sword; and as to the military, though I would be willing to stake every thing on their *valour*, yet valour alone without skillful commanders and soldier[s] well disciplined, is like a razor in the hands of a child.

But, what renders the situation of America more favourable to the views of France than any other country, is, the *negro slavery* to the Southward. On this it is that the villains ground their hope. It is said that some of the *free* negroes have already been admitted into the conspiracy of the UNITED IRISHMEN, and that some slave holders either in Carolina or Virginia have engaged, in "*a case of* URGENCY," to set their negroes free, in order to excite discontents amongst those of their neighbours, and thus involve the whole country in rebellion and bloodshed. I do not take upon me to say that these preparatory steps have been taken, but this I know, that nothing could be thought more hellish or better calculated to insure success.

There are two sorts of people who will *smile* at all this, and will call it a mere bug bear: these are, the muddy-headed men of indifference and the jacobins themselves. But, I trust the real friends of government will see it in its true light, and will not suffer themselves to be lulled asleep by the songs of Doctor "REPOSE"[10] and his adherents. All these people want for the present is, to see the government *quiet*, dull, and unsuspecting. This is what they wished in Britain and Ireland. Every precautionary measure of the legislature or the executive; every *inquiry*, however legal, and however delicately conducted, they brand with the name of "jealous tyranny;" and to every honest man, who has the zeal to come forward in the discovery of their infernal plots, they give the appellation of SPY. This has had much influence on weak minds. Your *good-natured peaceable* man cannot bear the name of *spy* or *informer*; he would sooner see his neighbours burnt in their beds, and his own wife and children along them. I hope, however, that there is yet a good sense and spirit enough left amongst us to despise everything these artful treacherous villains can say, and to defeat every thing they shall attempt. The man, who shall bring the leaders of this conspiracy to the halter, will deserve as well of his country as those who shall shed their blood in its defence.[11]

I should here dismiss the subject for the present; but, apprized of the dreadful effects which the UNITED IRISHMEN have produced in their own country, it is impossible for me to suppress a hope, that the above proofs of their dangerous, deceitful, and indefatigable villany may reach their deluded adherents there; and, should this be the case, there is a remark or two, which it may not be amiss to add, though not necessary on this side the Atlantic.

That the impious and rebellious crew, called the UNITED IRISHMEN, have been organized and are maintained by, and act under the directions of the savage tyrants of France, every person in Ireland must have had repeated assurances; if, however, there are any who really doubt of this, and are not yet quite dead to conviction, their doubts must certainly be removed by the evidence which is now laid before them.

The perfidious French, who have constantly undermined by their intrigues, before they have dared to hoist their bloody standard, saw, in the associations of WHITEBOYS and VOLUNTEERS,[12] a set of most excellent recruits for a *Jacobin affiliation*, which were very soon and very easily formed, under the name of UNITED IRISHMEN.

Numerous have been the arts by which these nefarious hirelings of France have seduced the ignorant from their attachment to their Government and their King. Amongst these, extolling the *liberty* and *happiness* of the people of America, has not been the least successful. This liberty, and this happiness, they have held up to their deluded followers as the rich fruits of a successful opposition to the parent country, as the fruit of rebellion, revolution, independence; and, in the style of the modern "JOCKEY OF NORFOLK," they have told them to "*make the application.*"

I could produce many instances of their hypocritical efforts of this sort; but I shall content myself with one, taken from their address to PRIESTLEY, on his departure for America, which I select, because it was signed by the villain REYNOLDS himself.

"You are going," say they, "to *a happier world*, the world of Washington and Franklin.—Yes! the Volunteers of Ireland still live. They live across the Atlantic! Let this idea animate us in our sufferings; and may *the pure principles and genuine lustre of Freedom, reflected from the* AMERICAN COASTS, *penetrate into our cells and our dungeons!*"

After this, who would not have expected to see them satisfied with the Government of America? They assuredly ought to have been contented, or at least *quiet*, when basking under the full blaze of that precious, cheering freedom, the reflexion of whose rays they so anxiously and piously prayed for. But how has it turned out? NAPPER TANDY behaved in such a turbulent manner, he vented such savage abuse on all branches of the Government, that he was very soon driven from his lodgings as a monster. People would not remain under the same roof with him; and this too, when sans-culottism was far from being obsolete. HAMILTON ROWAN,[13] in three days after his arrival in the city of Philadelphia, became one of the leaders of a mob of malcontents, assembled on purpose to overawe General Washington, and deter him from signing the commercial treaty with Great

Britain. REYNOLDS, still more boldly and industriously seditious, after having long contributed to a print in the pay of France, in which the Government was daily traduced, published a most false and wicked libel against Mr. PICKERING, the principal Secretary of State, directly accusing him with malversation in his office. The falsehood was proved upon him, and he is now under a criminal prosecution for the offence. Thus, the man who inhabited Kilmainham gaol for seditious practices and contumacy to the House of Lords in Ireland, can also make shift to get seized by the sheriff in America. And this is the very identical REYNOLDS too, who prayed so sincerely for the reflexion of the "pure principles and genuine lustre of freedom from the American coasts!"

Nothing short of a state of rebellion can content these wretches. All governments are to them alike hateful. Like Lucifer, they carry a hell about with them in their own minds; and thus they prowl from country to country. When in Ireland, *reform* was their *stalking-horse*. Give them but *universal suffrage*, and they would be content. For this they associated—for this they swore—and for this they murdered. Well, *here* they found it, in all its mobbish glory. Here every man, however ignorant, poor, or infamous, had a vote, and every office was elective, from the President to the petty constable. In fact, they found here every regulation, and every principle of political liberty which they pretended it was the end of their combination to enforce in their own country; but they did not find here what it was their real wish to effect in Ireland, namely, *a complete subjection to the will of Jacobin France*; and for this reason, and for this alone, they have never ceased to manifest their hostility to the Government, from the first moment of their landing to the present hour; and they are now just as busy and as indefatigable in the work of rebellion and bloodshed *here*, as ever they were in Ireland.

Miscreants! they have poisoned the domestic harmony of this country, and have for ever blasted the character of their own. The name of *Irishman* is become, and not without reason, detestable in the ears of Americans. Justice, however, forbids us to carry this resentment to any thing like a *general prejudice*. The innocent are never to be condemned with the guilty.

Ireland, owing to a combination of untoward circumstances, offered a favourable prospect to the views of the Jacobins; these circumstances have been improved to the greatest possible extent; but it would be unjust—it would be barbarous in the extreme, to impute to the whole nation the crimes of the infamous few; crimes in which their fidelity had scorned to participate, and which their zeal and courage have detected and brought to punishment. Sufficiently great is the misfortune to be the countryman of a traitor, without being loaded with a share of his guilt.

The great body of the Irish, instead of contempt and reproach, merit admiration and applause. They have had greater temptations to resist, and a more formidable conspiracy to combat, than any other people in Europe; yet their loyalty has triumphed, still triumphs, and I trust it ever will triumph, over every art and violence, to which it has been or shall be opposed.

[9]

Farewell Address

COBBETT WROTE THIS ADDRESS JUST BEFORE HE SAILED FOR England on June 1, 1800. He had several reasons for leaving: his attempt to bring about an Anglo-American military alliance against France had failed; Thomas Jefferson had been elected President; his old enemy, Thomas McKean, had been elected governor of Pennsylvania; and he was angry at the $5,000 fine he had received for libeling Benjamin Rush. With this defiant departure, Cobbett embarked on his new career in England, which began with an attempt to warn his countrymen against the dangers of American republicanism. He would not set foot in the United States again for another seventeen years—when he had become a political refugee very much like the "Emigrated Patriots" he had condemned during the 1790s. But no one—least of all Cobbett himself—could have foreseen such an ironic twist of fate on the day that he penned these words.

Farewell Address

YOU WILL, DOUBTLESS, BE ASTONISHED, THAT AFTER HAVING HAD SUCH A smack of the sweets of *liberty*, I should think of rising thus abruptly from the feast; but this astonishment will cease, when you consider, that, under a general term, things diametrically opposite in their natures are frequently included, and that flavours are not more various than tastes. Thus, for instance, nourishment of every species is called *food*, and we *all* like food; but while one is partial to roast beef and plumb pudding, another is distractedly fond of flummery and mush; so is it with respect to *liberty*, of which, out of its infinite variety of sorts, yours unfortunately happens to be precisely that sort which I do not like.

When people care not two straws for each other, ceremony at parting is mere grimace; and as I have long felt the most perfect indifference with regard to a vast majority of those whom I now address, I shall spare myself the trouble of a ceremonious farewell. Let me not, however, depart from you with indiscriminating contempt. If no man ever had so many and such malignant foes, no one ever had more friends, and those more kind, more sincere, and more faithful. If I have been unjustly vilified by some, others have extolled me far beyond my merits; if the savages of the city have scared my children in the cradle, those children have, for their father's sake, been soothed and caressed by the affectionate, the gentle, the generous inhabitants of the country, under whose hospitable roofs I have spent some of the happiest hours of my life.

Thus and *thus*, Americans, will I ever speak of you. In a very little time, I shall be beyond the reach of your friendship, or your malice; beyond the hearing of your commendations or your curses; but being out of your power will alter neither my sentiments nor my words. As I have never spoken any thing but truth to you, so I will never speak any thing but truth of you: the heart of a Briton revolts at an emulation in baseness; and though you have, as a nation, treated me most ungratefully and unjustly, I scorn to repay you with ingratitude and injustice.

To my friends, who are also the real friends of America, I wish that peace and happiness which virtue ought to ensure, but which, I greatly fear, they will not find; and as to my enemies, I can wish them no severer scourge than that which they are preparing for themselves and their country. With this I depart for my native land, where neither the moth of *Democracy*, nor the rust of *Federalism* doth corrupt, and where thieves do not, with impunity, break through and steal five thousand dollars at a time.

Notes

1. Observations on the Emigration of Dr. Joseph Priestley

1. Cobbett is referring to Abraham Cowley, the seventeenth-century poet and royalist.

2. For the full text of these addresses and Priestley's replies, see Edgar F. Smith, *Priestley in America, 1794–1804* (Philadelphia, 1920), pp. 22–40.

3. For a modern scholarly analysis of these riots, see Richard Rose, "The Priestley Riots of 1791," *Past and Present* 18 (1960), pp. 68–88.

4. In fact, Priestley believed that Unitarianism was the true, uncorrupted form of Christianity, and was strongly opposed to deism. See Joseph Priestley, *Letters to a Philosophical Unbeliever* (Birmingham, 1787), and *An Answer to Mr. Paine's Age of Reason; Being a Continuation of Letters to the Philosophers and Unbelievers of France, on the Subject of Religion, and of the Letters to a Philosophical Unbeliever* (London, 1794).

5. There are echoes here of Burke's attack on Richard Price's mixture of religious dissent and political radicalism. In his response to Price, Burke wrote of the "dislike I feel to revolutions, the signals for which have so often been given from pulpits." See Burke, *Reflections on the Revolution in France* (London, 1790; reprint, Harmondsworth, 1968), p. 110.

6. In taking this position, Cobbett was following the English Loyalist stereotype of Priestley as a violent revolutionary. In 1790, Priestley had argued that the established clergy, by refusing to support civil rights for dissenters, were "laying gunpowder, grain by grain, under the old building of error and superstition" that might blow up the church establishment "as suddenly, as unexpectedly, and as completely, as the . . . late arbitrary government in France." His enemies seized on these words, labelled him "Gunpowder Priestley," and pilloried him in the press. Priestley's claims that his meaning

had been distorted, and that he had only been warning the clergy about the potentially disastrous consequences of intransigence, fell on deaf Tory ears. See Arthur Sheps, "Public Perception of Joseph Priestley, the Birmingham Dissenters, and the Church-and-King Riots of 1791," *Eighteenth-Century Life* 13, no. 2 (1989), pp. 46–64.

7. In fact, three Tory magistrates in Birmingham either tacitly approved of or surreptitiously encouraged the rioters' attacks on dissenting meeting houses. See Rose, "Priestley Riots," pp. 80–82.

8. Richard Rose has shown that although the government wanted to prosecute the rioters to the full extent of the law, the Tory magistrates in Birmingham took a deliberately lax attitude and acquiesced in attempts to intimidate witnesses from testifying in the trials. He concluded that the riots were "an episode in which the 'country gentlemen' called out the urban mob to draw the dissenting teeth of the aggressive and successful Birmingham bourgeoisie." See Rose, "Priestley Riots," pp. 80–82.

9. A "hundred" was a unit of local government—the subdivision of a county, overseen by justices of the peace and a high constable.

10. Cobbett is alluding to the Jacobins' punishment of Lyons for the city's part in the "Federalist" revolt against central control from Paris during 1793. On October 12, 1793, when Lyons was recaptured by the revolutionaries, the Committee of Public Safety decreed that the city should be destroyed. Its name was to disappear, except on a monument among the ruins which would proclaim "Lyons made war on Liberty. Lyons is no more." See William Doyle, *The Oxford History of the French Revolution* (Oxford, 1989), p. 254.

11. This handbill, described by Richard Rose as "ultra-revolutionary," was written by John Hobson, minister of the Kingswood Unitarian Chapel. It was published at the same time that the Bastille Day dinner was announced in the press, and it incensed the local Loyalists. Birmingham's magistrates offered a reward of 100 guineas for the name of anyone associated with its publication; Hobson prudently kept his authorship quiet. See Rose, "Priestley Riots," p. 72, and James Belcher, *An Authentic Account of the Riots in Birmingham* (Birmingham, n.d.), p. 2.

12. Priestley, "Letter to the Inhabitants of Birmingham," in J. T. Rutt, ed., *The Theological and Miscellaneous Works of Joseph Priestley* (reprint, New York, 1972), vol. 19, pp. 540–42.

13. Priestley, "Answer to the Students at New College, Hackney," in Belcher, "Appendix," in *Authentic Account of the Riots*, p. 11.

14. Samuel Butler, *Hudibras* (1664), Second Part, Canto II, lines 451–54.

15. The Marquis de Lafayette, who was a constitutional monarchist, attempted to prevent the republican revolution of August 10, 1792; he defected to the Prussians a week later, only to be imprisoned by them for five years. Jacques-Pierre Brissot, a leading Girondin, was destroyed by the war which he had helped to start; the Jacobins guillotined him and his principal allies after a show trial in October 1793. Anacharsis Clootz was a Prussian nobleman who supported the revolution as a means of liberating all Europe;

amid Jacobin fears of a foreign conspiracy, he was executed in March 1794. Thomas Paine narrowly escaped the same fate; he was imprisoned for ten months for his links with the Girondins and nearly died in jail.

16. M.-J. Jourdan was a leader of the radical pro-French party in Avignon; he played a central part in the Glacière Massacre of October 1791, when sixty papal supporters were killed.

17. Michel Gentil was one of the moderate deputies in the Legislative Assembly.

18. On August 10, the monarchy was overthrown, paving the way for the National Convention and the declaration of the republic. In the fighting, 600 Swiss Guards were killed, as were about 250 revolutionaries. "It was," commented William Doyle, "the bloodiest day of the Revolution so far, but also one of the most decisive." Doyle, *French Revolution*, p. 189.

19. The words "his colleagues" were carefully chosen; Priestley had been elected (in his absence) to the National Convention in September 1792. Pierre-Louis Manuel, a Girondin deputy, was guillotined in November 1793; Charles Lacroix (or Delacroix), Georges Jacques Danton and François Chabot followed him in April 1794.

20. The Princess de Lamballe, a close friend of Marie-Antoinette, was killed in the September Massacres of 1792. These massacres were triggered by rumors of a "prison plot" against the revolution during the Prussian advance on Paris; between September 3 and September 7, between 1,100 and 1,400 prisoners were massacred. Many of them, like the princess herself, were executed after being found guilty by kangaroo courts dispensing the "people's justice." Cobbett's comments about the Princess de Lamballe are analogous to Burke's remarks in the *Reflections* about Marie-Antoinette. For Cobbett and Burke, the treatment of these women graphically illustrated the death of honor and decency in France, and the triumph of the brutal, vindictive and bloodthirsty mob. See also *Porcupine's Works*, vol. 3, pp. 91–93.

21. Paine *Rights of Man*, in Philip Foner, ed., *The Complete Writings of Thomas Paine* (New York, 1945), vol. 1, p. 283. Paine's words were: "They order these things better in France"; he was comparing the French Constitution's provisions preventing placemen and pensioners from sitting in the National Assembly with the English government's use of placemen and pensioners to build support in Parliament. Cobbett was quoting him out of context.

22. When Cobbett wrote these words, Paine was in the Luxembourg Prison in Paris, jailed by the Jacobins and close to death. See Paine to James Monroe, 18 August 1794 and 13 October 1794, in Foner, *Complete Writings of Thomas Paine*, vol. 2, pp. 1343, 1359.

23. John Sheffield, *An Essay on Poetry* (London, 1709), p. 12.

24. In 1791, a slave rebellion broke out in the French colony of San Domingo; the following year, the Legislative Assembly gave full rights to free coloreds. By 1793, French commissioners in the colony offered freedom to all

blacks who would fight for the Republic against the white planters; by October, the commissioners proclaimed general freedom for San Domingo. The National Convention, responding to these events, formally decreed in February 1794 the abolition of slavery in all French colonies.

25. The Democratic Societies attacked Washington for introducing "courtly forms, etiquettes and manners" into government circles. The criticism of Washington's "aristocratic" tendencies became more pronounced after Washington condemned the clubs as "self-created societies" and implicated them in the Whiskey Rebellion. See Foner, ed., *Democratic-Republican Societies*, pp. 71, 414, and passim.

26. Cobbett is referring to the condition of the refugees from the slave rising in San Domingo; he had taught English to many of these émigrés, and was directly acquainted with their experiences and condition.

27. Cobbett was thinking primarily of Burke's writings, including not only the *Reflections*, but also Burke's famous speech in Parliament during the debate on the Quebec government bill. See *Parliamentary History of England* (London, 1817), vol. 29, pp. 365–68.

28. Jean Paul Marat was the editor of the extremist newspaper *L'Ami du Peuple*. He thrived on conspiracies and plots, supported the September Massacres, and earned notoriety as a *buveur de sang*.

29. Paine's actual words were "That which a whole nation chooses to do, it has a right to do." See *Rights of Man, Part One* in Foner, *Complete Writings of Thomas Paine*, vol. 1, p. 251.

30. "Hence, in order that the social pact shall not be an empty formula, it is tacitly implied in that commitment—which alone can give force to all others—that whoever refuses to obey the general will shall be constrained to do so by the whole body, which means nothing other than that he shall be forced to be free." Jean-Jacques Rousseau, *The Social Contract* (Harmondsworth, 1968), p. 64.

31. Bertrand Barère was a member of the revolutionary Committee of Public Safety; these words come from his "Report on the Navy of the Republic in the Mediterranean," as translated in the *Aurora*, April 26, 1794.

32. The "authoress of the *rights of women*" was Olympe de Gouges; she argued in 1791 that women should have equal political rights with men. During the terror, her attacks on Robespierre brought her to the guillotine in November 1793. The "poor unfortunate Goddess," Madame Hébert, was the wife of the sansculotte journalist Jacques-René Hébert; she followed her husband to the guillotine in April 1794.

33. The Tammany Society of New York began in 1787 as a fraternal order; strongly opposed to monarchy and hereditary succession, the society combined American nationalism with support for the French Revolution and hostility to Britain. See Jerome Mushkat, *Tammany: The Evolution of a Political Machine, 1789–1865* (Syracuse, 1971).

34. These words should be compared with his private opinion that the people of the United States were a "cheating, sly, roguish gang." Cobbett to

Rachel Smither, July 7, 1794, in Lewis Melville, ed., *The Life and Letters of William Cobbett in England and America* (London, 1913), vol. 1, p. 87.

35. Priestley, "Address to the Jews," in Rutt, *Theological and Miscellaneous Works*, vol. 20, p. 280.

36. Ibid., vol. 25, p. 335.

37. Cobbett is referring to the persecution of priests during the revolution. Priests who refused to swear allegiance to the Civil Constitution of the Clergy (1790) became increasingly identified with the counterrevolution. As opinions polarized and feelings intensified, the clergy in general bore the brunt of the dechristianization campaign which gathered momentum during the Terror of 1793–94.

38. The Test Act of 1673 prevented Dissenters and Roman Catholics from holding offices under the Crown; it was part of a series of acts designed to strengthen the established Church of England. Contrary to Cobbett, Priestley's famous sermon on the Test Act, "The Conduct to be Observed by Dissenters," did not argue that tithes should be reapportioned. In fact, Priestley wanted the entire system of tithe payments to be abolished, and replaced by the principle of voluntary support for churches. See Rutt, *Theological and Miscellaneous Works*, vol. 15, pp. 391–92, and vol. 19, pp. 129–30.

39. The argument here is similar to that of David Hume, "Dialogues concerning Natural Reason," in A. Wayne Colver and John Vladimir Price, eds., *The Natural History of Religion and Dialogues concerning Natural Religion* (Oxford, 1976), p. 160: "Nothing exists without a Cause; and the original Cause of this Universe (whatever it be) we call GOD; and piously ascribe to him every Species of Perfection." I have not, however, been able to trace the specific source of Cobbett's quotation.

40. In taking this position, Cobbett shared Edmund Burke's view that an anti-Christian conspiracy lay behind the French Revolution. "It seems to me," Burke had written of the Civil Constitution of the Clergy, "that this new ecclesiastical establishment is intended only to be temporary, and preparatory to the utter abolition, under any of its forms, of the Christian religion." See Burke, *Reflections*, p. 256.

41. See the *Philadelphia Gazette*, June 20, 1794.

42. Thomas Muir founded the Society of the Friends of the People in Edinburgh, and helped to organize the General Convention of Scottish reformers which met in December 1792. On the radical wing of the reform movement, he was tried for seditious libel in August 1793 and was sentenced to fourteen years in Botany Bay. His "patriotic associates" included Thomas Palmer, who got seven years for spreading Paineite literature. In 1794, Maurice Margarot, Joseph Gerrald, and William Skirving were each given fourteen years' transportation for their part in the General Convention of British reformers, held in November 1793.

43. Léger Félicité Sonthonax and Etienne Polverel were French commissioners sent in 1792 to deal with the slave rebellion in San Domingo; in 1793, Sonthonax decreed the abolition of slavery in the colony. See Robert Louis

Stein, *Léger Félicité Sonthonax: The Lost Sentinel of the Republic* (London and Toronto, 1985).

44. In fact, Priestley and Bewley were friends who corresponded with each other about the properties of air. See Jack Lindsay, ed., *Autobiography of Joseph Priestley* (Teaneck, N.J., 1970), p. 96.

45. Robert François Damien stabbed Louis XV with a penknife in 1757; for his attempted regicide, he was tortured, pinched with red-hot irons, torn between four horses, and executed.

46. I have not yet been able to trace this quotation.

47. "Love of one's country"—clearly something that Cobbett himself felt deeply.

48. Priestley's son, Joseph junior, had been involved in a land company in the Susquehanna region; when it became apparent that much of the land was difficult to sell, Priestley believed that the proprietors had swindled his son. See F. W. Gibbs, *Joseph Priestley: Adventurer in Science and Champion of Truth* (London, 1965), p. 228. Cobbett's comments on land-jobbers in America anticipate his attitude toward financial speculators in Britain after 1800.

49. Oliver Goldsmith, *The Traveller* (London, 1764), lines 317–22:

> Fired at the sound, my genius spreads her wing,
> And flies where Britain courts the western spring;
> Where lawns extend that scorn Arcadian pride,
> And brighter streams than famed Hydaspes glide:
> There all around the gentlest breezes stray,
> There gentle music melts on every spray.

50. Dr. Vicesimus Knox was a minister and teacher who was well known in the late eighteenth century for his writings on religion and morality.

51. Cobbett was alluding to Priestley's chemistry experiments in general and discovery of oxygen in particular.

2. A Bone to Gnaw, for the Democrats

1. Mary Wollstonecraft replied to Burke's attack on the French Revolution in her *Vindication of the Rights of Men* (London, 1790), and established herself as a pioneer of feminism with her *Vindication of the Rights of Women* (London, 1792).

2. James Ridgway and H. D. Symons were the London publishers of Callender's book. In 1793, they were each sentenced to four years' imprisonment for their role in distributing democratic literature.

3. "Charley" refers to Bonnie Prince Charlie, the Young Pretender; "George" is King George III.

4. Literally translated, to be *sans culotte* was to be "without knee-britches"; the expression was used to describe the common people of Paris who saw themselves as the vanguard of the revolution.

5. "Sawney" was a derogatory term for a Scot.

6. The "Murderer's Hymn" was the "Marseillaise"; "Ça Ira" was another prominent song of the French Revolution ("Ah ça ira, ça ira, ça ira / Les aristocrats, à la lanterne"). The story of William Tell was a popular symbol in the 1790s of the deliverance of a people from tyranny. This "modernized" version was not actually performed, although an American version of the play was put on in New York in 1796, under the title *The Archers*. See William Dunlap, *History of the American Theatre* (reprint, New York, 1963), p. 285.

7. Joel Barlow was an American democrat and revolutionary who linked up with the radical Society for Constitutional Information in London, mixed with British and Irish émigrés in Paris, and became well known as the author of the *Advice to the Privileged Orders* (London, 1792).

8. In fact, Cobbett had been in Philadelphia for less than thirty weeks; at this stage in his career, he was pretending to be an American.

9. Cobbett is referring to the Whiskey Rebellion of 1794, which broke out in western Pennsylvania.

10. The "back-door clubs" were the Democratic Societies that sprang up in 1793, characterized by their commitment to political equality, their broad-based membership, and their support for the French Revolution.

11. For a corrective to Cobbett's conspiratorial caricature of the Democratic Societies' attitude to the Whiskey Rebellion, see Roland Baumann, "The Democratic-Republicans of Philadelphia," (Ph.D. dissertation, Pennsylvania State University, 1970), pp. 488–90.

12. Jack Straw was one of the leaders of the Peasants' Revolt of 1381; he was executed after the failure of the uprising. Charles James Fox was a leading Whig politician in Britain during the late eighteenth century.

13. Cobbett repeatedly—and incorrectly—asserted that Genet was the founder of the Democratic Societies in America; it was part of his campaign to portray American democrats as French puppets. After the Federalists had rejected him and the Republicans had abandoned him, Genet took refuge in Long Island—hence the reference to the "Island of Bliss." Genet wound up marrying the daughter of New York's Governor Clinton and settled down as an obscure but prosperous country gentleman. Ironically, Cobbett himself would seek sanctuary in Long Island between 1817 and 1819 to escape the British government's repression of radicalism after the Napoleonic Wars.

14. In their efforts both to encourage recruitment into the militia and to outflank their Federalist opponents, Philadelphia democrats like John Swanwick portrayed the whiskey rebels as crypto-Royalists who wanted to link up with the British Empire. Although such claims reveal more about democratic political tactics than western ideological realities, it was true that British agents had opened up negotiations with western sympathizers. John Graves Simcoe, the lieutenant governor of Upper Canada, believed that Britain could exploit antieastern sentiment and detach the western "colonies" of the United States from the union. The British government treated Simcoe's reports with skepticism; the American government took them very seriously indeed. See

Thomas Slaughter, *The Whiskey Rebellion* (Oxford, 1986), pp. 190–91, and J. Leitch Wright, Jr., *Britain and the American Frontier, 1783–1815* (Athens, Ga., 1975), pp. 98–99.

15. The whiskey rebels in 1794 described themselves as supporters of "Tom the Tinker"; threatening letters to government informers would be signed with the name. See Hugh Henry Brackenridge, *Incidents of the Insurrection* (Philadelphia, 1796), p. 79. "Tom the Tinker" was widely believed to be John Holcroft, one of the radical leaders of the Rebellion; his "prevaricating Coadjutor" was probably the more moderate Hugh Henry Brackenridge. "Old foxy Dorchester" was Lord Dorchester, the governor general of Canada.

16. Goldsmith's actual words were: "I have known many of these pretended champions for liberty in my time, yet do I not remember one that was not in his heart and in his family a tyrant." See *The Vicar of Wakefield* (London, 1766; reprint, Oxford, 1981), p. 98.

17. In other words, as if he had been a French Jacobin. Tallien had earned notoriety as a terrorist for his role in suppressing the provincial revolt against Parisian rule in 1793; for Barère, see "Observations on the Emigration of Dr. Joseph Priestley," Chapter 1, this volume, n. 31.

18. The reference here is to Chief Justice John Jay, who in 1794 had been sent to London as minister plenipotentiary with instructions to negotiate a commercial treaty with Britain.

19. The "Carmagnole" was a popular French revolutionary song that appeared shortly after the *journée* of August 10, 1792, and was sung throughout the terror. The tune was lively; the lyrics were bloodthirsty. See James A. Leith, *Media and Revolution* (Toronto, 1968), pp. 53–63.

20. The Marquis de Lafayette was a prominent figure during the constitutional monarchy of 1789–92, but was swept aside by the republican revolution in August 1792; see "Observations on the Emigration," n. 15. Philippe-Egalité, a prince of the royal blood who was formerly known as the Duc d'Orléans, remained popular after the republican revolution, but was guillotined by the Jacobins in November 1793. Georges Jacques Danton was a revolutionary hero during the terror, but was guillotined by Robespierre in April 1794. Robespierre presided over the attempt to create a terror-driven Republic of Virtue in the spring and early summer of 1794, until he himself was guillotined after the counterrevolutionary coup of the ninth of Thermidor (July 27, 1794).

21. Cobbett is alluding to Robespierre's attempt to replace the dechristianization movement in France with the officially organized cult of the Supreme Being. The "unfortunate catastrophe" to which Cobbett sarcastically refers was the overthrow of Robespierre in the Thermidorian coup; the date was July 27, not July 18.

22. The proposal to exclude from citizenship foreign noblemen who retained their titles came from Virginia's William Branch Giles. The slavery amendment was introduced by Samuel Dexter from Massachusetts; the "member from Carolina" was Joseph McDowell. For the debate over the Natu-

ralization Bill, see *Debates and Proceedings in the Congress of the United States (Third Congress)* (Washington, D.C., 1849), pp. 1030–66.

23. "Mundungus" was a foul-smelling tobacco; Cobbett is referring to the Southern planter-democrats who welcomed the American edition of Callender's book.

24. For "*Tom* the Tinker," see n. 15 above; "*Tom* the Devil" was one of Cobbett's nicknames for Thomas Paine.

25. John Dryden, "The Cock and the Fox," in *Fables, Ancient and Modern* (London, 1700), lines 742–43.

26. Ibid., lines 732–33.

27. Pope's actual words were:

> So schismatics the plain believers quit
> And are but damned for having too much wit.

See Pope, "An Essay on Criticism," in John Wilson Croker, ed., *The Works of Alexander Pope* (New York, 1967), vol. 2, p. 60.

28. The "projector" was William Thornton, author of *Cadmus: or, a Treatise on the Elements of Written Language* (Philadelphia, 1793).

29. This was a common counterrevolutionary theme; conservative writers frequently dismissed the women who represented the Goddess of Liberty in French revolutionary festivals as prostitutes in fancy clothes.

30. Cobbett is referring to John Swanwick, a radical Philadelphia merchant who, among other things, started up a school for young ladies in the city. Described by one historian as "a pompous, vain little man who wore big cravats" (Baumann, "Democratic Societies of Philadelphia," p. 497), Swanwick became one of Cobbett's principal targets in the 1790s.

31. "Even had he come out of Epeiros, even had he served the gods, / Even had he been born of the Trident, he droops if he is old!" The sexual connotation is clear; the source, however, is unknown.

32. David Bradford was generally regarded as the leader of the Whiskey Rebellion; Wat Tyler led the Peasants' Revolt of 1381.

3. A Kick for a Bite

1. Andrew Brown was the editor of the *Philadelphia Gazette*, a leading Jeffersonian newspaper.

2. Cicero, *De Oratore* III.165: "The metaphor ought to have an apologetic air."

3. On Susanna Rowson's career, see Dorothy Weil, *In Defense of Women: Susanna Rowson, 1762–1824* (University Park, Pa., 1976), and Patricia L. Parker, *Susanna Rowson* (Boston, 1986).

4. The reference is to Shakespeare's *Twelfth Night*, Act Three, Scene Two, ll. 24–28.

5. Eliza Whitlock was a leading English actress who arrived in the United States in 1793; she performed regularly at the New Theatre in Philadelphia.

6. Susanna Rowson's *Slaves in Algiers; or, a Struggle for Freedom* (Phila-

delphia, 1794) was first performed at Philadelphia's New Theatre in the summer of 1794. A dramatic fantasy about the American hostages who had been captured by the Barbary pirates, the play was well received by audiences in the United States.

7. Quintilian, *Institutio Oratoria* Book I.v.5: "In the first place, solecisms must not be allowed to intrude their offensive presence."

8. *Mentoria; or, The Young Lady's Friend* and *Charlotte: A Tale of Truth* were novels that Rowson published in London in 1791, two years before her arrival in the United States. *Charlotte* would eventually become America's first bestseller.

9. The notion that Americans breathed the air of liberty was commonplace in Patriotic literature during the revolutionary and early republican era. Thomas Paine, for example, remarked shortly after his arrival in America in 1774 that "Those who are conversant with Europe would be tempted to believe that even the air of the Atlantic disagrees with the constitution of foreign vices" (Paine, "Utility of this Work Evinced," *Pennsylvania Magazine*, January 1775). Cobbett found such sentiments irresistible invitations to sarcasm.

10. In John Gay's *The Beggar's Opera* (1728), Act One, Scene One: "We and the Surgeons are more beholding to women than all the professions besides."

11. The reference is to Matthew Prior's poem "Hans Carvel" (1700), in which Satan gives the "Impotent and Old" Hans a magic ring to keep his young wife. See H. Bunker Wright and Monroe K. Spears, eds., *The Literary Works of Matthew Prior* (Oxford, 1959), vol. 1, pp. 184–88.

12. Cobbett is referring to John Swanwick, who had defended Susanna Rowson in a pamphlet entitled *A Rub from Snub* (Philadelphia, 1795); Cobbett decided that "Scrub" was a more appropriate name for his adversary.

13. In his *Rub from Snub*, p. 46, Swanwick had made mildly disparaging remarks about the wife of the Federalist congressman Elias Boudinot.

4. The Bloody Buoy

1. The editor in question was Benjamin Franklin Bache, grandson of Benjamin Franklin and proprietor of the radical Philadelphia *Aurora*; see George Spater, *William Cobbett: The Poor Man's Friend* (Cambridge, Mass., 1982), p. 58.

2. The Comte de Mirabeau was a pamphleteer and brilliant orator in the National Assembly; among other things, he excelled in denunciations of the nonjuring clergy. For Marat, see "Observations on the Emigration of Dr. Joseph Priestley," Chapter 1, this volume, n. 28. The Marquis de Condorcet was a leading philosophe and revolutionary who attacked revealed religion. Jacques-René Hébert's *Père Duchesne* was a popular, scurrilous sansculotte newspaper which strongly supported the dechristianization movement.

3. Cobbett is referring to the new republican calendar that the French

Convention adopted in October 1793. The years were numbered from the birth of the French Republic rather than the birth of Christ; the weeks were ten days long, with rest days three times each month in place of Sundays. The calendar, remarks William Doyle, "marked a further stage in the divorce between the French State and any sort of religion." See *Oxford History of the French Revolution*, p. 260.

4. Foucault was one of the members of the Revolutionary Committee at Nantes; his order to throw the women over the cliff was revealed during the Thermidorian reaction against the terror, and was reprinted in *PW*, vol. 3, p. 116.

5. The Marquis de Condorcet had been associated with the Brissotin faction, and went into hiding to avoid arrest after the Jacobins came to power. He was caught in March 1794 and died in prison; according to some accounts, he took poison to avoid the guillotine. Although Cobbett accused him of atheism, it is not clear whether Condorcet was an atheist or a deist. See J. Salwyn Schapiro, *Condorcet and the Rise of Liberalism* (New York, 1963), pp. 178–80. In Cobbett's view, of course, atheism and deism amounted to the same thing.

6. Jean-Baptiste Louvet was a revolutionary writer and politician who aligned himself with the Girondins; Henri-Baptiste Grégoire was a cleric who emerged as a spokesperson for the lower clergy in the National Assembly, supported the Civil Constitution of the Clergy, and became a bishop in the new revolutionary order.

7. Berthier de Sauvigny, the intendant of Paris, had been caught in the act of emigration in July 1789; along with his father-in-law, Joseph François Foulon, he was lynched and decapitated. "When Berthier was murdered," wrote historian Norman Hampson, "a fanatic tore out his heart and thrust it at the horrified municipality" (*A Social History of the French Revolution*, p. 75).

5. The Life and Adventures of Peter Porcupine

1. See Benjamin Franklin, "The Autobiography," in Jesse Lemisch, ed., *Benjamin Franklin: The Autobiography and Other Writings* (New York, 1961), pp. 17–18; Samuel Johnson's definition appears in his *Dictionary* (London, 1755).

2. In fact, Cobbett was born on March 9, 1763; see E. I. Carlyle, *William Cobbett* (London, 1904), pp. 303–4.

3. For John Swanwick, see "A Bone to Gnaw, for the Democrats," Chapter 2, this volume, n. 30.

4. Colonel Hugh Debbieg, an expert on fortifications, was tried for insubordination in 1784 after writing a hostile letter to his commanding officer the Duke of Richmond; five years later, following another written attack on the Duke, Debbieg was deprived of his rank and pay for six months. George Spater suggested that Debbieg's example may have strengthened Cobbett's

own belligerent tendencies; see Spater, *William Cobbett: The Poor Man's Friend* (Cambridge, Mass., 1982), pp. 20, 91.

5. Written by Bishop Robert Lowth in 1762, the *Grammar* became the standard late eighteenth century text on the subject.

6. Cobbett's account is more significant for what it omits rather than for what it includes. There is no mention of corruption in the army, his attempt to court-martial four of his officers, or his authorship of *The Soldier's Friend*. In 1805 he commented that "here, in the printed account of my life, there is a small chasm. When I published that account, I was in the midst of the revilers of England, and particularly of the English army; or, I should then have stated, that the primary cause of my leaving the army . . . was, the abuses, the shocking abuses as to money matters, the *peculation*, in short, which I had witnessed in it, and which I had, in vain, endeavoured to correct." See *PR*, October 5, 1805.

7. Cobbett's nickname for John Swanwick; see also Cobbett's remarks in *A New Year's Gift to the Democrats* (Philadelphia, 1796), pp. 66–67.

8. Cobbett is referring to the Abbé Raynal's *The Revolution of America* (London, 1781).

9. This was William Short. The circumstances in which Cobbett obtained this letter of recommendation remain unclear, but see Spater, *William Cobbett*, pp. 41–42.

10. William Keteltas was a leading New York Republican. John Oldden, Cobbett's landlord, received an anonymous letter threatening to destroy Cobbett's publishing and bookselling shop unless Cobbett was evicted. Oldden refused; Cobbett used the incident to depict democrats in general as intolerant, violent men who believed that "the press is free for them, and them alone." See Cobbett, *The Scare-Crow* (Philadelphia, 1796), esp. p. 19.

11. Thomas Bradford was Cobbett's first printer and publisher; the two men fell out in 1796.

12. Matthew Carey was a leading Irish-American democrat and publisher in Philadelphia.

13. Phineas Bond was the British consul in the United States. In Europe at this time, rumours were circulating that Bond himself was Peter Porcupine. See Paine, "Letter to George Washington," in Philip S. Foner, ed., *The Complete Writings of Thomas Paine*, vol. 2, pp. 709–10n.

14. Andrew Allen was a Philadelphia Loyalist who fled to England during the War of Independence; his daughter married George Hammond, the British undersecretary for foreign affairs.

15. The "American Envoy" was John Jay; his treaty with Britain had been ratified by the Senate in June 1795.

16. Cobbett's *Political Censor* was published in eight numbers between March 1796 and March 1797; it provided a running commentary on the proceedings of Congress and the central political issues of the day.

17. "Citizen Hint" was the author of the letter that had threatened John Oldden, Cobbett's landlord.

6. History of the American Jacobins

1. On Brissot, see "Observations on the Emigration of Dr. Joseph Priestley," Chapter 1, this volume, n. 15.

2. Cobbett's attempt to portray American democrats as anti-federalists, and consequently as enemies of the federal constitution, sacrificed accuracy for polemical purposes. In fact, many of the artisans who joined the American Democratic Societies had supported the Constitution of 1787. See, for example, John R. Nelson, Jr., *Liberty and Property* (Baltimore, 1987), pp. 15–21.

3. For a scholarly corrective to Cobbett's treatment of Genet, see Harry Ammon, *The Genet Mission* (New York, 1973).

4. In fact, the French government neither expected nor wanted the United States to join France in the war against Britain. Aware that the United States was not of major military significance, the French believed that a neutral America that carried grain to its "sister republic" across the Atlantic would best meet the needs of the revolution. See Ammon, *Genet Mission*, pp. 21–31.

5. Once again, Cobbett is caricaturing the activities of his opponents. Genet did not "create" the Democratic Societies; in fact, the first such organization, the German Republican Society of Philadelphia, was formed shortly before Genet's arrival. It is true that Genet suggested the name of the Democratic Society of Pennsylvania—but the original idea had been to call the association the Sons of Liberty, not the Jacobins. See Philip S. Foner, "Introduction," *The Democratic-Republican Societies, 1790–1800* (Westport, Conn., 1976), pp. 6–7, Eugene Link, *Democratic-Republican Societies 1790–1800* (New York, 1942), pp. 19–43; and "A Bone to Gnaw, for the Democrats," Chapter 2, this volume, n. 13. In the words of Roland Baumann, "Although Genet played a large part in Philadelphia's politics between May and August 1793, his presence served only to stimulate an already existing political acrimony." See Baumann, "The Democratic-Republicans of Philadelphia: The Origins, 1776–1797" (Ph.D. dissertation, Pennsylvania State University, 1970), pp. 439, 440–45.

6. Presumably a misprint; the actual date, of course, was July 1789.

7. Pearce may have been John Pierce, ropemaker, who appears in the membership list of the Democratic Society of Pennsylvania; Elhanan Winchester was an American Universalist minister and abolitionist who preached in Philadelphia and London during the 1780s and 1790s.

8. Jean Antoine Joseph Fauchet, Genet's Jacobin replacement as minister to the United States, arrived in Philadelphia along with three fellow commissioners in February 1794.

9. On this question, see "Bone to Gnaw," n. 11.

10. Cobbett is quoting from Fauchet's dispatches to the French government, which were intercepted by the Royal Navy and released to the American government in the summer of 1795, during the debate over Jay's Treaty. See the Introduction.

11. Alexander Dallas, the Secretary of the Commonwealth of Pennsylvania, also served as vice president of the Democratic Society of Pennsylvania, which Cobbett had dubbed the "Mother Club" of American Jacobinism.

12. The governor of Pennsylvania was Thomas Mifflin; the Secretary of the Treasury was Alexander Hamilton; the Secretary of the Commonwealth of Pennsylvania was Alexander Dallas; Edmund Randolph was Secretary of State at the federal level. The proclamation to which Fauchet refers was Washington's demand that the whiskey rebels disperse.

13. See William Findley, *History of the Insurrection* (Philadelphia, 1796), p. 74; Cobbett is, in characteristic fashion, completely misrepresenting the position of his opponent, who only argued that the hot weather contributed to short tempers during the summer of 1794.

14. Pierre Samuel Dupont de Nemours was an eminent physiocrat and a leading orator in the National Assembly; he would eventually become the founder of the Dupont industrial dynasty in the United States. Cobbett repeated his attack on the "infamous Dupont" in *Porcupine's Works*, vol. 5, pp. 300–302.

15. The French Republic was proclaimed on September 22, 1792; the monarchy had been overthrown on August 10.

7. Pen Portraits

1. Cobbett's attack on Thomas Paine appeared in the *Political Censor*, May 1796, pp. 196–204. Paine's *Age of Reason* (Paris, 1794), a populist deist work that attacked both revealed religion and atheism was one of the most controversial books written in the Age of Revolution. It offended Christians everywhere, it deeply divided the democratic movement in Britain, and it severely damaged Paine's reputation in America. Not surprisingly, Cobbett singled out the book for special attention.

2. Literally translated as "hitherto," this expression was used by French revolutionaries to dismiss their opponents as "has-beens."

3. Many of Paine's opponents at this time accused him of hypocrisy for defending in the *Rights of Man* the Constitution of 1791 and then helping to draft its successor in late 1792. Paine himself believed that general principles were more important than specific constitutional arrangements and argued that the art of constitution-making was still in its infancy. "The best constitution that could now be devised consistent with the conditions of the present moment," he wrote in the spring of 1792, "may be far short of that excellence which a few years may afford." Paine, *Rights of Man, Part 2*, in Philip S. Foner, ed., *The Complete Writings of Thomas Paine* (New York, 1945), vol. 1, p. 396.

4. These words are a parody of the radical revolutionaries' references to "la sainte insurrection"; they were not used by Paine himself.

5. In fact, Paine had begun the first part of the *Age of Reason* in the spring of 1793, before the dechristianization movement in France had gathered

momentum; he completed it that fall, shortly before his arrest at the end of December.

6. Paine's actual words in the *Rights of Man* were "*that every religion is good that teaches man to be good*" (Foner, *Complete Writings*, vol. 1, p. 451). Nevertheless, it is clear that Paine either concealed his deist views before the *Age of Reason*, or came to embrace deism after he wrote the *Rights of Man*.

7. In fact, Paine had written that the Constitution of 1795 was the "*best organized system* the human mind has yet produced," although he continued to oppose its restricted property qualifications. See Paine, *Agrarian Justice*, in Foner, *Complete Writings*, vol. 1, p. 607.

8. These character sketches of British and Irish democrats are taken from *Porcupine's Gazette*, February 2, 1798, and *Porcupine's Works*, vol. 9, pp. 257–58n. Hancock and Harper were both in prison in 1798, when Cobbett penned these lines. On James Thomson Callender, see Michael Durey, *With the Hammer of Truth: James Thomson Callender and America's Early National Heroes* (Charlottesville, Va., 1990). James Reynolds, the revolutionary Irish physician who fled to America in 1794, was the author of the first socialist utopian tract in the United States. See Richard Twomey, "Jacobins and Jeffersonians" (Ph.D. dissertation, University of Northern Illinois, 1974), pp. 214–40. Matthew Lyon, the Republican congressman from Vermont, earned notoriety for spitting at and fighting with the Federalist Roger Griswold in the House of Representatives in 1798.

9. Archibald Hamilton Rowan was a leading United Irishman who escaped from Dublin's Newgate Prison in 1794, witnessed the terror in France, and arrived in Philadelphia in the summer of 1795. Plunged into poverty, he did indeed try to survive by making and selling spruce beer in Wilmington. See Harold Nicolson, *The Desire to Please* (London, 1943), esp. p. 166.

10. Daniel Isaac Eaton was an English Jacobin bookseller who published Paine's writings and edited *Hog's Wash*, a democratic newspaper whose title snorted at Edmund Burke's remark about a "swinish multitude." He moved to the United States in 1798 and returned to England in 1801, where he resumed his career as a radical.

11. Citizen Richard Lee, one of the most extreme republicans in London, wrote pamphlets with such titles as *King Killing* and *The Happy Reign of George the Last*. After fleeing the country in 1796 with the wife of a government spy, he resurfaced in Philadelphia as the publisher of the *American Universal Magazine*. See Twomey, "Jacobins and Jeffersonians," pp. 27, 58.

12. Thomas Muir became a democratic hero and martyr after his trial for sedition in 1793 and his sentence to fourteen years' transportation; see "Observations on the Emigration of Dr. Joseph Priestley," Chapter 1, this volume, n. 41. He escaped from Botany Bay, only to be maimed in a naval conflict; Cobbett began by quoting a report of Muir's arrival at Cadiz and then commented on the story. See *Porcupine's Gazette*, September 15, 1797.

13. Cobbett's comments on Noah Webster came from *Porcupine's Works*, vol. 7, p. 4n; *Porcupine's Gazette*, July 17, 1798; and *The Rush-Light*, February 28,

1800. A moderate Federalist, Webster was the editor of the *Minerva*, a newspaper, and author of the widely used *American Spelling Book*, which attempted to establish a new, simplified spelling system for the New World; the idea was to reduce America's cultural dependence on Britain. He earned Cobbett's enmity in 1797 for refusing to take a strong pro-British position against the French Revolution.

14. Benjamin Franklin Bache edited the Philadelphia *Aurora* and was a leading member of the Democratic Society of Pennsylvania (see "The Bloody Buoy," Chapter 4, this volume, n. 1); Thomas Greenleaf was the editor of the New York *Journal* and the *Argus*, as well as a member of the Democratic Society of New York.

15. In 1797, during the second yellow fever epidemic to hit Philadelphia in the decade, Cobbett attacked Dr. Rush's treatment of bleeding his patients. Rush sued for libel; the case came to court in 1799 and resulted in the $5,000 fine that helped drive Cobbett out of the United States. See the Introduction. These extracts are from *The Rush-Light* (February 15, 1800, and February 28, 1800) in which Cobbett attacked the proceedings of the trial in general and the defense's portrayal of Rush's character in particular.

16. Joseph Hopkinson, the composer of *Hail Columbia*, was Rush's defense counsel; Dr. James Mease was a student and friend of Rush who testified on Rush's behalf during the trial.

17. These attacks on Thomas McKean were published in Cobbett, "The Republican Judge," in *Porcupine's Works*, vol. 7, pp. 333–34; *Political Censor*, January 1797, p. 39; and *Porcupine's Gazette*, April 29, 1799. McKean was the chief justice of Philadelphia; in 1799 he was elected governor of Pennsylvania. A democrat, a drinker, and a domineering man who rewarded his friends and punished his enemies, McKean exemplified for Cobbett the kind of petty tyranny and abuse of power that masqueraded under the name of liberty. For a modern assessment of McKean's career, see G. S. Rowe, *Thomas McKean* (Boulder, Colo., 1978).

18. See Captain John Ferdinand Dalziel Smyth, *Narrative* (New York, 1778), p. 17.

19. Antoine Quentin Fouquier-Tinville earned notoriety as the public prosecutor in France during the Reign of Terror. On McKean's role in the execution of Abraham Carlisle and John Roberts during the War of Independence, see Rowe, *Thomas McKean*, pp. 115–20.

20. The Chief Justice of England.

21. This piece first appeared in *Political Censor*, March 1797, pp. 107–15. Dr. Michael Leib was one of Philadelphia's leading democrats and represented Germantown in the state legislature. Among other things, Cobbett accused him of getting rich on the backs of yellow fever victims. "This Leib," he wrote on another occasion, "is one of the most infamous wretches that ever existed. He now [September 1797] stands charged with purloining the property of children, whose father he visited on his death-bed; yet this man is a member of Congress!" (*Porcupine's Works*, vol. 7, pp. 185–86n.).

22. The "five Sultans of France" were the five directors who constituted the executive under the Constitution of 1795; the governor of Pennsylvania at this time was Thomas Mifflin; James Madison, William Branch Giles, and Albert Gallatin had established themselves as the leading Republican politicians in the House of Representatives during the 1790s.

23. Benjamin Banneker has been described as "the first American black scholar"; he was, among other things, an astronomer, mathematician, surveyor, poet, mechanic, philosopher, clock maker, and zoologist. See Lerone Bennett, Jr., *Pioneers in Protest* (Chicago, 1968), pp. 13–26.

24. Cobbett is referring to William Thornton's *Cadmus: or, a Treatise on the Elements of Written Language*, which remodelled the alphabet with a system of phonetics and received first prize in 1793 from the American Philosophical Society. See "A Bone to Gnaw for the Democrats," Chapter 2, this volume, pp. 111–12.

25. Cobbett is alluding to Rush's eulogium on David Rittenhouse, the Philadelphia radical and scientist who had been president of both the Democratic Society of Pennsylvania and the American Philosophical Society. Rush's words, commented Cobbett on another occasion, were full of "hyperbolic bombast." See *Porcupine's Works*, vol. 4, p. 361.

26. Frederick Muhlenberg had been the Republican chairman of the House of Representatives during the debate over Jay's Treaty; when it came to the crunch, he cast his deciding vote in favor of the treaty. Rather than praising his action, Cobbett dismissed Muhlenberg as a vacillating, two-faced politician.

27. See "Bone to Gnaw," n. 15.

28. Thomas Mifflin and John Barclay, the Irish-American merchant who served as the first president of the Bank of Pennsylvania.

29. Formerly the Assistant Secretary of the Treasury under Hamilton, Coxe had moved into the Republican camp by the mid-1790s. During the first years of the War of Independence, Coxe had been a Loyalist, and had returned to his native Philadelphia with General Howe's army—hence Cobbett's jibe about the crown.

30. Cobbett's first publisher, with whom he had fallen out in 1796. See "Life and Adventures of Peter Porcupine," Chapter 5, this volume, pp. 175–76.

31. These pages in the original edition of "Life and Adventures" described Cobbett's treatment at the hands of Bradford. See Chapter 5, this volume, pp. 175–76.

32. In which it appeared that Randolph had appealed to Fauchet to bribe Mifflin and Dallas to restore peace in western Pennsylvania during the Whiskey Rebellion. See John C. Miller, *The Federalist Era* (New York, 1960), pp. 169–70.

33. For Cobbett's earlier attacks on Swanwick, see "Bone to Gnaw," pp. 113–14. Swanwick's father had been a customs officer in Philadelphia, and was a Loyalist wagon master during the War of Independence; Cobbett enjoyed rubbing this background in Swanwick's face.

34. Bache was experiencing financial difficulties in running the *Aurora*; he had also been beaten up in the Southwark district of Philadelphia for his attacks on George Washington. See Jeffery A. Smith, *Franklin and Bache* (New York, 1990), pp. 159–60.

35. James Monroe had recently returned to the United States after spending two years in Paris as the American minister to France. Strongly critical of Washington's foreign policy, he wrote in 1797 the angry *View of the Conduct of the Executive of the United States*, which blamed the American government for the deterioration of Franco-American relations.

36. Cobbett's nickname for Albert Gallatin, the Pennsylvania congressman who in 1797 took over the leadership of the Republican party in the House of Representatives from James Madison.

8. Detection of a Conspiracy

1. See "History of the American Jacobins," Chapter 6, this volume, n. 11.

2. On James Reynolds, see "Pen Portraits," Chapter 7, this volume, n. 8.

3. In a footnote to the edition of this pamphlet in *Porcupine's Works*, Cobbett commented that "These two questions, 4 and 5, are well worth the attention of the reader, particularly if he be an Irishman. The answer to question 4, is to be in the *negative*, and that to question 5, in the *affirmative*; consequently, the initiated swears, 'that he does *not think that Great Britain ought to govern Ireland*; and that he will do to the utmost of his power for the establishment of *a republican form of government there*.' Now, mark: When these miscreants were in Ireland, they were seditious, to be sure; but they never openly avowed their intentions. On the contrary, they wished, they said, to preserve *the essence of the British Constitution*; this Constitution they were everlastingly *extolling*; they frequently expressed the warmest *attachment to his Majesty*; and when they were called *Republicans*, and told that their intention was to effect *a separation from the sister kingdom*, they called it a '*gross slander!!*' This has been the constant practice of all the runaway patriots, from PRIESTLEY to REYNOLDS. Surely, such proofs of their duplicity must in time open the eyes of their deluded adherents!"

4. William Playfair, the author of the *History of Jacobinism, Its Crimes, Cruelties, and Perfidies*; see "History of the American Jacobins," Chapter 6, this volume, n. 1.

5. Cobbett was referring to Benjamin Franklin Bache, editor of the *Aurora*; the charge was just as baseless as Bache's accusation that Cobbett had been bought by Pitt's gold.

6. James Napper Tandy was a leading United Irishman who temporarily took refuge in the United States before joining the community of Irish radicals in Paris; he pressed for a French invasion of Ireland in support of the Rebellion of 1798.

7. Reynolds's letter to Secretary of State Timothy Pickering is no longer

extant. But see James Callender, *Sedgwick & Co.* (Philadelphia, 1798), and *The Prospect Before Us* (Richmond, 1800–1801), vol. 1, p. 149, for the Federalist attempt to prosecute Reynolds for seditious libel.

8. In *Porcupine's Works*, Cobbett added these comments: "While I am writing this note, there is a bill passing through the lower House of Congress, authorizing the President to cause to be seized and sent out of the country, all such *aliens* as have been convicted of *treason* or *sedition* in other countries, or are *known to have fled hither to escape from the hands of justice*. This is a very wise, and absolutely a necessary measure. Citizen REYNOLDS may probably be forced back again to his offended country, to receive sentence in those courts which he fled from! All mankind will rise united against these treacherous wretches; they will be driven from shore to shore; the indignant waves will at last hurl them on some desert strand to perish and become food for the fowls of the air. The '*Monthly Review Enlarged*' will doubtless find in their fate, an excellent subject for an elegy."

9. Cobbett is referring to the XYZ dispatches, which had been made public in April 1798, just before *Detection of a Conspiracy* was published.

10. Cobbett's nickname for James Reynolds.

11. This is where the original pamphlet ended. The following section was added by Cobbett in *Porcupine's Works*.

12. The Whiteboys were agrarian secret societies operating in Ireland during the 1760s and 1770s; the Volunteers formed the nucleus of the Irish reform movement during the American War of Independence. In the 1790s, the United Irishmen—many of whose members had been in the Volunteers—recruited former Whiteboys in the struggle against British rule.

13. On Rowan, see "Pen Portraits," n. 9.

Index

Abercrombie, James, 209
Adams, Abigail, 36–37
Adams, John, 14, 23, 34
Adet, Pierre-Auguste, 23, 36
"Agricola," 51, 81
Alien and Sedition Acts (1798), 23, 48, 239, 279n8
　inadequate to deal with United Irishmen, 251–53
　intimidating to Daniel Isaac Eaton, 225–26
Allen, Andrew, 176, 272n14
American Constitution:
　attacked by democrats, 186–87, 197
　as bulwark against democracy, 26, 182, 187
　defended by Cobbett, 24, 155, 178
　denounced by Cobbett, 24
　English foundations of, 66
American Monthly Review, 121–34
American Philosophical Society, 78, 234–35, 277nn24–25
American Revolution:
　denounced by Cobbett, 41–42
　praised by Cobbett for its moderation, 209
　supported by Cobbett's father, 4, 160–161
Ames, Fisher, 14, 36
Appleby, Joyce, 17
Associated Teachers (New York), 68n, 76–77, 79
Atheism:
　in America, 152–53, 209–11
　and Condorcet, 149, 271n5
　and deism, 73, 146, 208–9
　in French Revolution, 71n, 137, 146–47, 149

　and Priestley, 71
　and rejection of all authority, secular and spiritual, 26, 137, 147

Bache, Benjamin Franklin, 36, 141, 180n, 210, 227, 236, 249, 278n35
　assaulted, 278n34
　attacked by Cobbett for supporting the French Revolution, 140, 204n, 227, 236, 270n1
　on funding system, 207–8
　on monarchical tendencies in American government, 207
　on Washington's proclamation against Whiskey Rebellion, 207
　See also [Philadelphia] *Aurora*
Bacon, Francis, 30
Banneker, Benjamin, 234, 277n23
Barclay, John, 277n28
Barère, Bertrand, 70, 97n, 102, 204n, 264n31, 268n17
Barlow, Joel, 95, 99, 267n7
Barruel, Abbé, 143
　History of the French Clergy, 143–44
Berkley, George, 162–63
Berthier de Sauvigny, 152, 271n7
Bettertout, Lord, 198
Bewley, Doctor, 77, 266n44
Biddle, Charles, 197n
Billaud-Varenne, Jean Nicolas, 204n
Blount, William, 24
Bolingbroke, Henry St. John, Viscount, 40, 43
Bompard, Citizen, 116
Bond, Phineas, 176, 272n13
Boudinot, Elias, 270n13
Bournonville, Citizen, 191
Bowles, William, 24

[281]

Brackenridge, Hugh Henry, 268n15
Bradford, David, 116, 269n32
Bradford, Thomas, 51, 155, 173–77, 235, 272n11, 277n31
Brissot de Warville, Jacques-Pierre, 61, 112–13, 185, 204, 220, 262n15
Brown, Andrew, 124, 209n, 269n1. *See also Philadelphia Gazette*
Burdett, Sir Francis, 44
Burke, Edmund, 37–38, 184, 264n27, 275n10
  on anti-Christian conspiracy behind French Revolution, 265n40
  and community values, 27
  on dissenters, 261n5
  influence on Cobbett, 25–27, 32
  on limitations of reason, 26
  and Marie-Antoinette, 263n20
  prediction of increasing violence in France, 25
  Reflections on the Revolution in France, 25, 27, 35, 38
  and tyranny of the majority, 24–25
Butler, Samuel, 262n14

Callender, James Thomson, 209n, 224, 237–38, 275n8
  afflicted by *mania reformatio*, 93
  attacked by Cobbett, 90–94
  on British government, 87
  compared to Paine, 111
  Political Progress of Britain, 87, 89–95, 101, 103, 108–11, 114–17, 122, 124
  prediction of revolution in Britain and Ireland, 87, 114–17
  on Tories in America, 35n, 36
  and Whiskey Rebellion, 108–10
Carey, Matthew, 38–39, 45, 173, 176, 272n12
Carlisle, Abraham, 231, 276n19
Carrier, Jean Baptiste, 144
Chabot, François, 63, 263n19
Charles I, 65
Chatham, Lord, 98, 102, 198
Christ, Jesus, 71n, 73–74, 105, 118n, 138, 209n
Christianity:
  attacked by Paine, 219, 221–23
  attacked in America, 74
  attacked in France, 28, 72–74, 137–38, 146–47, 221–22
  as bulwark of social order, 26–27, 72
  embraced by Cobbett, 3, 160
Cicero, 269n2

Clinton, George, 267n13
Clootz, Anacharsis, 61, 278n15
Coates, William, 197n
Cobbett, William:
  career and characteristics:
    anti-intellectualism, 39–40, 48
    in army, 3, 5–7, 155, 166–69, 272n6
    consistency, 12, 24–30, 50–51
    conversion to conservatism (1792–94), 8–13
    conversion to political radicalism (c. 1802–6), 42–44
    court-martial case (1792), 5–6, 8, 12, 155, 272n6
    early republicanism, 3, 7–8, 155, 171
    English patriotism, 4, 12, 27, 29–30, 34, 43, 46–47, 51, 83–86, 156–57, 162
    later radicalism, 1, 12–13, 39, 44–46
    libel trial (1799), 41
    literary style, 37–40, 46, 119, 125–27
    personality, 1–2
    personalization of politics, 10, 12, 52–53, 217–38
    popular appeal, 2, 35–38, 47
    pragmatism, 24
    pretense of being American (1794–95), 24, 98, 110, 116
    return to America (1817–19), 45
    tension between the ideal and the real, 7–8, 10, 12, 49
    upbringing, 4, 158–64
  views:
    abstract rights, 25, 28, 47–48, 50, 64, 66, 70
    abuse of power, 7–8, 12, 39
    Anglo-American military alliance, 32–34
    British interests in America, 2–3, 24, 32–34, 37, 46
    Burke's influence on, 25–27, 32
    corruption, 1, 3–7, 10, 26–27, 43–44
    culture of democracy, 3, 87–88, 95–99, 104, 111–12, 183, 198–201, 208
    demagogues, 26, 80
    democratic ideology, 2, 10, 25–29, 47–48, 64–68, 260
    equality, 28, 51, 67, 70, 88, 137–38, 145–46, 196

Cobbett, William (*cont.*)
  family values, 3, 27–28, 48, 232
  French revolutionary ideology in America, 3, 18–19, 29–31, 47, 74–75, 95, 138, 140, 150, 152–54, 185–87, 198, 241–42, 255
  French revolutionary imperialism in America, 30–34, 252–53
  hypocrisy, 6, 28, 39, 48–49, 87–88, 107, 196, 202, 210
  later attitude (c. 1811–35) to American empire, 45–46
  later attitude (c. 1811–35) to American liberty, 44–46
  liberty, 10, 12, 27–28, 30, 43–46, 50, 65, 67, 70, 88, 95, 103–4, 115, 133–34, 137–38, 142, 145–46, 151, 156, 178–80, 184–85, 189, 196, 199, 259
  liberty of the press, 40, 44, 140–41, 147, 153, 155, 174–75, 179–80
  literary style of opponents, 78–79, 119, 122–32
  nativism, 48, 110, 200, 239–57
  property relations, 26–27, 145, 147, 149
  rule of the mob, 25–26, 28, 42, 56, 60–63
  terror, 25, 28–29, 137, 143–45
  women, 27, 47–48, 61, 67, 70, 89–90, 112–13, 126, 130–31, 135–36, 183, 199
  writings:
    The American Rush-Light, 44
    "The Bloody Buoy," xiii, 137–54
    "A Bone to Gnaw, for the Democrats," 87–118, 121–22, 126, 175
    "A Bone to Gnaw, for the Democrats, Part II," 120, 135–36
    The Cannibals' Progress, 141
    Cobbett's Parliamentary Debates, 1
    Country Porcupine, 35
    English Grammar, 119
    "History of the American Jacobins," 182–216
    "A Kick for a Bite," 37, 119–34
    "The Life and Adventures of Peter Porcupine," xiii, 155–81
    "Observations on the Emigration of Dr. Joseph Priestley," 25, 50–86, 173–75
    Political Censor, 177, 234, 272
    Political Register, 1, 156
    The Porcupine, 41
    Porcupine's Gazette, 33–35, 37–38
    Rural Rides, 1, 156
    The Scare-Crow, 180–81
    The Soldier's Friend, 6–8, 155
Collot d'Herbois, Jean Marie, 204n
Condorcet, Marquis de, 147, 149, 270n2, 271n5
Cowley, Abraham, 52, 261n1
Coxe, Tench, 235, 277n29
Cruikshank, Isaac, 69

Dallas, Alexander, 22, 197, 201, 206, 235, 242, 274nn11–12, 277n32
Damien, Robert François, 79, 266n45
Danton, Georges Jacques, 63, 105, 204, 208–9, 221, 231, 263n19, 268n20
David, Jacques Louis, 95n
Debbieg, Colonel Hugh, 167, 271n4
Deism:
  in America, 208–9
  and atheism, 73, 146, 208–9
  in French Revolution, 146–47
  and Paine, 26, 222–23
  and Priestley, 53, 71, 261n4
  and rejection of all authority, secular and spiritual, 26
Delacroix, Charles. *See* Lacroix, Charles
Democratic Societies, 106, 115, 122, 124, 127, 212, 267n10
  and Afro-Americans, 113, 202–3
  and American government, 196–97, 215–16, 264n25
  caricatured as anti-federalist, 186–87, 193, 273n5
  on the defensive, 32, 216, 242
  and Fauchet, 203–5
  and Genet, 18–19, 30–31, 193–94, 201–3, 205, 267n13, 273n5
  and Jay's Treaty, 215–16
  poisoning the minds of the people, 198–201
  and Proclamation of Neutrality, 215
  and Whiskey Rebellion, 21, 31, 99–100, 205–8, 215–16, 267n11
  and women, 112–13
  See also Jacobins
Democratic Society of New York, 52, 58, 63, 66–67, 68n, 69–70, 79, 82, 276n14
Democratic Society of Pennsylvania, 194–97, 205–6, 274n11, 276n14
Dexter, Samuel, 268n22
Dick, Doctor, 230
Dissenters, 26, 53–55, 261n5, 265n38
Dorchester, Lord, 101, 268n15
Drinker, Elizabeth, 35, 37

Dryden, John, 269n25
Duane, William, 45
Du Ponceau, Stephen, 191, 197n
Dupont de Nemours, Pierre Samuel, 208, 274n14

Eaton, Daniel Isaac, 225–26, 275n10
English radicals in America, 81–82, 133, 197, 202–3. *See also* Eaton, Daniel Isaac; Hancock; Harper; Lee, Citizen Richard; Priestley, Joseph; Rowson, Susanna; Transatlantic Radicalism
Exeter, Earl of, 40

Fauchet, Jean Antoine Joseph, 22, 203, 205–6, 216, 235, 273n10, 277n32
Federalists (U.S.A.), 14–17, 24, 34–37, 40, 47–48, 260
Findley, William, 208
Fitzgerald, Lord Edward, 168–69
Foucault, M., 148, 271n4
Foulon, Joseph François, 271n7
Fouquier-Tinville, Antoine Quentin, 231, 276n19
Fox, Charles James, 99, 107, 108n, 116, 267n12
Franklin, Benjamin, 40, 47, 158, 160, 181n, 204n, 271n1
    Autobiography, 155
Frederick, General, 168–69
Freneau, Philip, 191
French Revolution:
    and Cobbett's conversion to conservatism, 11–12
    disastrous consequences in France, 28, 67–68, 140, 149–50, 170–71
    horrors of, and Constituent Assembly, 147–49
    as inspiration for radicals in England, 5–6, 54–55
    and irreligion, 137–38, 142–47
    and mob violence, 61–64, 137, 142–45
    and Paine, 219–23
    and Priestley, 55, 61, 67–68, 263n19
    support for, in America, 18, 74, 138, 150–54, 209
    See also Cobbett, William: views; Jacobins

Gallatin, Albert, 141, 233, 237–38, 277n22, 278n36
Gay, John, 270n10

Genet, Edmund:
    adulation in America, 19, 104, 106, 188–92
    attempts to strengthen Franco-American ties, 18–19, 30, 182, 187–88
    enlistment of volunteers in America, 28, 188–89, 201
    failure of his mission, 19, 32, 99–100, 201–3
    snubbed by Washington, 192–93
    See also Democratic Societies
Gentil, Michel, 62, 263n17
George II, 98, 209–10
George III, 21
Gerrald, Joseph, 265n42
Gibbon, Edward, 74
Gifford, William, 2
Giles, William Branch, 233, 268n22, 277n22
Gillray, James, 9, 49
Glacière Massacre (1791), 263n16
Glentworth, Doctor, 229
"God Save the Guilliotine" (song), 96
Goldsmith, Oliver, 39, 102, 266n48, 268n16
Gouges, Olympe de, 264n32
Gould, Sir Charles, 9
Grattan, Henry, 107
Graydon, Alexander, 35
Greenleaf, Thomas, 227, 276n14
Grégoire, Henri-Baptiste, 151, 209, 271n6
Griswold, Roger, 275

Hamilton, Alexander, 14–17, 19, 274n12, 277n29
Hammond, George, 176, 272n14
Hancock (English radical), 224
Hardy, Thomas, 5
Harmar, General Josiah, 20
Harper (English radical), 224
Hazlitt, William, 35
Hébert, Jacques-René, 38, 147, 264n32, 270n2
Hébert, Madame, 70, 264n32
Hobson, John, 262n11
Holcroft, John, 268n15. *See also* "Tom the Tinker"
Holland, Mr., 164–65, 167
Hopkinson, Joseph, 228, 276n16
Howe, General, 235, 277n29
Howe, Lord, 213
Hume, David, 123, 265n39
Hutchinson, James, 197n

Irish in America, 10, 74, 133, 239–57.
  See also Reynolds, James; Rowan,
  Archibald Hamilton; Tandy,
  James Napper; Tone, Wolfe;
  Transatlantic Radicalism; United
  Irishmen
Israel, Israel, 197n

Jackson, David, 197n
Jacobins, 3, 26, 226, 254
  in America, 15, 51, 88, 93, 137–38,
    182–216, 245, 247, 251
  attacked by Cobbett, 24, 29–30, 36,
    51, 181, 182–216
  in England, 55, 196–97, 220
  in French Revolution, 11, 28, 55, 98,
    102, 111, 196–97, 247
  international network, 23, 30–31,
    182–83, 220, 239, 251–52, 255–
    56
  and women, 183, 198–99
  See also Democratic Societies; French
  Revolution
Jay, John, 21, 102, 177, 268n18, 272n15
Jay's Treaty, 21–23, 31–32, 49, 215–16,
  237, 255–56, 268n18, 272n15,
  273n10
Jefferson, Thomas:
  approached by Cobbett (1792), 3,
    171–72
  approval of Callender, *Political Progress
    of Britain*, 91–93, 224
  Federalist images of, 16, 141
  and Genet, 19
  and Republican political economy, 18
  and "revolution of 1800," 23, 34, 258
  ridiculed by Cobbett, 233–34
  and Tories in America, 36
Johnson, Samuel, 158, 271n1
Jourdan, M-J, 61–63, 263n16

Keteltas, William, 172, 272n10
Know-Nothing Party, 48
Knox, Vicesimus, 85, 266n50
Kuhn, Doctor, 229

Lacroix, Charles, 63, 263n19
Lafayette, Marquis de, 11, 61, 97, 104,
  104–5n, 204, 262n, 268n20
La Fontaine, Jean de, 113
Lamballe, Princess de, 63, 263n20
Lee, Citizen Richard, 226, 275n11
Leib, Michael, 197n, 233, 276n21
Liston, Robert, 37

Louis XVI:
  and American independence, 88, 97,
    106n
  attacked by Paine, 26
  and democratic ingratitude, 88, 97
  execution welcomed by American
    democrats, 88, 97, 99, 199–200,
    204; but abhorred by most Americans, 215
  guillotined in effigy in Philadelphia,
    18, 200
  treatment in France compared to
    treatment of Washington in
    America, 138, 153–54
  Washington's friendship for, 192
Louvet, Jean-Baptiste, 151, 204, 271n6
Lowth, Bishop Robert, 5, 167, 272n5
Loyalist Claims Commission (British
    North America, 1785–87), 5
Loyalists in the United States, 36–37
Lyon, Matthew, 224–25, 275n8

Mackintosh, James, 59
Madison, James, 18, 106, 115, 141, 233,
  277n22, 278n36
Mansfield, Lord, 232
Manuel, Pierre-Louis, 63, 263n19
Marat, Jean-Paul, 118, 147, 203–4
  adored by Philadelphia democrats,
    105
  compared to Franklin, 47
  compared to Jesus, 74, 118n, 138,
    152, 209n
  compared to McKean, 231
  compared to Priestley, 68
  and Democratic Society of New York,
    79
  and September Massacres, 105n,
    264n28
Margarot, Maurice, 265n42
Marie-Antoinette, 263n20
Marx, Karl, 2
Maury, Abbé, 139
McDowell, Joseph, 268n22
McKean, Thomas, 41, 49, 218, 230–32,
  258, 276n17, 276n19
McKnight, Reverend, 211
Mease, James, 228, 276n16
Melville, Lord, 8
Mifflin, Thomas, 100, 106n, 206, 235,
  274, 277n22, 277n28, 277n32
Miller, John C., 22
Mingo Creek Society, 21
Mirabeau, Compte de, 147, 204, 270n2

Mohammed, 71n
Molière, 104, 174
Monroe, James, 236, 278n35
Monvel, M., 71
Moore, Doctor, 105n, 118n
Morse, Jedidiah, 239
Muhlenberg, Frederick, 22, 234–35, 277n26
Muir, Thomas, 74, 80, 94n, 226, 265n42, 275n12

New Theatre (Philadelphia), 119, 129, 134–36, 269n5, 270n6

Oldden, John, 172, 272n10, 272n17
Orléans, Louis Philippe Joseph, Duc d' (Philippe-Egalité), 105, 268n20
Orwell, George: *Road to Wigan Pier*, 1

Paine, Thomas, 68–69, 170, 217, 238, 263nn21–22, 264n29, 269n24, 270n9, 274nn3–5, 275nn6–7
  admired by Cobbett (1792), 7–8
  and America's future, 14
  character assassinated by Cobbett, 219–23
  on Cobbett, 38
  deism, 219, 221–23. See also Paine, Thomas: *Age of Reason*
  image of America rejected by Cobbett, 10
  influences Cobbett's writing style, 39
  revolutionary in England, 65
  victim of French Revolution, 61, 64, 220–23, 263n15
  writings:
    Age of Reason, 26, 53n, 111, 118, 219, 221–23, 238, 274n1, 274n5
    Common Sense, 219, 238
    Decline and Fall of the English System of Finance, 43
    Letter to George Washington, 238
    Rights of Man, 3, 6, 8, 59, 104n, 219n, 220, 222, 223n, 238, 274n3, 275n6
Palmer, Thomas F., 94n, 265n42
Pearce (John Pierce?), 202, 273n7
Penn, William, 157
[Philadelphia] *Aurora*, 36, 169, 171, 181, 236, 270n1, 276n14, 278n34, 278n5. *See also* Bache, Benjamin Franklin
Philadelphia Gazette, 90, 105, 209n, 212, 269n1. *See also* Brown, Andrew
Pickering, Thomas, 250, 256, 279n7

Pierce, John. *See* Pearce
Pitt, William, 45, 177, 181
  "Pitt system," 38
Playfair, William, 182, 184–85, 247
  History of Jacobinism, 182, 184
Plymouth, Earl of, 56
Polverel, Etienne, 75, 265n43
Pope, Alexander, 43, 111, 269n27
Porter, John, 197n
Prentiss, Reverend, 211
Price, Richard, 261n5
Priestley, Joseph, 129, 217, 236, 255
  arrival in New York, 50, 52–53, 173
  on Cobbett, 40–41
  democratic addresses to, 51, 68–80
  and democratic principles, 25, 64, 66
  and French Revolution, 55, 61, 67–68, 263n19
  and religion, 53–55, 72–74, 77, 105, 261n4
  and revolutionary republicanism, 54–55, 65–66, 69, 114, 261–62n6, 278n3
  utopian image of America, 82–83, 266n48
  writing style attacked by Cobbett, 78–79
Priestley Riots (1791), 30, 50, 53, 55–63, 262nn7–8
Prior, Matthew, 270n11
Proclamation of Neutrality (1793), 102, 193, 205, 207, 215

Quasi-War (1798–99), 23, 33–34, 239
Quintilian, 270

Randolph, Edmund, 22, 206, 216, 235, 274n12, 277n32
Raynal, Abbé, 10, 40, 171, 272n8
Reeves, John, 30
Republican Natives of Great Britain and Ireland, 50, 65, 68n, 74–75, 79–80, 114
Republicans (U.S.A.), 10, 17–18, 24, 31, 35
Reynolds, James, 224, 243, 250–51, 253–56, 275n8, 278n3, 279nn7–8, 279n10
Richmond, Duke of, 167
Ridgway, James, 8, 91, 266n2
Rittenhouse, David, 197, 277n25
Roberts, John, 231, 276n19
Robespierre, Maximilien, 28, 79n, 97, 105, 203–4, 208, 214n, 221, 268nn20–21

Robison, Doctor, 239
Rogers, Doctor, 211
Rousseau, Jean-Jacques, 40, 68, 74, 264n30
Rowan, Archibald Hamilton, 225, 255, 275n9
Rowson, Susanna, 27, 47, 119, 121, 128–36, 269n3, 269–70n6
   Charlotte: A Tale of Truth, 133, 270n8
   Mentoria: or, The Young Lady's Friend, 133, 270n8
   Slaves in Algiers, 130–32, 135, 269–70n6
   The Volunteers, 136
Royal Society, 39, 77, 173
Rush, Benjamin, 36, 40–41, 218, 228–30, 234, 258, 276nn15–16, 277n25

St. Clair, General Arthur, 20
St. Paul, 74, 209
Scottish radicals in America, 74, 93n, 265n42. *See also* Callender, James Thomson; Thornton, William; Transatlantic Radicalism
September Massacres (1792), 11, 105n, 137, 263n20, 264n28
Sergeant, Jonathan, 197n
Shakespeare, William, 104, 157, 183, 211, 269n4
Sheffield, John, 263n23
Sheridan, Richard Brinsley, 116
Shippen, Edward, 41
Short, William, 172, 272n9
Simcoe, John Graves, 267n14
Skirving, William, 265n42
Slavery, 28, 47, 49, 66, 75, 88, 107–8, 151, 254
Smith, Samuel Harrison, 119. *See also* American Monthly Review
Smyth, John Ferdinand Dalziel, 231, 276n18
Society of the Illuminati, 239
Society of United Irishmen. *See* United Irishmen
Sonthonax, Léger Félicité, 75, 265n43
Spater, George, 156
Sprat, Thomas, 39
Stanhope, Charles, 107, 108n, 116
Stevens, Doctor, 229
Straw, Jack, 99, 110, 267n12
Swanwick, John, 49, 167–68, 179, 267n14, 270nn12–13, 271n3, 272n7, 277n33
   defense of Susanna Rowson, 135–36

and female education, 120, 269n30
ridiculed by Cobbett, 113–14, 136, 163, 169, 235–36
Swift, Jonathan, 37, 39–40, 43, 92
Tale of a Tub, 4
Symons, H. D., 91, 266n2

Tallien, Jean Lambert, 102, 204, 268n17
Tammany Society (New York), 68n, 70–74, 79, 82, 264n33
Tandy, James Napper, 249, 255, 278–79n6
Taylor, A.J.P., 6
Ternant, Jean de, 187
Test Act (1673), 73, 265n38
Thornton, William, 88, 111–12, 234, 269n28
   Cadmus: or, a Treatise on the Elements of Written Language, 269n28, 277n24
"Tom the Tinker," 101–2, 109, 235, 268n15
Tone, Wolfe, 10
Transatlantic Radicalism, 8–9, 45, 47, 65–66, 74–75, 79–80, 110, 118, 138, 152, 180, 200, 217–18, 224–26, 236–37. *See also* English radicals in America; Irish in America; Republican Natives of Great Britain and Ireland; Scottish radicals in America; United Irishmen
Tyler, Wat, 116, 269n32

Unitarianism, 53–55, 71, 93, 261n4
United Irishmen, 224, 239–57

Volney, Compte de, 40
Voltaire, François, 40, 74, 181n, 204
Volunteers (Ireland), 255, 279n12

War of 1812, 45–46
Washington, George, 11, 157, 182, 220, 230
   attacked by American democrats, 67, 118, 138, 153–54, 161, 235, 264n25, 278nn34–35
   on Cobbett, 36–37
   defense of America from Jacobinism, 141
   and Genet, 19, 106n, 192, 201
   and Jay's Treaty, 22, 255–56
   and neutrality, 102, 207
   and Whiskey Rebellion, 20, 31, 208, 274n12
Watts, Isaac, 96n

Webster, Noah, 37, 218, 227–28, 234, 275–76n13
Whiskey Rebellion (1794), 20–21, 30–32, 88, 94n, 99–102, 182, 205–8, 210–11, 216, 264n25, 267n9, 267n11, 267n14. *See also* Democratic Societies
Whiteboys, 255, 279n12
Whitlock (student, University of Philadelphia), 211
Whitlock, Eliza, 129, 269n5
Wilberforce, William, 43, 46

Williams, Gwyn, 6
Winchester, Elhanan, 202, 273n7
Winterbotham, William, 10
Wistar, Doctor, 229
Wollstonecraft, Mary, 27, 38, 266n1
  Vindication of the Rights of Women, 90
Women's rights, 3, 27, 47–48, 70, 119–20, 130–31

XYZ affair (1798), 23, 33, 279n9

Yonge, Sir George, 6